WRITER IDENTITY AND THE TEACHING AND LEARNING OF WRITING

Writer Identity and the Teaching and Learning of Writing is a groundbreaking book which addresses what it really means to identify as a writer in educational contexts and the implications for writing pedagogy. It conceptualises writers' identities, and draws upon empirical studies to explore their construction, enactment and performance. Focusing largely on teachers' identities and practices as writers and the writer identities of primary and secondary students, it also encompasses the perspectives of professional writers and highlights promising new directions for research. With four interlinked sections, this book offers:

- Nuanced understandings of how writer identities are shaped and formed;
- Insights into how classroom practice changes when teachers position themselves as writers alongside their students;
- New understandings of what this positioning means for students' identities as writers and writing pedagogy; and
- Illuminating case studies mapping young people's writing trajectories.

With an international team of contributors, the book offers a global perspective on this vital topic, and makes a new and strongly theorised contribution to the field. Viewing writer identity as fluid and multifaceted, this book is important reading for practising teachers, student teachers, educational researchers and practitioners currently undertaking postgraduate studies.

Contributors include: Teresa Cremin, Terry Locke, Sally Baker, Josephine Brady, Diane Collier, Nikolaj Elf, Ian Eyres, Theresa Lillis, Marilyn McKinney, Denise Morgan, Debra Myhill, Mary Ryan, Kristin Stang, Chris Street, Anne Whitney and Rebecca Woodard.

Teresa Cremin is Professor of Education (Literacy) at The Open University, UK.

Terry Locke is Professor of Arts and Language Education at the University of Waikato, New Zealand.

WRITER IDENTITY AND THE TEACHING AND LEARNING OF WRITING

*Edited by Teresa Cremin and
Terry Locke*

Routledge
Taylor & Francis Group

LONDON AND NEW YORK

First published 2017
by Routledge
2 Park Square, Milton Park, Abingdon, Oxon OX14 4RN

and by Routledge
711 Third Avenue, New York, NY 10017

Routledge is an imprint of the Taylor & Francis Group, an informa business

British Library Cataloguing in Publication Data
A catalogue record for this book is available from the British Library

Library of Congress Cataloging in Publication Data
A catalog record for this book has been requested

ISBN: 978-1-138-94571-5 (hbk)
ISBN: 978-1-138-94890-7 (pbk)
ISBN: 978-1-315-66937-3 (ebk)

Typeset in Bembo
by Swales & Willis Ltd, Exeter, Devon, UK
Printed by Ashford Colour Press Ltd.

CONTENTS

CONTRIBUTORS

The editors

Teresa Cremin is Professor of Education (Literacy) at The Open University, UK. Her socio-cultural research focuses mainly on the consequences of teachers' literate identities and practices, and creative pedagogies in literacy, the arts and the sciences from the early years through to higher education. She has a particular interest in volitional reading and writing. Her research is frequently co-participative, involving teachers as researchers both in school and children's homes. A Fellow of the English Association, the Academy of Social Sciences and the Royal Society of the Arts, Teresa is also a Director of the Cambridge Primary Review Trust and a Trustee of the UK Literacy Association (UKLA). Teresa co-convenes the British Educational Research Association's Creativity Special Interest Group and is a member of the Economic and Social Research Council's Peer Review College. Previously she has served as a President of the UK Reading Association and the UKLA and as a Trustee of the Society for Educational Studies, and as a Board Member of BookTrust and the Poetry Archive. Recent publications include: *Researching Literacy Lives: Building Home School Communities* (2015, Routledge); *Building Communities of Engaged Readers: Reading for Pleasure* (2014, Routledge); and *The International Handbook of Research into Children's Literacy, Learning and Culture* (2013, Wiley Blackwell), edited with Kathy Hall, Barbara Comber and Luis Moll. Teresa is editor of the Routledge series *Teaching Creatively in the Primary School*.

Terry Locke is Professor of Arts and Language Education at the University of Waikato, New Zealand. His research interests include the teaching of writing, teacher identity, disciplinary literacies, teaching literature and music education research. His current research is action-research based and involves working with groups of teachers in secondary schools with a view to developing a culture of writing in the school. Since 2002, Terry has been Editor-in-Chief of the journal *English Teaching: Practice and Critique*. Recent publications include: *Developing Writing Teachers: Practical Ways for Teacher-Writers to Transform their Classroom Practice* (2015, Routledge) and the edited book, *Beyond the Grammar Wars: A Resource for Teachers and Students on Developing Language Knowledge in the English/Literacy Classroom* (2010, Routledge).

Contributors

Sally Baker is Research Associate in the Centre of Excellence for Equity in Higher Education at the University of Newcastle, Australia. She is interested in exploring students' literacies, particularly experiences of reading, in the context of transition. Her current research examines how students from refugee backgrounds experience cultural and linguistic change in the context of their transitions into and through higher education. She is also interested in how language and literacies are positioned and taught in pre-university contexts and how this relates to the positioning in the undergraduate context. Recent publications can be found in *Assessment and Evaluation in Higher Education* and *Ethnography and Education*.

Josephine Brady is Lecturer in Education (Primary English) at the University of Birmingham, UK. She is interested in children and young people's writing outside of school, and also the processes of learning poetry by heart for primary-aged children. Her wider research interests include the development of teachers' expertise in poetry teaching and the use of children's literature to explore sensitive issues in the primary classroom.

Diane R. Collier is Assistant Professor of Education (Early Literacy) at Brock University, Canada. She researches multimodality, literacies and literate identities. Using critical qualitative and ethnographic methodologies, she focuses on processes of textmaking, children's use of community resources (particularly popular culture) and what can be learned from children about their consumption and production of texts. Her research interests also include ethical considerations of children's participation in research, teaching for social justice and the use of children's literature in classrooms. Most recent projects examine how gender and class might influence how children see themselves as literate beings, and how children visualise their families through photographs and through visual and digital literacy practices. Diane serves as Vice-President of Language and Literacy Researchers of Canada (LLRC) and North American Book Reviews editor of the *Journal of Early Childhood Literacy*. Some recent publications include: 'I wish I was a~lion, a puppy: a multimodal view of writing-process assessment' in the journal *Pedagogies*; 'A room with a view: revisiting the multiliteracies manifesto, twenty years on' in the multilingual journal *Fremdsprachen Lehren und Lernen*; and '"I'm just trying to be tough, okay": masculine performances of everyday practices' in the *Journal of Early Childhood Literacy*.

Nikolaj Elf is Associate Professor at the Department for the Study of Culture, University of Southern Denmark, and Senior Lecturer II (10%) at University of Stavanger, Norway. His socio-cultural research focuses on longitudinal ethnographic studies of local school writing cultures, students' writer development and multimodal literacy practices within and across the disciplines, including L1, science, social science and interdisciplinary writing. From 2009 to now, he has worked with the longitudinal project Writing to Learn, Learning to Write (see www.sdu.dk/wllw) funded by the Danish Research Council. He is a research consultant for the Norwegian research project Responsive Literacy Practices in Digitalized Classrooms (RESPONS) funded by the Norwegian Research Council. Elf is co-editor of the journal *L1 – Educational Studies in Language and Literature* and co-coordinator of a Special Interest Group on Technology and Literacy Education (SIG TALE) within The International Association for Research in L1 Education (ARLE). He is a member of the editorial board of *Nordic Journal of Literacy Research* and a reviewer for several journals. His recent publications include 'Technology in L1: a review of empirical research projects in Scandinavia 1992–2014' in *L1 – Educational Studies in Language and Literature* (with Hanghøj, Erixon and Skaar, 2015).

Ian Eyres is Senior Lecturer in Education at The Open University, UK, where he currently works mostly on primary and early years modules. His wide-ranging work in the fields of language in primary education and teacher development has included research and teaching in both literacy and second-language learning. He has been involved in a number of international education projects in South Asia, Africa and South America. Until recently he played a leading role in a long-term project to improve the quality of English teaching in government schools across Bangladesh, where he also played a major part in the development of a new national initial teacher education programme. Much of his work has focused on the development of teachers' expertise within their own classrooms. His PhD focused on teachers as writers.

Theresa Lillis is Professor of English Language and Applied Linguistics at The Open University, UK. Her research interest in writing across a range of domains centres on the politics of production and participation. She has authored and co-authored books include *Student Writing: Access, Regulation, and Desire* (2001, Routledge), *Academic Writing in a Global Context* (with Mary Jane Curry, 2010, Routledge) and *The Sociolinguistics of Writing* (2013, Edinburgh University Press). She has published articles in journals such as *Language and Education, Written Communication, Revista Canaria de Estudios Ingleses, International Journal of Applied Linguistics* and *TESOL Quarterly*.

Marilyn McKinney is Professor of Literacy Education at the University of Nevada, Las Vegas, USA, and Director of the Southern Nevada Writing Project. Her current research and professional work explore intersections of teachers' writing identities, teacher preparation and retention, and teacher learning communities. Recently she was invited, with writing project site leaders from across the US, to participate in the National Writing Project (NWP)'s *Building New Pathways to Leadership* grant aimed at testing new models in an effort to expand NWP communities of practice to develop leadership opportunities for under-served teachers. Locally, Marilyn is working with colleagues and doctoral students to investigate the potential of collaborative informal learning (e.g., e-mentoring cohorts, educator meet-ups, digital assessment of teaching and learning) to support and encourage retention among novice teachers and those prepared through alternative routes. Publications include 'Teacher inquiry for equity: Collaborating to improve teaching and learning' (2010, *Language Arts*) and 'Narrating and performing identity: An exploration of literacy specialists' writing identities' (2009, *Journal of Literacy Research*).

Denise N. Morgan is Assistant Professor of Literacy Education at Kent State University in Ohio, USA. Since 2010, Denise has served as Director of the Reading and Writing Centre. Denise completed a three-year post-doctoral fellowship at the University of South Carolina on a federally funded grant studying teacher change in beliefs and practices. Her research focuses on reading and writing instruction, teacher preparation and professional development. She often writes and presents with the classroom teachers with whom she works. In 2015, Denise and her colleague were awarded the Janet Emig research award by the National Council of Teachers of English for their review on preparing pre-service teachers to teach writing in *English Education*. Her research has appeared in outlets such as *Voices from the Middle*, *Middle School Journal*, *Journal of Literacy Research*, *The Reading Teacher*, *Action in Teacher Education*, *Journal of Early Childhood Teacher Education*, *Journal of Early Childhood Teacher Education* and *Language Arts*.

Debra Myhill is Professor of Education at the University of Exeter, UK. Her research has focused particularly on young people's composing processes and their metacognitive awareness of them; the inter-relationship between metalinguistic understanding and writing; the talk-writing interface; and the teaching of writing. She is Director of the Centre for Research in Writing, which promotes interdisciplinary research, drawing on psychological, socio-cultural and linguistic perspectives on writing. Over the past fifteen years, she has led a series of research projects in these areas, in both primary and secondary schools, and has conducted several commissioned research studies for the government, including the national evaluation of the Every Child a Writer intervention. She is regularly invited to undertake commissioned research or advisory roles for professional bodies, policy-makers and examination boards. Debra runs numerous professional education courses for teachers, examining the practical classroom implications of her research on the teaching of writing, and, in 2014, her research team was awarded the Economic and Social Research Council Award for Outstanding Impact in Society.

Mary Ryan is the Assistant Dean (Research) in the Faculty of Education at Queensland University of Technology in Brisbane, Australia. Her research investigates discourses of literacy, learning, youth culture and teachers' work. She applies theories of reflexivity, socio-spatiality and criticality to the 'texts' produced in classrooms, schools, higher education institutions, workplace learning and in social media. She is a Principal Fellow of the UK Higher Education Academy and is Associate Editor for a number of international journals. Mary led an Australian Learning and Teaching Council competitive research grant focused on developing a research-based approach to teaching and assessing reflective writing, which resulted in conceptual models and strategies for reflective learning. She is the editor of a recent book from this project, *Teaching Reflective Learning in Higher Education: A Systematic Approach using Pedagogic Patterns* (2015, Springer). She has led a number of research projects on writing practices and pedagogies for linguistically and culturally diverse students and has written over sixty publications in the past decade in the areas of literacy, teachers' work and reflective practice and learning.

Kristin K. Stang is Professor of Special Education at California State University, Fullerton, USA. She received her PhD from Northwestern University in Communication Disorders with an emphasis on learning disabilities. Kristin currently serves as the primary investigator/project director on a $1.5-million federal special education programme improvement grant and is Co-PI of CSUF Project TitanPRIDE, a project designed to transform teacher preparation across all university preparation programmes. Kristin has also served as the CSUF coordinator of the Accessible Technology Initiative, director of the Academic Technology Center, interim director of Academic Technology and interim director of the Faculty Development Center. Kristin's research interests include teacher preparation, special education at the middle and secondary level, and faculty support for online and hybrid instruction, especially in the area of writing. She has published multiple peer-reviewed articles, an edited book, editorials and book reviews, while frequently presenting at international and national conferences. Kristin's work has appeared in a variety of journals, including *Teacher Education Quarterly, American Secondary Education, International Journal of Online Pedagogy and Course Design, Action in Teacher Education, Exceptional Children* and *Teacher Education and Special Education.*

Chris Street is Professor of Secondary Education at Cal State Fullerton, USA, where he directs the master's programme in secondary education. Chris's current research focuses on the development of teachers' identities as writers. His research interests also include adolescent literacy, college readiness, and the teaching of reading and writing. He developed and teaches the graduate-level course upon which this chapter is based. He also founded and directs a campus writing centre at a local high-needs high school in southern California. Chris is actively involved with many professional organisations, most notably the International Reading Association, where he serves on the editorial advisory board for the *Journal of Content Area Reading*. He is also a teacher consultant with the National Writing Project. His work has appeared in a variety of journals and books, including *Teacher Education Quarterly, Journal of Content Area Reading, Voices from the Middle, Mentoring & Tutoring, Comprehending Nonfiction 6-8,*

Multicultural Education, Journal of College Reading and Learning, Teaching Developmental Reading: Historical, Theoretical, and Practical Background Readings (2nd edn) and *Journal of Adolescent & Adult Literacy*. He co-authored (with Ellen and Jeffrey Kottler) *English Language Learners in Your Classroom: Strategies that Really Work* (2008, Corwin Press).

Anne Whitney is Associate Professor of Education at Pennsylvania State University, USA. Her research focuses on how writing fits into lives inside and outside of the classroom. A former high-school English teacher, she has spent much of her career studying the writing lives of teachers, investigating how writing in professional development can transform both how teachers work with students and how they are positioned as possessing education knowledge. She has also studied student writers from elementary school through college, writing in religious settings and emotions in writing. She received the Steve Cahir Award for research from the American Educational Research Association's Writing and Literacies SIG (2008), the Janet Emig Award from the Conference on English Education of the National Council of Teachers of English (2009) and the Best Article Award from the Conference on English Leadership of the National Council of Teachers of English (2010). She currently serves on the Executive Committee of the Conference on English Education of the National Council of Teachers of English. Her research has been published in such forums as *Research in the Teaching of English, Teachers College Record, English Education, Teachers and Teaching* and *English Journal*.

Rebecca Woodard is Assistant Professor of Curriculum and Instruction (Language, Literacy, and Culture) at the University of Illinois, Chicago, USA. Her research takes a socio-cultural perspective to explore how to make writing instruction in schools more meaningful, equitable and humane for teachers and students. Recent projects have looked at how writing teachers' participation across literacy practices and networks enriches and transforms their instructional practices, as well as culturally relevant/sustaining writing practices. Recent publications can be found in *Research in the Teaching of English, E-Learning and Digital Media* and *Written Communication*.

FOREWORD

We would expect young people to be taught to play a musical instrument by someone who could play that musical instrument. We expect writing to be taught in schools, colleges and universities by teachers and lecturers, but we don't have the same expectations of them as writers. Indeed, many of those teachers and lecturers may not feel confident about themselves as writers. Whatever their subject or discipline, the majority of teachers/lecturers do not practise the communicative art that is essential to their students' success: writing.

Teresa Cremin and Terry Locke – both distinguished practitioners of the arts of writing themselves – have put together a book that addresses this very problem. They recognize that most *English* teachers/lecturers, for example, are drawn into teaching their subject through a love of *reading* rather than writing. Such teachers have often taught writing by demonstrating sophisticated theoretical knowledge of writing processes, re-drafting, editing and proofreading; and knowledge about writing, like awareness of coherence and cohesion in whole texts, syntactic rules for composing sentences, and morphological and phonemic rules for word formation. But these same teachers, who might be excellent practitioners of the art of teaching (pedagogy), may rarely compose works of writing themselves other than for purely pragmatic purposes. Their identities as professionals, and specifically as teachers, are not necessarily bound up with actual practice of the art they profess to teach.

The notion of writer identity is a relatively recent one, at least explicitly. Some professional writers see themselves as 'writers'; others, like journalists, report writers and those who write text for the 'real world', don't tend to give themselves the recognition and status they deserve as practitioners of the art. By extending the mantle of 'writer' to include documentary genres as well as fictional ones, we do a service to writing by acknowledging the wide range of types of writing that are practised. We also move writing away from a mysterious, quasi-Romantic practice to a *métier*: an art practice in which many can excel. Furthermore, we can bring the practices and processes of professional writers closer to the practices of teachers, classrooms and students: each can speak to the other about common challenges of writing, as well as the specific challenges of writing in particular genres.

Like 'voice' and *voices*, writing and the *range of writing practices* carry the signature of identity/*identities*. The emphasis on the pluralistic notion of voices, writing practices and multiple selves reflects a move away from a Romantic notion of a single voice and a single self, and towards 'identity' being formed socially by our engagement in a range of social communities and networks in the latter part of the twentieth/first part of the twenty-first century. Such a shift is particularly in tune with the experience of young adults who try on a range of different selves as they develop confidence in 'who they are' in adulthood. Recognition and expression of those different voices and kinds of writing are crucial factors in young people's development as people and as writers.

We know, for example, that narrative plays a significant part in the development of young people's identity and in their thinking. It also provides the structures to organize and make sense of experience and/or to chart imaginative possible worlds that can be used for pleasure and to gain perspective on the 'real world'. But so, too, can other kinds of writing. We know much more about expositional and argumentational writing, and their relation to speech, than we did a generation ago. What we have learnt is that exposition and argument can start as early as explorations in narrative; that these modes or meta-genres can be combined into hybrid forms; and that direct engagement with the real world can often be better handled through exposition and argument. Identities can be forged as much through what you argue for and against as through narrative.

Such exploration of the relationship between meta-genres, between genres and of the hybrid forms that particular rhetorical situations can generate is central to the writing curriculum in schools and colleges, and part of the excitement of writing for young people. The development of student writer identities – of students seeing themselves as writers – is part of a long journey of learning the art. Chaucer's 'the lyf so short, the craft so longe to lerne' sums up the challenge well. The act of positioning oneself and then seeing oneself as a writer should start early, and develop through primary and secondary school, through college and in later life. The confidence that comes of such an apprenticeship in the art can have other benefits too: in a complex relationship with speech and other modes; in finding one's way socially and politically (and thus in terms of emerging identities); and in expression.

If learning is an effect of community, then various aspects of a working community can help to enhance the development of writing. One of these is peer review and support for teachers' writing, modelling how the pedagogy of the writing classroom might be shaped to maximize the social/interactive/learning dynamic. The US-based National Writing Project (now with over 40 years' experience of working with teachers) and younger networks in other countries are prime examples of writing communities for teachers. Another example of an approach to understanding the complexity of writing in higher education is the work of the

Thinking Writing Group at Queen Mary University of London, which works to develop and enhance lecturers' and students' writing across the disciplines.

What the present book also brings to the fore is the fact that composing academic essays, dissertations and theses, as well as writing in a range of subjects at school level, is a *creative* act. The term 'creative writing' is often used to draw a line round a particular kind of writing: the production of fictional and lyric genres. Creativity, however, is present in any compositional act, requiring applied imaginative energy, the ability to arrange and re-arrange written text (and often images too), and the development of a sharp sense of audience.

Implicit in the development of teachers' thinking and practice in writing is the need for time and space in a busy professional life for continuing professional development. One of the unforeseen advantages of the National Writing Project is not only its focus on teachers-as-writers, but also its intense and sustained support for teachers as teachers. There is a need for writing practice, but also for reflection about that practice and about how reflection and practice can be used to benefit students. What this book does very well is to map the various stages of teacher-writer/writer-teacher development, from engaging with one's own writing through peer discussion and review; from the transitions and transformations that result from thinking about how writing experiences can be used pedagogically in the classroom; through teachers writing alongside their students and sharing knowledge about writing processes; and through re-conceptions of the very nature of teaching itself. The structure of the book into its four sections models the cyclical nature of engaging in writing as a teacher, and how personal and professional identity/identities mesh with each other.

Finally, reflexivity is mentioned as a key dimension in the development of teachers and students as writers, and of teachers as teachers of writing. Although the act of writing is one that engages all the faculties at once, the possibility of stepping back from the intense heat of creation into a more reflexive mode allows editorial insights, re-visioning of the writing, the addressing of structural issues, attention to clarity and audience consideration to take place. It also enables both a narrower focus on accuracy and a wider aperture on the social dynamics and functions of writing. Part of the wider picture is the place of writing with a multimodal conception of communication and composition; part of a wider socially and politically informed contemporary rhetoric of writing.

This book contributes to this new and emerging field in an incisive, research-based and illuminating way. It deserves to be read widely, and to inspire teachers, lecturers, students and others not only to write as well as to read, but also to *see themselves* as writers.

Richard Andrews
Professor in Education
University of East Anglia

ACKNOWLEDGEMENTS

The editors are indebted to the sixteen authors who have contributed to this cutting-edge volume, many of whom have undertaken new empirical studies for the purpose, adding to their own work and that within the field. Others have seized the opportunity to summarise their work and advance new arguments about the potential significance of writing identities and why they matter for teachers and students. We recognise, too, the many researchers whose work in the related fields of literacy, disciplinary literacy, applied linguistics, writing and identities has been seminal to the development of this as a current, and we believe enduring, focus in education. While these scholars are far too numerous to mention by name, their work is evidenced in the pages that follow. We also wish to thank the team of reviewers from three continents who assiduously offered constructive criticism and detailed advice as the draft chapters were submitted. Lastly, we recognise the contribution of the Routledge team, of Clare Ashworth and Sarah Tuckwell in particular, for their support and attention to detail.

INTRODUCTION

Teresa Cremin and Terry Locke

In the light of increasing international interest in teachers' and students' literate identities and practices, this book addresses the under-researched area of teachers' and students' writer identities and in so doing seeks to advance the field. The volume is premised upon two key assertions, namely that writer identity matters and needs recognition and development in educational contexts, and that young people's writer identities are influenced by the ways in which their teachers identify as writers. It brings together new empirical studies and scholarly reviews on writer identity and the teaching and learning of writing from researchers working in Australia, Canada, Denmark, New Zealand, the UK and the USA. The volume explores what it means to identify as a writer, the issues that surround the concept of 'being a writer', and the consequences that arise when teachers and students do or do not identify as writers. Several contributors also conceive of and examine writing as a significant form of identity work.

It is only relatively recently that an identity lens has been employed by school-focused writing researchers such that teachers' and students' writer identity enactments have been studied in classrooms or professional learning contexts (e.g. McKinney and Giorgis, 2009; Locke et al., 2011; Cremin and Baker, 2010, 2014; Ryan, 2014). Teachers in many countries are expected to model writing and demonstrate their proficiency as writers, even though modelling certain techniques and strategies is a far cry from modelling being a writer in the classroom. Enacting the dual roles of teacher and writer is potentially problematic in school if, as research indicates, practitioners lack self-assurance and positive writing identities (e.g. Luce-Kapler et al., 2001; Gannon and Davies, 2007; Cremin and Oliver, 2016). It is equally problematic if teachers are unsure about what it might mean to model a writer identity.

Such issues are compounded by the fact that historically in the high-school context many teachers report being drawn to teach English by a love of reading, not writing, and whilst many associate reading with pleasure and satisfaction, few view writing in the same way (Peel, 1995; Gannon and Davies, 2007). In their Australian study, Gannon and Davies (2007) found that a love of literature or an inspirational English teacher prompted most of the respondents to teach the subject, not an interest in writing. Canadian research in the elementary phase also reveals that reading, not writing, forms the backbone of teachers' literacy experiences and that this impacts upon their classroom practice where reading is profiled over composition (Yeo, 2007). In addition there has been a growing call for teachers of all disciplinary areas to view themselves as teachers of writing (Shanahan and Shanahan, 2008; Grimberg and Hand, 2009). However, there is widespread recognition that such teachers are reluctant to assume the mantle of either teacher of writing or disciplinary writer (Carney and Indrisano, 2013; Locke and Johnston, 2016). Alongside this it is argued that performativity discourses have distorted professional understanding of the nature and purpose of composition (Cremin and Myhill, 2012; Locke, 2013).

A recent systematic review of research into teachers as writers (from 1990–2015) underscores these difficulties. It suggests there are multiple difficulties and tensions including practitioners' low self-assurance as writers, adverse writing histories, and limited conceptions of writing and being a writer, such that there is a genuine challenge in composing and enacting the positions of teacher and writer in the classroom (Cremin and Oliver, 2016). The review concludes that:

> Pre-service and in-service training programmes appear to have important roles to play in developing teachers' conceptions of writing and sense of self as writer. Findings suggest that sustained opportunities to reflect on personal writing histories, engage in writing, discuss textual processes and participate in a community of practice can influence teachers' self-assurance as writers and their pedagogical approaches.
>
> *(Cremin and Oliver, 2016)*

However, the review states that the evidence base in relation to the pedagogical consequences of whether teachers identify as writers and the influence of their understanding of and attitudes towards teaching writing remains 'extremely thin, particularly regarding impact on student outcomes' (Cremin and Oliver, 2016).

To examine these complex, potentially interrelated issues more closely, we invited scholars researching in the field to contribute to this volume and to share their new data and current perspectives on writer identity. We divided the resultant text into four sections. In turn these examine: conceptions of writing, writers and identities; the development of teachers' writer identities; the shifting practices and positions adopted by teachers in classrooms; and students' identities as writers, both within and beyond school. Working mainly but not exclusively from a sociocultural perspective, the contributing scholars employ a range of methodological approaches and timescales. Most use multiple-method qualitative strategies such as case study, ethnography and naturalistic inquiry, whilst others combine qualitative and quantitative methods. In relation to their research instruments, interviews, observations, questionnaires and scrutiny of writing samples are commonly used to explore the ways in which writers perform and enact their identities in different contexts. Some of the contributors offer diverse perspectives on the common-sense, yet much debated, contention that to teach writing, teachers need to 'be writers', or in some sense to identify themselves as writers. Other contributors focus on students' writer identities and the ways young people position themselves and are positioned as writers within and beyond school. Professional writers' identities are also examined with a view to illuminating possible consequences for the teaching of writing and young writers' identities.

Section A: Writing, writers and identity

Commencing the examination of identity and writing which threads through the volume, Eyres offers a conceptual examination of these terms, drawing on multiple theoretical perspectives and standpoints. Initially he contrasts different conceptualisations of literacy, recognising that policy-makers and educators who adopt traditionally 'asocial' and 'autonomous' models (Street, 1984) of literacy tend to dislodge cognitive skills 'from their socio-cultural moorings in human relationships and communities of practice' (Richardson, 1998, p. 116). Eyres takes a sociocultural view of literacy, recognising it is embedded within specific social and cultural contexts and is underpinned by an 'ideological' model in Street's (1984, 2008) terms. He links this social model to the ways in which participants in any community of practice move from peripheral participation to full membership (Lave and Wenger, 1991) and highlights the influence of classroom literacy/writing practices which have a direct bearing on the literate identities of all involved. Consistent with this standpoint, Eyres then examines identity as situated performance, and considers the influence of culture and context upon individuals' identity enactments. He also considers various frameworks to account for the fluidity and multiplicity of identities, including that of 'figured worlds' and identity positioning (Holland et al., 1998; Holland and Lave, 2001).

Whilst recognising the socially ascribed and constructed nature of identity, Eyres also draws attention to identity as an internalised process and the role of personal agency. In examining the significance of autobiographical narrative (written or spoken), he posits this can be seen as identity performance rather than text. Additionally Eyres considers connections and intersections between writing, identity and learning to write. He argues that learning to write involves the adoption of a writer identity through inter- and intrapersonal identity work, and engagement in literacy practices and with cultural artefacts. He furthers highlights the role of agency and personal subjectivity, as well as the interplay between teachers' own identities as writers, their perceptions of students and their students' own sense of themselves as writers. His exploration of the multiple conceptualisations of writing and identity establishes a focused context for the volume.

The first empirically based chapter attends to the voices, not of teachers or young novice writers, but of highly experienced professional writers. Cremin,

Lillis, Myhill and Eyres draw upon a cross-university study to reflect upon these professionals' histories and identities as writers. Their subjects have published widely and are both well known and well respected within their primary writing domain. The range includes novelists, a poet, journalists, screen-writers, magazine columnists and academic writers (all of the last group are UK science professors). The team adopted a biographical approach to examine the professional writers' identities as expressed and constructed in interviews. In this chapter they focus on the writers' memories of formal education and the influence of childhood reading. In so doing, Cremin and colleagues ensure that the writers' voices and views complement those offered elsewhere in the volume from an educational perspective. They analyse the professional writers' 'master narratives' (Hammack, 2011) as revealing identity enactments in their own right and also as a form of exploration to consider possible implications for the development of young writers and the teaching of writing.

Reflecting upon their experience of formal education, the professional writers reported a range of constraints on their early development as writers: a systemic lack of attention to and interest in imaginative writing in classroom settings and some challenging and discouraging relationships with teachers, many of whom expressed scant interest in their writing. In addition, specific, negative, school-based writing memories appeared salient in their narrated life stories. Many of the professional writers described their childhood determination to succeed against these odds, fuelled it appeared by a deep pleasure in reading and a desire to make and shape their own narratives, though play, talk and writing. Indeed, despite their adverse recollections, most of the participants positioned themselves as having been child writers, although some acknowledged that this may have been partly a retrospective re-construction. The writers' memories of early reading were detailed and specific, encompassing both books and other media, and they frequently referred to drawing upon childhood favourites in their later writing, naming particular texts that they perceived had influenced their later writing. This study, in highlighting the motivating power of narrative and the impact of early reading and listening-to-print practices, demonstrates the shaping influence of writers' early and social experiences of learning to write and becoming writers, and underscores the value of adopting an identity lens to understand writers and writing.

Section B: Writing identity and the development of teachers

The next section of the book focuses its attention on the formation of teachers' identities as writers in both pre-service and in-service settings. Three chapters explore this, both through new empirical studies with teachers engaging in pre-service and in-service learning (Morgan, and Street and Stang) and through a reflective examination and re-conceptualisation of work in this area (Whitney).

The starting point of Morgan's chapter is that many teachers are not well prepared to teach writing, and often demonstrate negative attitudes to writing stemming from their own schooling experiences, together with a lack of actual, recent, positive writing experiences. 'I argue', she writes, 'that the writing identity that may be most helpful to teachers is one where they identify as a writer who understands *how* and *why* writers enact their craft'. Morgan's study set out to explore how teachers (both pre-service and in-service) participating in a US graduate education course, designed and delivered by herself, came to develop or modify understandings of writing and teaching writing. Cognisant that many teachers express concerns about teaching writing and that pre-service courses offer relatively limited preparation in this area (Morgan and Pytash, 2014), she sought to enable her course members to develop their identities as writers. The course afforded opportunities for participants to engage in process writing in a programme of study, in which multiple goals were manifest, including: reading as a writer, textual study, the use of mentor texts and writing, as well as planning a unit of work on a self-chosen genre. In essence, Morgan aimed to 'help teachers rediscover writing while developing their understandings of principles, practices, theories, and research related to writing development and instruction'.

Her findings indicated that the lines between what the teachers learned as writers and as teachers of writing were often blurred, and that as teachers and writers, the participants identified common ground in respect of these two identity positions. As a result of their involvement in the project, some if not all of the participants were better able to articulate aspects of the writing process itself, to make use of 'mentor texts' to support their own and their students' growth as writers, to help students in choice-making around writing, and to view themselves as writers. For Morgan, the participants learned both from living inside the process and from seeing the ways in which their fellow writers in the group were influenced, but particularly in and through critical conversations about writing which were at the core of their work as an emerging community of writers. As a consequence, she argues, some of the teachers' previously held conceptions about writing, their awareness and ability to talk about writing craft, and to see themselves as writers were modified and enhanced.

Street and Stang also focus on the importance of developing communities of writing practice. However, their emphasis is more on writing across the curriculum and the resistance to assuming identities as teachers of writing and writers we alluded to earlier, attributable in part to teachers' own writer biographies. Their premise is that if teachers are going to view themselves as members of writing and teaching communities, 'teacher educators would do well to consider issues of biography, self-confidence, and proficiency with writing in undergraduate and graduate courses'. Based on a National Writing Workshop model, Street and Stang developed and evaluated a US in-service graduate writing course aimed at changing the attitudes, skills and practices of a cross-disciplinary group of middle- and high-school teachers. As an initial activity, participants wrote and shared a 'writing autobiography' as a community-building exercise and as an induction into the productive use of peer-response practices, which became a cornerstone for additional written assignments. Response groups often formed spontaneously in response to a shared content area and/or a shared work setting and became the source of collegial support and constructive criticism. Through the experience of being student-writers again, the teachers, Stang and Street argue, working alongside their colleagues, developed their confidence as writers. In their evaluation of the course, the authors found that, in particular, participants viewed peer sharing and peer response positively, saw their own writing as evolving over time, and indicated certain changes in their attitudes to writing itself (including changes in self-confidence).

For Street and Stang, the study findings were a powerful reminder of the importance of acknowledging teachers' biographies as writers as a first step in their 'escaping' them. Like other contributors to this book, they highlight the importance of exposing pre-service teachers to supportive communities of practice models of induction, where the affective domain is acknowledged and respected. They claim that the existence of the University's unlimited revision policy enabled the teachers to make real gains as they sought to continually revise and redraft their work. For some of the teachers on the course, this mediating tool contributed to a new-found pleasure in writing and an enhanced sense of self-efficacy as writers. Their work suggests that within communities of practice, peer feedback plays a vital part in supporting the development of positive attitudes to writing.

In the last chapter in this section, Whitney extends the argument that 'teachers must be writers' by situating historically the growth of the teacher-as-writer movement in the US, offering an informed analysis of what she perceives as a conceptual shift from 'teachers as writers' to 'teachers as researchers', and more recently to 'teacher-writers'. In doing so, she adopts a broad stance on the National Writing Project referred to by Street and Stang in the previous chapter. She begins by observing that while the notion that 'the teacher of writing should also write' has become a commonplace, the reality in many classrooms is that many teachers both dread and avoid writing. At the same time, she asserts, a growing number of teachers are assuming the identity of 'teacher-writers' who not only model writer identities in their classrooms, but manifest writing practices in both professional and political spheres as a means of reclaiming and asserting their autonomy. In particular, she highlights the value of teachers writing for publication, and widening their knowledge and influence as pedagogues supporting their colleagues.

The main emphasis of Whitney's chapter is to argue for a range of in-service teacher education strategies that can contribute to the formation of such teacher-writer identities. When students are taught by a teacher-writer, she contends, they are more likely to experience someone who empathises with their writing difficulties and understands the writing process. However, there are also benefits for the teacher when they assume the identity of teacher-writer. The identity, she contends, offers an expansion of the self, and allows for an enrichment of one's classroom experiences. Whitney argues for two avenues whereby teachers might develop identities as teacher-writers: National Writing Project involvement and participation in teacher writing groups. Finally, she draws attention to the crucial role being a teacher-writer can play in fostering a teacher's professional agency as someone who writes back to some of the policies and practices currently working to the detriment of teachers and students. Describing teacher writing as 'disruptive', she stresses the significance of teacher-writers' voices and their role in challenging the prevailing performative orthodoxy in education. Alongside other contributors to this volume, Whitney recognises writing as a significant form of identity work. She believes that through their writing, teacher-writers can work to reject the persistent policy positioning of pedagogues as 'technicians' who merely deliver the given curriculum, and that they can both voice and demonstrate that there are alternative, more effective and more humane ways to enable learning.

Section C: Teachers as writers – shifting practices and positions in the classroom

Practitioners are often supported in developing their identities as writers through involvement in university credit-bearing courses such as those run by Street, Stang, Morgan and our next contributor, McKinney. Her work, alongside four other contributors in this next section, focuses on investigating teachers' practices and positions as writers and as teachers, both those reported and those enacted and observed in the classroom.

In her study, McKinney examined the views and reported practices of six novice teachers (four male and two female), whom she believed had identified themselves as writers through various assignments and activities during her US Teaching Writing course the previous semester. Nonetheless she recognises that teachers are 'positioned and position themselves as capable or not capable, and agentive in some spaces but not in others depending on contexts, time and space, resources, mentors and a host of other factors'. Through the dual lenses of Ellsworth's (1997) concept of pedagogical mode of address and Phelan's (1993) conception of the politics of performance, McKinney examines the teachers' perceptions of being a writer and teaching writing. In particular, through close analysis of interview data and their reflections on teaching writing (submitted as part of the course), McKinney seeks to explore the reported intersections between writing identity and classroom performance with regard to pedagogical relationships.

McKinney's participants clearly demonstrate that they are, in Whitney's earlier terms, 'teacher-writers'; these novice teachers saw themselves as writers and asserted their professional autonomy in different contexts to nurture positive writer identities in the young. All wrote with enthusiasm about writing lessons, units or experiences that fostered a sense of creativity, agency and empowerment of their students' voices. All were committed to their students and to building classroom writing communities which specifically included practices that demonstrated connections between their writing and their teaching identities; their teaching encompassed reciprocal intersections between their identity positions as teachers and as writers. The examples illuminating this are highly engaging, as are the ways in which these novice teachers seek to offer relational spaces for themselves and their students as writers. McKinney highlights the salience of developing a pedagogical mode of address in the classroom from a writer's perspective and the potential of teachers using their experiences as writers, especially in the US system which she argues, through the narrow and prescribed curriculum, limits opportunities for students to engage in writing for real purposes.

In the following chapter, drawing on observational data gathered in the classroom, Baker and Cremin focus their lens on the affective dimension of writing and identifying oneself, or being identified by others, as a teacher-writer. In an earlier study by these UK authors, emotion had emerged as a salient intrapersonal force shaping how teachers position themselves and are positioned in their roles as teacher-writers/writer-teachers in the classroom (Cremin and Baker, 2010). In particular, teachers' relationships with their unfolding compositions and their emotional engagement/disengagement with their writing had influenced their situated sense of self-as-writers in this classroom. Their chapter revisits this earlier dataset and offers a multi-agent account of the emotional experience of participating in a writing classroom. It explores the experiences of a teacher, Jeff, the teaching/support staff sitting amongst the pupils and the pupils themselves. As the authors observe, there is relatively little research which addresses the emotional involvement of teachers or students as writers, although studies of teachers writing in pre-/in-service programmes evidence considerable insecurity, anxiety and discomfort (e.g. Cremin, 2006; Gardner, 2014; Morgan, 2006; Whitney, 2008). Through an analysis of Jeff's talk and actions during demonstration writing, the authors seek to make manifest his anxiety and genuine nervousness in composing a particular piece about his gran in the public forum of the classroom and they document how he handles this.

Baker and Cremin argue that the pedagogy of spontaneously composing texts as a teacher in front of a class may support children to develop their nascent authorial confidence, but it also poses an open risk for teachers who are emotionally invested in their roles as writers and teachers. Throughout the observed session, the teacher in this study experienced writing as a struggle. As he moved across the teacher-writer/writer-teacher continuum (Cremin and Baker, 2010), he experienced a not dissimilar continuum of positive and negative feelings about his writing. Nonetheless, as the voices of the teaching assistant, class teacher and pupils indicate, by composing authentically and revealing his concerns, Jeff was not only successfully positioning himself as a writer-teacher at moments during demonstration writing and when writing alongside his pupils, but was also helping to build a classroom community of writers. His vulnerability was not echoed in the reflections of the others present, but his intention to create a community of writers was both recognised and celebrated. In particular, Jeff's written comments on the children's writing illustrated his engagement, empathy and desire to understand and validate their life experiences and authorial voices. In the highly performative culture characterising compulsory education in the UK, Baker and Cremin posit that the work of teachers who are emotionally invested in writing and teaching writing may offer a more 'human and humane' way forward, which recognises the place of affect and seeks to foster children's own identities as writers with something to say.

Extending this exploration of the consequences of teachers positioning them-selves as writers in the classroom, Woodard offers a case study of a teacher, Hannah, who had participated in a four-week US National Writing Project Summer Institute programme and was subsequently observed in her classroom over a period of seven months. Also adopting a positional view of identity which reflects its situ-ated nature, Woodard uses Bucholtz and Hall's (2005) 'tactics of intersubjectivity' analytical framework to examine specific relational processes through which iden-tities are narrated and performed across contexts and over time. The six relational processes comprise: adequation and distinction, authentication and denaturalisa-tion, and authorisation and illegitimation. These are used to analyse and interpret Hannah's journeys as a writing teacher. Woodard's analysis reveals that whilst this English as a Second Language (ESL) teacher never saw herself as a particularly good writer, lacked self-assurance as a writer (due to negative past experiences) and rarely wrote volitionally for her own pleasure before the NWP Summer Institute, she worked hard to create a palpably different school experience for her students.

In a manner not dissimilar to McKinney's study, Woodard analyses the ways in which Hannah sought to authorise her young students' writerly identities. These included legitimising their diverse personal experiences, their fan writing and their drawing. Examples of these strategies are offered, including, for example, a coun-try project which positioned the students as experts on their cultures and enabled them to draw on their funds of knowledge (Moll et al., 1992). Students also had the opportunity to draw and compose speech bubbles, which Hannah found was particularly important for her emergent ESL writers. In the process of legitimising such practices, Hannah appeared to be redefining, for her students, what counts as writing in her classroom and also reshaping the students' relationship to writ-ing and potentially their views of themselves as writers. The extent to which this influenced her view of herself as a writer is not known, but the study reveals the kinds of practices which may emerge when teachers work intentionally to legiti-mise students' writerly identities and raises a number of questions for research and practice. As Woodard observes, 'for teachers interested in authenticating identities as writers and writing teachers, it might be productive to closely examine their own beliefs about what counts as writing and who counts as writers, as well as tensions in those beliefs'.

In the following chapter, Locke, drawing on studies from a range of schools and with teachers representing different subject areas and disciplines, also examines teachers' classroom practices and the consequences for students as writers. These New Zealand-based studies examine connections between teachers' engagement in writing workshop-based professional learning experiences and their shifting identities as writers. In addition, the chapter offers instances of classroom practice that evidence the impact of subsequent, changed pedagogical practice on students as writers. Initially Locke explores the concept of writer identity, and argues that Ivanič's (2004) seminal framework does not sufficiently 'tell a story about what it means to write or be a writer'. He offers his own definition of writer identity as 'the subscribed-to discourse or story about what it means to be a writer that is implicit in one's own beliefs and practices' and links this to notions of teacher professional identity and disciplinary literacy. In recognition of the disciplinary diversity in his data, gathered from two projects with a total of 21 teachers, Locke argues that there is a need to expand the mantra that 'every teacher is a teacher of writing' to 'every teacher is a teacher of certain types of writing'. Alongside attention to the transformative potential of sustained writing workshops as part of professional learning and a focus on cross-disciplinarity, he examines the challenges secondary schools face in becoming cultures of writing, the importance of classroom inquiry, and the need for whole-school and community commitment.

The interviews with the teacher-researchers from the schools after they had experienced the first year of their respective projects indicate a gradual shift in their identities both as writers and teachers of writing. These teachers had, Locke asserts, developed a deeper understanding of writing and the writing process, and they expressed more empathy for students' challenges as writers. Additionally their classroom practices had changed. Many were more willing to write alongside students, and spent more time on process and the use of subject-specific meta-languages, all of which the teachers perceived impacted on students themselves, in terms of motivation, performance and identity. Locke argues that to move the research and practice agenda forward at the level of each school, the value of intensive transformational professional experiences, such as writing workshops aligned with opportunities for critical inquiry and the facilitation of cross-disciplinary dialogue within and beyond the school, need to be integrated into the development of professional learning communities as change-agents. Only then, Locke suggests, will a school culture of writing be achieved in which teachers' and students' own identities as writers are nurtured.

Section D: Students' writing identities

In the concluding section of the volume, the focus is on students' identities as writers and the interplay between teacher positioning (and being positioned) and the identity positions adopted and made available to students as writers in the classroom. As noted earlier, there is very little research which explicitly examines the interplay between teachers' and students' identities as writers, and documents the consequences with regard to students' writing competence and confidence. Three chapters examine these issues following an opening chapter in which Brady explores students' writing identities in the world beyond school.

Drawing upon a study which investigated the role of writing in the lives of 15 self-identified home writers (aged 7–13 years) in the north of England, Brady explores the experiences and understandings of these young writers, and examines if their attitudes towards home and school writing differ. Atypically, she positioned this work in out-of-school contexts and located her sample through the library system and writing events for children. Brady commences by debating the concept of 'home', explores connections with Bhabha's (1994) third-space theory and argues that home writing can take place anywhere and at any time an individual feels 'at home'. The significance, she asserts, rests in the conceptual aspects of home (security, warmth, feeling comfortable) and 'the way of inhabiting it' (Boym, 1994: 166). This may offer a useful description for those teachers who write volitionally at NWP institutes, on university writing courses and in teachers' writing groups, for example, as detailed in several previous chapters. Brady's focus, however, is on the students themselves – those young writers who choose to write 'at home'. She employs Archer's (2003; 2007) work on reflexivity and the concepts of agency and structure to undergird her analysis of the multiple interviews and pieces of home writing gathered over a year.

The findings from this ethnographically styled study indicate that the young people had markedly different relationships with home and school writing. These were distinctively described as 'writing for self' and 'writing for others'. The former was characterised by a sense of personal agency; the latter by a perceived lack of choice and control. Brady argues that the former emerged from a space where the young people felt empowered and the latter was required in a space in which they often felt powerless. Based on this research, Brady offers a newly conceived home/writing continuum which seeks to capture and display information about an individual's home writing, the individual home writer and, most importantly, the relationship between each home writer and their home writing. Applying this to a 13-year-old home writer, Brady demonstrates that for this teenager home writing represents a source of empowerment; it offers her an outlet to explore challenging issues, reflect upon them and then move forwards. Her relationship with her poetry in particular is powerful and dynamic, existing in the present rather than the past. Through this analysis Brady evidences the critical role that reflexivity plays in the process of writing.

Collier too employed ethnographic methods to understand the writing practices and identities of two young 'becoming' writers – Kyle and Stephanie – in the middle years of elementary school. Although she visited the children at home, Collier mostly moved in and out of observer and participant roles in their school, where she positioned herself as a becoming writer too. During a two-year longitudinal study of Canadian children's text-making, Collier wrote alongside Kyle and Stephanie in the classroom and in the computer lab at school. This involved her in 'glancing sideways' at the children and making detailed observational notes to view these young writers' multiple identities through the intersection of their writing, their social identities and their talk about both of these. This concept of 'glancing sideways' as a method of data collection draws on Kendrick's (2005) study of a five-year-old at play, and focuses on ongoing processes. Collier asserts that change and flux are normal. She also seized opportunities for informal ongoing, sideways conversations with the young writers and examined the processes of writing drafts and polishing final products.

Viewing writer identities as fluid and multiple, Collier conceives of writing as a form of narrative play and an expression of literate identity (Kendrick, 2005; Wohlwend, 2009, 2011). This latter focus enables her to document what happens in the children's literacy classrooms, even during conventional literacy practices when they are writing in more formalised and potentially routinised ways about set themes. Collier's analysis offers a detailed sense of the two writers as unique individuals with different interests, passions and preferences. It also reveals how these writers are constructed and construct themselves through particular practices. Both seemed concerned to follow conventions and expectations as they perceived them, and both were positioned by their teacher in different ways according to their perceived academic abilities. As Collier observes, learning from children through glancing sideways is reminiscent of the work of early educators who conceptualised 'kidwatching' (Owoki and Goodman, 2002). Such observations facilitate the recognition of difference and enable Collier to highlight the shaping influence of relationships on the children's developing social and academic identities. Such informal yet formative documentation and the detailed knowledge of each writer which accrues over time are, as Collier also notes, a far cry from more usual standardised or mandated assessments. It allows nuanced details of the complex relationship between writing identities, texts and contexts to be understood as part of children's journeys of becoming.

The next chapter also draws on a longitudinal case study, this time in the context of Danish middle- and high-school education with students aged 14–18 years. Elf examines the development of the writer identity of Amalie, an adolescent Danish student, and in so doing debates what is meant by this, theoretically and empirically/analytically. The case study he presents is part of a four-year ethnographic study of adolescent writers (2009–2013). Theoretically, Elf, like Collier and most of the other contributors to the current volume, positions his work within a sociocultural approach to writing, emphasising that learning about writing occurs through participation and the use of mediating tools in a situated community. Regarding writers' development, Elf draws on Lemke's (2000) claim, further developed by Burgess and Ivanič (2010), that student-writers coordinate writing and identification processes that unfold on many timescales in contexts inside and outside school. This theoretical framework informs the heuristic model and tool for analysing writer development as a sociocultural and textual practice in school which Elf employs.

In following the teenager Amalie from her last year in middle school and into the high-school education programme called *htx*, a three-year higher technical education programme, Elf engaged in intensive field work, including participant observation of her writing at school, collecting all writing prompts for and the actual written assignments, all the feedback she received on these assignments, and ongoing interviews. Elf conducted a timescales analysis of how and why this young adolescent develops as a writer and found that Amalie was 'taught by bitter experience' to write, as she reflects in a late interview. She makes some rather dramatic turns in terms of writer identification, from 'loving' writing in science in middle school to 'hating it' in high school, due to a lack of feedback, amongst other reasons. However, at the end of high school, Elf indicates that there are signs that Amalie is restoring her old interest through the writing of and reflection upon an interdisciplinary writing project that includes social science and science. On the basis of this case study, Elf argues that both researchers and teachers need to be wary of making any absolute conclusions about students' 'linear' development of writer identity; rather, he asserts, the evidence reveals their fluid, idiosyncratic and patterned nature (Andrews and Smith, 2011). Additionally, Elf's timescales approach to writer development offers new methodological and empirical insights into how to understand such developments in practice.

The final chapter by Ryan considers the ways in which students and teachers shape texts and identities together. Drawing on data from linguistically and culturally diverse primary-phase children in Australia, Ryan focuses on writing as a social performance and as a significant form of identity work. Conscious that young people perform their identities through writing in diverse ways and particularly in incongruent and fluid social media contexts beyond school, she argues that the teaching of writing in school needs to support students in navigating such highly visible contexts to make writing decisions that represent themselves and others in appropriate and intended ways. She posits that students need to be enabled as reflexive writers with access to diverse repertoires from which they can choose, and with an accompanying self-awareness of the implications of writing choices in different contexts. Drawing on the work of Archer's (2007, 2012) critical realist theory of reflexivity (as Brady also does), Ryan further argues that teachers need to understand their own and their students' modes of reflexivity so they can create enabling pedagogic conditions that prompt the reflexive processes of action and re-action, and engender satisfying and successful writing practices for all.

Illustrative examples of children's writing samples and interviews are presented through Ryan's examination of Archer's (2007) four reflexive modes: communicative, autonomous, meta-reflexive and fractured. She notes that whilst writers may use all four, each tends to have a predominant mode. Ryan highlights the indicators that constitute each mode and reflects upon the conditions that may produce and/or perpetuate it. Importantly, she also considers the potential constraints for students who enact that mode. For example, she demonstrates that when students who tend to be communicative reflexives are given constant guidance and direction about every aspect of writing, their reflexivity may only be 'enabled' to rely on their teacher's suggestions. Ryan recognises the many tensions and complexities involved and makes recommendations for the teaching of writing that enable a meta-reflexive approach to the identity work involved. She argues that developing students' reflexive writing identities is an imperative for contemporary times and asserts that meta-reflexivity is the mode that will most enable students to negotiate variable conditions of writing and develop identities as writers with something to say.

The volume as a whole adopts the view that reflexive debate amongst scholars about writer identity and the teaching and learning of writing will likewise enhance the potential for developing young writers with something to say and the assurance to say it, in part through generating intellectual energy and discussion about teachers', professional writers' and students' writer identities and continued exploration of the consequences for pedagogy and practice. Additionally it is hoped that through the identification of alternative approaches to examining writers' identities and the opening up of compelling new lines of inquiry, the volume will make a valuable contribution to the field.

References

Andrews, R., and Smith, A. (2011) *Developing Writers: Teaching and Learning in the Digital Age*. Milton Keynes: McGraw-Hill/Open University Press.

Archer, M. S. (2003) *Structure, Agency and the Internal Conversation*. Cambridge: Cambridge University Press.

Archer, M. S. (2007) *Making Our Way Through the World: Human Reflexivity and Social Mobility*. Cambridge: Cambridge University Press.

Archer, M. S. (2012) *The Reflexive Imperative in Late Modernity*. Cambridge: Cambridge University Press.

Bhabha, H. K. (1994) *The Location of Culture*. London: Routledge.

Boym, S. (1994) *Common Places: Mythologies of Everyday Life in Russia*. Cambridge, MA: Harvard University Press.

Bucholtz, M., and Hall, K. (2005) 'Language and identity', in Duranti, A. (ed.), *A Companion to Linguistic Anthropology*. Malden, MA: Blackwell, pp. 369–394.

Burgess, A., and Ivanič, R. (2010) 'Writing and being written: issues of identity across time-scales'. *Written Communication, 27*, 228–255.

Carney, M., and Indrisano, R. (2013) 'Disciplinary literacy and pedagogical content knowledge'. *Journal of Education, 193*, 3, 39–49.

Cremin, T. (2006) 'Creativity, uncertainty and discomfort: teachers as writers'. *Cambridge Journal of Education, 36*, 3, 415–433.

Cremin, T., and Baker, S. (2010) 'Exploring teacher-writer identities in the classroom: conceptualising the struggle'. *English Teaching: Practice and Critique, 9*, 3, 8–25.

Cremin, T., and Myhill, D. (2012) Writing Voices: Creating Communities of Writers, London, Routledge.

Cremin, T., and Baker, S. (2014) 'Exploring the discursively constructed identities of a teacher-writer teaching writing'. *English Teaching: Practice and Critique, 13*, 3, 28–53.

Cremin, T., and Oliver, J. (2016) 'Teachers as writers: a systematic review'. *Research Papers in Education*. Retrieved from http://dx.doi.org/10.1080/02671522.2016.1187664.

Ellsworth, E. (1997) *Teaching Positions: Difference, Pedagogy, and the Power of Address*. New York: Teachers College Press.

Gannon, S., and Davies, C. (2007) 'For love of the word: English teaching, affect and writing'. *Changing English, 14*, 1, 87–98.

Gardner, P. (2014) 'Becoming a teacher of writing: primary student teachers reviewing their relationship with writing'. *English in Education, 48*, 2, 128–148.

Grimberg, B., and Hand, B. (2009) 'Cognitive pathways: analysis of students' written texts for science understanding'. *International Journal of Science Education, 31*, 4, 503–521.

Hammack, P. (2011) 'Narrative and the politics of meaning'. *Narrative Inquiry, 21*, 2, 311–318.

Holland, D., Lachicotte, W., Skinner, D., and Cain, C. (1998) *Identity and Agency in Cultural Worlds*. Cambridge, MA: Harvard.

Holland, D., and Lave, J. (2001) 'History in person: an introduction', in Holland, D., and Lave, J. (eds), *History in Person: Enduring Struggles, Contentious Practice, Intimate Identities*. Sante Fe, NM: School of American Research Press, pp. 1–32.

Ivanič, R. (1998) *Writing and Identity: The Discoursal Construction of Identity in Academic Writing*. Amsterdam: Benjamins.

Ivanič, R. (2004) 'Discourses of writing and learning to write'. *Language and Education, 18*, 3, 220–245.

Kendrick, M. (2005) 'Playing house: a "sideways" glance at literacy and identity in early childhood'. *Journal of Early Childhood Literacy, 5*, 1, 5–28.

Lave, J., and Wenger, E. (1991) *Situated Learning: Legitimate Peripheral Participation*. Cambridge: Cambridge University Press.

Lemke, J. L. (2000) 'Across the scales of time: artifacts, activities, and meanings in ecosocial systems'. *Mind, Culture, and Activity, 7*, 273–290.

Locke, T., Whitehead, D., Dix, S., and Cawkwell, G. (2011) 'New Zealand teachers respond to the 'National Writing Project' experience'. *Teacher Development, 15*, 3, 273–291.

Locke, T., and Kato, H. (2012) 'Poetry for the broken-hearted: how a marginal year 12 English class was turned on to writing'. *English in Australia, 47*, 1, 61–79.

Locke, T., Whitehead, D., and Dix, S. (2013) 'The impact of "Writing Project" professional development on teachers' self-efficacy as writers and teachers of writing'. *English in Australia, 48*, 2, 55–69.

Locke, T. (2013) 'Assessing student poetry: balancing the demands of two masters'. *English Teaching: Practice and Critique, 12*, 1, 23–45.

Locke, T., and Johnston, M. (2016) 'Developing an individual and collective self-efficacy scale for the teaching of writing in high schools'. *Assessing Writing, 28*, 1–14.

Lortie, D. (1975) *Schoolteacher: A Sociological Study*. Chicago, IL: University of Chicago Press.

Luce-Kapler, R., Chin, J., O'Donnell, E., and Stoch, S. (2001) 'The design of writing: unfolding systems of meaning'. *Changing English, 8*, 1, 43–52.

McKinney, M. and Giorgis, C. (2009) 'Narrating and performing identity: Literacy specialists' writing identities', *Journal of Literacy Research, 41*, 1, 104–149.

Moll, L., Amanti, C., Neff, D., and Gonzalez, N. (1992) 'Funds of knowledge for teaching: using a qualitative approach to connect homes and classrooms'. *Theory into Practice, 31*, 132–141.

Morgan, D. N., and Pytash, K. E. (2014) 'Preparing preservice teachers to become teachers of writing: a 20-year review of the research literature'. *English Education, 47*, 1, 6–32.

Morgan, W. (2006) '"Poetry makes nothing happen": creative writing and the English classroom'. *English Teaching: Practice and Critique, 5*, 2, 17–33.

Owocki, G., and Goodman, Y. (2002). *Kidwatching: Documenting Children's Literacy Development*. Portsmouth, NH: Heinemann.

Peel, R. (1995) 'Primary teachers as writers: a preliminary survey of B.Ed English students perceptions of writing'. *Reading, 29*, 2, 23–26.

Phelan, P. (1993) *Unmarked: The Politics of Performance*. New York: Routledge.

Richardson, P. (1998) 'Literacy, learning and teaching'. *Educational Review, 50*, 2, 115–134.

Riessman, C. K. (2003) 'Analysis of personal narratives', in Holstein, J., and Gubruium, J. F. (eds), *Inside Interviewing: New Lenses, New Concerns*. London: Sage, pp. 331–346.

Ryan, M. E. (2014) 'Writers as performers: developing reflexive and creative writing sidentities'. *English Teaching: Practice and Critique, 13*, 130–148.

Shanahan, T., and Shanahan, C. (2008) 'Teaching disciplinary literacy to adolescents: rethinking content-area literacy'. *Harvard Educational Review, 78*, 1, 40–59.

Street, B. V. (1984) *Literacy in Theory and Practice*. Cambridge: Cambridge University Press.

Street, B. V. (2008) 'New literacies, new times: developments in literacy studies', in Street, B. V., and Hornberger, N. (eds), *Literacy: Encyclopedia of Language and Education*, Vol. 2. New York: Springer, pp. 3–14.

Whitney, A. (2008) 'Teacher transformation in the national writing project'. *Research in the Teaching of English*, pp. 144–187.

Wohlwend, K. E. (2009) 'Damsels in discourse: girls consuming and producing identity texts through Disney princess play'. *Reading Research Quarterly, 44*, 1, 57–83.

Wohlwend, K. E. (2011) *Playing Their Way into Literacies: Reading, Writing, and Belonging in the Early Childhood Classroom*. New York: Teachers College Press.

Yagelski, R. P. (2011) *Writing As a Way of Being: Writing Instruction, Nonduality, and the Crisis of Sustainability*. New York: Hampton Press.

Yeo, M. (2007) 'New literacies, alternative texts: teachers' conceptualisations of composition and literacy'. *English Teaching: Practice and Critique, 6*, 1, 113–131.

SECTION A
Writing, writers and identity

1

CONCEPTUALISING WRITING AND IDENTITY

Ian Eyres

Conceptions of literacy

Traditional understandings of literacy

The idea that 'writing consists of applying knowledge of a set of linguistic patterns and rules for sound–symbol relationships and sentence construction' has underlain 'a great deal of policy and practice in literacy education' (Ivanič, 2004, p. 227) in many English-speaking countries. A traditional approach to teaching writing focuses on the teacher as authority, instructor and sole audience; the teacher of discrete skills, such as spelling and planning and the suppression of errors. Interaction, especially between learners, has not been encouraged (Smith and Elley, 1998). Implicit in such an approach is the idea that writing can be accounted for in purely cognitive terms, a matter of manipulating symbols, with the writer coordinating a complex variety of elements (Wray and Medwell, 2006). More recent psychologically based models of writing have cast the student writer in a more agentive, problem-solving role than in the traditional classroom, and afford some room for social context in terms of both the 'task environment' (Flower and Hayes, 1980) and the text's eventual audience. However, they persist in characterising the writing task as a matter of orchestrating cognitive processes (Flower and Hayes, 1980; Bereiter and Scardamalia, 1987), an endeavour to be undertaken, albeit with some teacher support, by the individual learner. Indeed, one model (Bereiter and Scardamalia, 1987) identifies the need to compose without the benefit of a conversational partner, as one of the key features of writing which the young writer needs to accommodate (Smith and Elley, 1998).

This conceptualisation of literacy learning as a matter of individuals acquiring 'asocial' cognitive skills which are 'dislodged from their socio-cultural moorings in human relationships and communities of practice' (Richardson, 1998, p. 116) has been called an 'autonomous' model (Street, 1984). This perspective takes little or no account of the role of immediate social and cultural contexts or the institution-alised nature of many forms of writing (Schultz and Fecho, 2000).

Through the years, curricula reflecting the autonomous model have enjoyed credence with education policymakers and in the current neoliberal climate it is easy to see why. The conception of literacy as a set of skills allows 'normative assumptions' (Luke and Woods, 2009, p. 198) and relatively easy regulation through the top-down imposition of policy strategies implemented by means of behavioural rewards and punishments linked to test scores (Luke and Woods, 2009). Such a view may also underpin 'a common matrix of premises about accountability as test-ing, standardization as uniformity of method, competitive marketization of schools, central surveillance of teachers' (Luke and Woods, 2009, p. 200). Moreover, a con-ception of literacy as a fixed code encourages the development of a teacher-proof literacy curriculum (Poulson and Avramidis, 2003).

The assumption of a straightforward connection between easily measurable levels of literacy attainment, and social progress, mental development and indi-viduals' economic fitness (Collins, 2000) enables the construction of 'perceived crises based on fears that poor teaching and unprepared graduates are causing an inability to compete economically with other nations' (Burns, 2012, p. 93). Such appeals can be practically irresistible: 'In simple terms how could any educational professional or politician stand against raising standards in literacy?' (Goodwyn and Findlay, 2003, p. 31).

The autonomous model, although presented as a 'a socially neutral "technology of the intellect"' (Collins, 2000, p. 71), serves to preserve the power of the domi-nant group by enabling them to 'view their literate practices as universal and to institutionalize them' (Burns, 2012, p. 94). Moreover, any responsibility to improve standards of literacy is placed squarely on schools without any consideration of wider social and economic factors (Luke and Woods, 2009).

A sociocultural view of literacy

An alternative standpoint holds that, as an activity which is always embedded within social and cultural interactions (MacCleod, 2004), literacy cannot be under-stood outside of its social and cultural context. Rather than simply being an abstract code to be learnt, literacy is something that happens in a unique way within each 'literacy event', and habitual ways of doing literacy constitute 'literacy practices' (Street, 2003). Both practices and events, while being situated within their imme-diate physical, social and cultural context, are also constructed by a wider political and ideological context (MacCleod, 2004). Proponents of a sociocultural literacies perspective take the view that any engagement with literacy is a social act since

> The ways in which teachers or facilitators and their students interact is already a social practice that affects the nature of the literacy being learned and the ideas about literacy held by the participants.
>
> *(Street, 2003, p. 78)*

Within a sociocultural perspective, literacy has been defined as 'the learning and use of symbols . . . mediated by and constituted in social systems and cultural practices' (Moje et al., 2008, p. 109) and understood 'principally as a form of social participation', with literacy learning seen 'principally as a form of socialisation' (Brandt and Clinton, 2002, p. 342). Ethnographic research has shown how children's conception of the social context of literacy has a bearing on their ability to adopt the literacy practices of school (Heath, 1983), and this entails an acceptance that children's developing control of the symbolic system of literacy is not a simple matter of solving a cognitive puzzle but also, simultaneously, 'the child's increasingly active participation in a cultural dialogue' (Dyson, 1991, p. 106) and the 'negotiation of social worlds' (Schultz and Fecho, 2000). The world is therefore seen as 'socially constructed, where knowledge is in flux and issues are complicated by deep structures of multiply-perceived meaning' (Schultz and Fecho, p. 51). As the learner strives to order personal thoughts to address others, the public nature of the linguistic signs means that they also represent aspects of societal order (Dyson, 1995).

Although this body of theory originated only towards the end of the twentieth century (Whitney, 2008), the idea that literacy is a situated social practice has been described as 'something of an orthodoxy' in current literacy research (Brandt and Clinton, 2002, p. 337). The concept of learning as a social practice, involving a growing relationship with a group until one has the capacity to become a full member, has been developed as a theory of 'communities of practice' (Lave and Wenger, 1991). Participants, through practice, learn to behave as other community members; to become a writer, therefore, is to join a community of writers (Street, 2003; Dix and Cawkwell, 2011). Thus, the literacy practices of any given classroom have a direct bearing on the literate identity of both teacher and learners, since 'how we believe, how we interact, what we value, what we think, what we believe, what we say, what we read and so on are all part of our identity' (MacCleod, 2004, p. 246).

Conceptualising identity

Self and identity

So far I have used the term identity without defining it, and it has perhaps been understood in the everyday meaning of a personal sense of self. In everyday thinking, personal identity or an essential self is a given (Gubrium and Holstein, 2000), and viewed as something both distinctive and constant. While such a conceptualisation is, as will become clear, problematic, personal belief in 'a singular authentic self', 'resolutely available as a beacon to guide us', remains 'the leading experiential project of our era' (Gubrium and Holstein, 2000, p. 96) and subjectivity remains an essential part of any more complex conception of identity. However, alongside the 'internalized process' of the personal sense of self, an individual's actions in social and cultural contexts can also be considered as 'situated performance' (Thorne 2004, p. 5). The inward and outward-facing nature of identity has also been characterised as a matter of operating at two levels, 'the interpersonal (seeming) and the intrapersonal (feeling)' (Bartlett, 2007, p. 35).

Identity as situated performance

Approaches to identity that draw upon sociocultural and critical theory highlight the role of individuals' relationship with 'people, institutions and practices' (Sarup, 1996, p. 102). Since individuals habitually adjust their behaviour actively to meet external demands (McAdams, 2001), identity is 'nurtured by a myriad of social affiliations' (Thorne, 2004, p. 364). Situated performance may express membership of such personal, social and cultural categories as race, class and gender (Hall, 1990; Wortham, 2004), affiliations which may often be assigned via power relations (Holland and Leander, 2004).

Rather than as a state or condition, identity can be seen as an active and continuing process of identification: solidarity or allegiance arising from the recognition of characteristics shared with other individuals, local social and cultural groups or wider categories such as race, class and gender, in a way which reflects the power relations of society (Hall, 1990; Wortham, 2004; Holland and Leander, 2004). Alternatively, identities may be constructed 'through difference'; that is, in relation to an (often more powerful) group with which an individual does not identify (Hall, 1990).

From this perspective, identities are enacted through the interaction of personal, social and cultural elements in different contexts and activities (Lewis et al., 2007). The need to negotiate one's position within activity means that identity is an active pursuit, the 'doing of identity' (Moje and Luke, 2009, p. 431) which takes place at the interface of individual, society and culture. Identification is thus 'never complete, always in process' (Hall, 1990, p. 222) and is 'something fluid and dynamic that is produced, generated, developed, or narrated over time' (Moje and Luke, 2009, p. 418).

One theoretical framework designed to account for this fluidity does so in terms of 'figured worlds' (Holland et al., 1998), social and cultural environments in which the individual must construct or 'figure' roles for themselves and others. Through improvising actions the individual comes to figure their personal identity as well as those of others. Roles are not fixed, but constantly in the process of being created (Urrieta, 2007). This allows roles both for personal agency and for culture, situation and other participants. Rather than simply being a feature of the 'internal state' of the individual concerned, different identities may arise from their recognition by others, in or observing interaction (Gee, 2000). Identity is both about 'the "kind of person" one is recognised as "being"' (Gee, 2000, p. 1) and the kind of person one feels oneself to be, with considerable interplay between the two.

A similar perspective draws on the idea of positioning, a process through which 'individuals dynamically position themselves both toward and against others and thereby construct their identities' (Thorne, 2004, p. 5). Positioning may be mediated by culture and cultural artefacts 'constructing and producing historically specific persons as complicated social, cultural, and psychological beings' (Holland and Leander, 2004, p. 137). In the course of a day, most people will position themselves variously, sometimes conflictingly, in relation to numerous others (Moje and Luke, 2009). Positioning may be seen as the result of interpellation (Althusser, 2006), an invitation to take up a particular social position (Moje and Luke, 2009). In Althusser's model, an individual is interpellated (or 'hailed') by ideology. If compliant, they are cast as a subject of the ideology. A refusal is also an act of identity formation, in a reciprocal 'microproduction' of both a social position and 'a self who inhabits and comes to personify it' (Holland and Leander, 2004, p. 128). Positioning always involves negotiation and this is often in respect of multiple parties (Cremin and Baker, 2010). Positions may be taken personally or generically (e.g. 'the position of women') and the accumulation of positions over a period can result in strongly felt and complex elements of identity (Satterfield, 2004).

Identity as internalised process

The above discussion has concerned ways in which a range of continuing interactions serves to shape identities. This relates well to the dynamic nature of individual lives lived within cultures and societies and also helps explain why people in similar circumstances develop similar identities. However, if taken to its extreme, underplaying the role of personal agency as a deterministic view of identity as ineluctably shaped by circumstances (Munro, 1998; Watson, 2006), the perspective would fail to account for the individual differences that underlie subjectivities and for any individually experienced sense of self or subjectivity (Moje and Luke, 2009), which the individual may consider a core identity (Alsup, 2006) or an 'authentic self' (Gergen, 1991, p. 7).

This relationship between the personal and the social may be seen as mutually constructive or antagonistic. Gergen portrays his own self as besieged by social and professional demands amounting to a state of 'social saturation' (Gergen, 1991, p. 3). Rather than this eroding the 'personal self', however, heightened interactive opportunities enhance it in 'a proliferating and variegated panorama of sites of self-knowledge' (Gubrium and Holstein, 2000, p. 96). In the context of the workplace, however, requirements to perform a particular kind of self, especially through 'deep acting' which involves deliberately evoking required feelings (rather than 'surface acting', simply behaving to order), may result in 'emotional stress and burnout' (Hochschild, 1979, p. 558), perhaps due to the suppression of personal agency.

From a more objective standpoint, core identity may be constituted by an individual's 'unique trajectory through "discourse space"' (Gee, 2000, p. 24). Experiences are not 'disjointed episodes' (Adawu and Martin-Beltrán, 2012, p. 378) and the connection goes beyond a simple accumulation of memories. Actions and choices are taken in the light of past experiences and imagined futures (Hinchman and Hinchman, 1997) and past and future identities may each shape the other (Mishler, 1999). The source of personal identity has been described as a 'narratively structured unity' (Polkinghorne, 1991, p. 143).

The notions of 'core identity' and 'personal subjectivity' do not contradict a dynamic and socially grounded view of identity; individual agency must be taken into account. Self and identity therefore emanate from 'the interplay among institutional demands, restraints, and resources, on the one hand, and biographically informed, self-constituting social actions, on the other' (Gubrium and Holstein, 2000, p. 102).

Multiple identities

Continuing interaction implies the continual production of new subjectivities (Moje and Luke, 2009) and identities. At its simplest level, a person may be different at home from 'how she or he "is" at work' (Mishler, 1999). If people position and reposition themselves continually, their identities are 'multiple and always in flux' (Moje and Luke, 2009). Over time the effects of interactions relate to and combine with each other to achieve a greater complexity (Holland and Leander, 2004).

A number of metaphors have been used to account for multiple identities. Some, including sedimentation (Rowsell and Pahl, 2007; Holland and Leander, 2004) and 'lamination' (Bendix and Brenneis, 2005), see dynamic processes resulting in a stable outcome (sedimentary rock and a resounding cymbal respectively), though certainly in the former case at least, further deformation and reformation are envisaged. In constructing identity, the individual must not only integrate (synchronically) differing roles and relationships experienced at a given point in time but also (diachronically) with past, identity-constructing experiences (McAdams, 2001).

Others, including the concept of 'borderlands' (Alsup, 2006), emphasise the dynamic and continuing nature of identity formation. In accounting for the situation of students who are constructing a 'teacher' identity which is quite different from their earlier identities, Alsup says they 'find themselves living at the intersection of multiple worlds and multiple ways of knowing'. Their goal in developing new identities is not to erase these borders but to find ways of existing in the space between them, 'in which to experience a richer, fuller and more complex understanding of self and other' (Alsup, 2006, p. 15).

Narrative and identity

Personal narrative is intimately linked both to the individual self and 'a fundamental means of social interaction' (Stanley and Temple, 2008, p. 279). Narration is a collaborative practice, involving empathy, reciprocation (Riessman, 2003) and positioning. Autobiographical narrative (written or spoken) therefore supports identity construction by allowing the narrator to adopt particular positions in relation to both listeners and other characters in the narrative (Wortham, 2001) and so is performance rather than text; the performance embraces both the spoken words and their enactment within a social and cultural context. Through the act of narration, relationships are established between the narrator and the audience

(Wortham, 2001). Speakers make claims and assertions which demonstrate and therefore fashion aspects of their identity (Bamberg, 2005). The process may also involve the re-evaluation of oneself in accordance with a growing apprehension of others' perspectives (McVee, 2004).

As noted earlier, narrative allows individuals to assemble the 'vast aggregation of . . . episodes and stories' which help them maintain a core identity (Polkinghorne, 1991, p. 143), giving experience 'a unity that neither nature nor the past possesses so clearly' (Cronon, 1992, p. 134). Narratives may also promote a related sense of social situations, and of history (Bamberg and McCabe, 1998, p. iii). Through recounting personal stories, narrators reveal much about social and historical context (Riessman, 2003), while the shortest of anecdotes may 'pay tribute to the grand narratives of a culture' (McVee, 2004, p. 896). If narratives have 'transformative potential' (Wortham, 2001) for their tellers then they have a role to play in learning. We do not simply learn from experience, but also from the repeated recounting of it, and from listeners' responses.

Writing, identity and learning

Identity and learning to write

Until very recently, identity has been a relatively neglected focus in writing research, with teachers' writing identities having received 'scant attention' (Cremin and Baker, 2010). Any link between a writer identity and pedagogy has been no more than an 'unexamined assumption' (McKinney and Giorgis, 2009). This seems strange, given the intimate relationship between writing and personal identity (Cazden, 2009).

Literacy may have a benign or malign impact on one's sense of identity (McCarthey, 2001). If literacy is 'a social process' whose various technologies are 'used within particular institutional frameworks for specific social purposes' (Street, 1984, p. 97), within literate societies there are many aspects of literacy and literacy practice which a person may be aligned with or alienated from. In a literate society, consciously not being a reader or writer can be as significant to identity as conscious proficiency or enthusiasm.

Agency, as well as being essential to identity construction, is central to the understanding of literacy teaching and learning. Agency allows learners to take ownership of their learning (Cremin et al., 2006) and construct personal identities (Van Sluys, 2004). Learning to write involves the opportunity to express one's own ideas in one's own way and to use the medium for one's own purposes (Fisher, 2006). The agency to adopt risky new identities is central to learning. The degree of learner agency in play is a significant factor in the nature of the classroom as a social and cultural environment. For the teacher's part, through acting in a creative way, characterised by spontaneity and flexibility, they are 'arguably . . . in a stronger position to develop the creative voice of the child' (Cremin, 2006).

The identities of learner writers

Learning has long been associated with the fashioning of identities (e.g. Lave and Wenger, 1991) and it has been argued that Vygotsky's (1978) conception of mental development occurring as individuals engage with the world around them is a matter of both 'awareness of self' and 'formation of self' (McCarthey and Moje, 2002).

Furthermore, literacy development cannot be understood without reference to 'the local culture of the classroom', which constitutes the environment in which literacy develops (Schultz and Fecho, 2000, p. 56). While this is often understood in terms of the individual learner being shaped by their experience, it has been argued that the interactions with teacher and peers which contribute to each writer's work mean that a more collective understanding is in order, with learning viewed as a social rather than a developmental process (Bourne, 2002).

Learning to write has been characterised as the adoption of a writer identity through inter- and intrapersonal identity work and engagement with a wide range of cultural artefacts, with learners working to enter the figured world of '"the educated person"' (Bartlett, 2007, p. 56) and to participate effectively in the cultural practices of literacy. Through such identity work, an individual comes to function in terms of the systems and practices of literacy. Thus, in the context of the discourses of classrooms, the learner-writer is entering into 'new signifying practices which produce new relations of meanings' (Bourne, 2002). Through the variety of discourses and discursive practices of the classroom, many positions are open to learners. The ways in which teachers and others frame the learner's work, challenge them to adopt the social conventions represented by written language. From this perspective, learning to write has been likened to the ways in which young children construct both oral language and subjectivity through interaction (Bourne, 2002). The social negotiation necessary to this process is of both a 'cognitive/strategic' and 'emotional/motivational' nature (McCarthey, 2001); the learner must solve the intellectual puzzle of literacy learning, but they must also want to join 'the literacy club' (Smith, 1988).

I have argued above that individuals use what they know about how others perceive them in the construction of their own subjectivities, and such a process has been observed in classrooms, with the perceptions communicated explicitly or implicitly through the actions of teachers, parents and peers all playing a role in identity construction. Students are well aware of how adults talk about them (McCarthey, 2001). Traditionally, many teachers have applied multiple essentialist judgements such as 'shy', 'aggressive', 'motivated' or 'lazy' to individuals (McCarthey and Moje, 2002; Bourne, 2002). Teachers may also have expectations according to a learner's race, class, culture and gender; for example, research suggests some take negative stereotypical attitudes about poorer families into the classroom with them (Redeaux, 2011). Perceptions such as these, and particularly judgements that a child is or is not 'bright' or a 'high-attainer', affect the nature of feedback given to an individual, with significant consequences for the student as a reader (e.g. Hall, 2012) and for their sense of self as a writer and the quality of a student's writing (e.g. Bourne, 2002). (See also Chapter 2 on the impact of teacher feedback on the emerging identities of children who later became respected professional writers.) Teachers' perceptions of individual children may also affect instructional decisions such as which texts children are required to read and for how long (McCarthey and Moje, 2002). Bourne (2002) and Hall (2012) offer empirical evidence that within the discourses of the classroom, such labelling means that access to certain roles or identities is restricted for certain children.

Moreover, young people's perceptions of who they are – whatever the extent to which these perceptions are influenced by the judgements of others – have an important bearing on how they respond, interact and learn in the classroom (McCarthey and Moje, 2002). Their personal sense of efficacy affects how an individual performs (McCarthey, 2001). In the context of literacy, McCarthey's research found students to have a sense both of 'who they were as readers and writers' but also of 'the value they placed on these activities' (2001, p. 143). Students' perceptions of other students were affected by their apparent degree of success in literacy and literacy played a part in how students viewed themselves, especially in the case of those who saw themselves as successful writers. McCarthey describes a virtuous progression for those frequent and fluent writers who came to see literacy as increasingly essential to their identity and to the cultural practices they engage in. On the other hand, those who saw themselves as slow performers tended to avoid writing (McCarthey, 2001). She also notes that ability grouping, a public formalisation of how teachers view students as writers, affects performance in just the same way that the highly visible assignation of children to colour-coded reading levels made a substantial contribution to how they saw themselves as readers (ibid., 2001).

Despite the power of teachers and others to influence identity formation, it is important to remember that learners position themselves agentively within the discourses of the classroom (Bourne, 2002). They do this in respect of a whole range of literacy practices in ways that may be influenced by cultural expectations from home (McCarthey and Moje, 2002). Bourne's close observation of children working together on a writing task showed interactions in which children differentially made demands on each other, 'defending or creating a place for themselves in the classroom "pecking order"' as they developed their text (2002, pp. 244–5). She argues that educators would do better to pay attention to this kind of social positioning than to individually located constructs of identity such as maturity and ability.

The identity of writer-teachers

Developments in theory and research that frame writing as socially and culturally situated and constructed have been linked to the much discussed proposition that it is important for writing teachers to be writers. A recent systematic review of the research in this area concludes that:

> teachers have narrow conceptions of what counts as writing and being a writer and that multiple tensions exist. These relate to low self-confidence,

negative writing histories, and the challenge of composing and enacting the positions of teacher and writer in the classroom. This suggests that for many teachers the teaching of writing is experienced as problematic. This is likely to have consequences for student motivation and achievement.

(Cremin and Oliver, 2016)

Indeed, even if writing is viewed as a freestanding cognitive process, a set of skills to be transferred from teacher to individual learner regardless of context or situation (Richardson, 1998), it is more than likely that teachers who personally possesses those skills – both at the level of knowing how texts and sentences are structured and words spelt and also at the level of familiarity with practical strategies related to the processes of composition – will be better equipped to explain and impart them to young learners.

The practice of a writer-teacher has the potential to be grounded in their experiences as an author and therefore the social and cultural practices of authors. Teacher and learners are able to take part in the classroom's cultural dialogue from a shared perspective. Learners taught by writer-teachers may be more concerned with 'how writers talk, act, and think, as well as issues concerning the content and mechanics of writing' (Frank, 2001, p. 469). Writer-teachers have the potential to help children as they become writers and develop their own writer identity. 'Instead of developing as writers who understand "writing" as spelling, editing, or grammar, these students use social and cultural practices that help them to develop identities as readers, writers, and speakers in a discourse of authors' (Frank, 2001, p. 472).

If teaching and learning are seen as socially and culturally situated and constructed, writer-teachers become both 'authors and authorities in the teaching of writing' (Whitney, 2008, p. 282) since their understanding of writing is grounded in 'what authors do as they write' rather than in the orthodoxies of writing pedagogy (Frank, 2001, p. 469). The three identified principles of 'authorship', 'authority' and 'authorisation' entail agency in terms of the use of personal knowledge and experience to construct knowledge (Wood and Lieberman, 2000). In classrooms where learners have the agency to choose how they write and learn, they are free to adopt (or not) the writing behaviours of their teachers. Claims, albeit contested ones, have been made for the benefits of teachers' simply allowing pupils to see them writing, both while the children write themselves (Graves, 1983) and as part of their daily routine (Bearne, 1998). It is argued that if teachers show writing to be part of their own lives, children will see 'writer' as a desirable role: 'teachers must show the advantages that membership in the club of writers offers' (Smith, 1988, p. 26). It has also been argued that through 'the act of living one's life under the gaze of another', as an active writer, a teacher may induct students to 'conduct their own lives in literate ways' (Kaufman, 2002, p. 56) and be perceived as a fellow writer (Augsburger, 1998; Cremin and Myhill, 2012). Such fellow writers are arguably repositioned in the classroom in a less traditionally hierarchical manner and may thus lend their authority to students and authorise alternative writing practices. (See Chapter 7 for an examination of a teacher who seeks to reposition himself as a writer in the classroom and Chapter 8 for a close analysis of authorisation in action.)

It is worth noting that for learners to be able to follow their teacher's example, they need a significant degree of choice or agency in the writing they undertake. This is not always evident in the genre and skills paradigms which have formed the basis of the English curriculum in England and other countries in recent decades (Beard, 1999). Indeed, it has been suggested that writing which has some personal value 'may have to be conducted outside the constraints of timetabled lessons and become part of the fabric of extra-curricula [sic] activities' (Domaille and Edwards, 2006, p. 75).

Teachers may choose to make their writer identity visible by sharing their own texts written outside the classroom (Street, 2003) and may earn the trust of younger learners by revealing something of themselves and their history as writers (Street and Stang, 2008). Teachers who are reflectively engaged as writers, through professional development or initial teacher education for example, may learn more about themselves as writers and about writing and from inside the process (e.g. Cremin and Myhill, 2012; McKinney and Giorgis, 2009). It has also been argued that students will be more motivated to write if their teachers are prepared to share the affective aspects of the writing experience – both the pain and joy (Gleeson and Prain, 1996) – and their passion for writing (Street, 2003). Sharing the agony may be of particular value since, as many researchers evidence, writing is an activity which can often leave teachers feeling vulnerable and anxious (Gannon and Davies, 2007; Cremin, 2006; Luce-Kapler et al., 2001). Through renewing their experience of writing and reflecting actively upon it, teachers may come to appreciate how difficult children can find it.

Notwithstanding these arguments about teachers as writers, Cremin and Oliver's (2016) systematic review of research in this area from 1990–2015 only identified 22 studies which 'were considered sufficiently rigorous for inclusion in the review; earlier studies tended to be anecdotal and lacked analytic detail'. In addition and significantly, with regard to the impact of teachers' writing on student outcomes, the review reveals this is both limited and inconclusive (Cremin and Oliver, 2016). In the light of this work, the current volume includes studies which offer new and carefully documented insights into teachers', professional writers' and students' histories and identities as writers. Some of them also explore the difference this makes in the classroom.

Conclusion

Although it can be thought of as an abstract code, in reality, writing only exists or takes place in the context of literacy events and practices. From this perspective, learning to write is less a matter of acquiring skills and habits than of becoming a writer or developing a writer identity. Writing is unavoidably a medium of (willing or unwilling) self-expression. Through their texts, each writer reveals much about personal identity, social affiliations and how they understand and respond to the world, since writing embodies both personal voice and stance. Writing also reveals the degree of the writer's skill in the medium itself.

Identity, in turn, is not a simple matter of personal essence but something that is constantly enacted and changing through each individual's encounters with society and culture. This dynamic conception of identity recognises the importance of agency and personal subjectivity, the latter growing and developing through interaction within social and cultural contexts. An essential way in which these interactions take place is through the use of narrative to present and position oneself towards others.

All writing pedagogies, even those that view writing as able to operate 'autonomously', function within the social and cultural context of the classroom, and therefore the identities of students and teachers have a significant role to play in the learning which takes place. Learners build a writing self as they establish personal positions within the discourses and literacy practices and events of the classroom and the wider world. Therefore research into the learning of writing needs a wide focus which seeks to understand how these classroom encounters play out and to explore writing as a social and cultural phenomenon as well as a personal one.

It has been argued that teachers are more effective in teaching writing if they are writers themselves and are able to share their writer identity with their pupils. While there are a variety of reasons why this may be true, it must be acknowledged that most teachers do not profess to be writers. However, the question of how those teachers who perceive themselves to be writers manage and exploit their dual identities in their classrooms is one that is beginning to be more extensively researched. This question, alongside others relating to students' identities as writers, is examined more fully in the chapters to come.

References

Adawu, A. and Martin-Beltrán, M. (2012) 'Points of transition: understanding the constructed identities of L2 learners/users across time and space', *Critical Inquiry in Language Studies*, vol. 9, no. 4, pp. 376–400.

Alsup, J. (2006) *Teacher Identity Discourses: Negotiating Personal and Professional Spaces*. London, Routledge.

Althusser, L. (2006) 'Ideology and ideological state apparatuses (notes towards an investigation)', in Sharma, A. and Gupta, A. (eds) *The Anthropology of the State: A Reader*, Oxford, Wiley Blackwell, pp. 86–111.

Augsburger, D. J. (1998) 'Teacher as writer: Remembering the agony, sharing the ecstasy', *Journal of Adolescent and Adult Literacy*, vol. 41, no. 7. Retrieved from http://eds.a.ebscohost.com.libezproxy.open.ac.uk/ehost/detail/detail?sid=f7f1ddd1-fe4b-4977-92e1-bc371c46002e%40sessionmgr4001&vid=3&hid=4211&bdata=JnNpdGU9Z Whvc3QtbGl2ZSZzY29wZT1zaXRl#db=a9h&AN=438030.

Bamberg, M. G. (2005) 'Narrative discourse and identities', in Kindt, T., Schernus, W. and Meister, J. C. (eds) *Narratology Beyond Literary Criticism: Mediality, Disciplinarity*, Berlin, De Gruyter, pp. 213–237.

Bamberg, M. G. and McCabe, A. (1998) 'Editorial', *Narrative Inquiry*, vol. 8, no. 1, pp. iii–v.

Bartlett, L. (2007) 'To seem and to feel: Situated identities and literacy practices', *The Teachers College Record*, vol. 109, no. 1, pp. 51–69.

Beard, R. (1999) *National Literacy Strategy: Review of Research and other Related Evidence*, London, Department for Education and Employment.

Bearne, E. (1998) *Making Progress in English*, London, Routledge.

Bendix, R. and Brenneis, D. (2005) *Senses*, Münster, LIT Verlag.

Bereiter, C. and Scardamalia, M. (1987) *The Psychology of Written Composition*, Hillsdale, NJ, Lawrence Erlbaum Associates.

Bourne, J. (2002) '"Oh what will miss say!" Constructing texts and identities in the discursive processes of classroom writing', *Language and Education* vol. 16, no. 4, pp. 241–259.

Brandt, D. and Clinton, K. (2002) 'Limits of the local: Expanding perspectives on literacy as a social practice', *Journal of Literacy Research*, vol. 34, no. 3, pp. 337–356.

Burns, L. D. (2012) 'Standards, policy paradoxes, and the new literacy studies: A call to professional political action', *Journal of Adolescent and Adult Literacy*, vol. 56, no. 2, pp. 93–97.

Cazden, C. (2009) 'Writing a narrative of multiple voices', in Carter, A., Lillis, T. and Parkin, S. (eds) *Why Writing Matters: Issues of Access and Identity in Writing Research and Pedagogy*, Amsterdam/Philadelphia, John Benjamins, pp. 3–5.

Collins, J. (2000) 'Bernstein, Bourdieu and the new literacy studies', *Linguistics and Education*, vol. 11, no. 1, pp. 65–78.

Cremin, T. (2006) 'Creativity, uncertainty and discomfort: Teachers as writers', *Cambridge Journal of Education*, vol. 36, no. 3, pp. 415–433.

Cremin, T. and Baker, S. (2010) 'Exploring writer-teacher identities in the classroom: Conceptualising the struggle', *English Teaching: Practice and Critique*, vol. 9, no. 3, pp. 8–25

Cremin, T. and Myhill, D. (2012) *Writing Voices: Creating Communities of Writers*, London, Routledge.

Cremin, T. and Baker, S. (2014) 'Exploring the discursively constructed identities of a teacher-writer teaching writing', *English Teaching: Practice and Critique*, vol. 13, no. 3, pp. 28–53.

Cremin, T. and Oliver, J. (2016) 'Teachers as writers: A systematic review', *Research Papers in Education*. Retrieved from http://dx.doi.org/10.1080/02671522.2016.1187664.

Cremin, T., Burnard, P. and Craft, A. (2006) 'Pedagogy and possibility thinking in the early years', *Thinking Skills and Creativity*, vol. 1, no. 2, pp. 108–119.

Cronon, W. (1992) 'A place for stories: Nature, history, and narrative', *The Journal of American History*, vol. 78, no. 4, pp. 1347–1376.

Dix, S. and Cawkwell, G. (2011) 'The influence of peer group response: Building a teacher and student expertise in the writing classroom', *English Teaching: Practice and Critique*, vol. 10, no. 4, pp. 41–57.

Domaille, K. and Edwards, J. (2006) 'Partnerships for learning: Extending knowledge and understanding of creative writing processes in the ITT year', *English in Education*, vol. 40, no. 2, pp. 71–84.

Dyson, A. H. (1991) 'Viewpoints: The word and the world – Reconceptualizing written language development or do rainbows mean a lot to little girls?', *Research in the Teaching of English*, vol. 25, no. 1, pp. 97–123.

Dyson, A. H. (1993) *Social Worlds of Children: Learning to Write in an Urban Primary School*, New York, Teachers College Press.

Dyson, A. H. (1995) 'Writing children reinventing the development of childhood literacy', *Written Communication*, vol. 12, no. 1, pp. 4–46.

Fisher, R. (2006) 'Whose writing is it anyway? Issues of control in the teaching of writing', *Cambridge Journal of Education*, vol. 36, no. 2, pp. 193–206.

Flower, L. and Hayes, J. R. (1980) 'A cognitive process theory of writing', *College Composition and Communication*, vol. 31, pp. 365–387.

Frank, C. R. (2001) 'What new things these words can do for you: A focus on one writing-project teacher and writing instruction', *Journal of Literacy Research*, vol. 33, no. 3, pp. 467–506.

Gannon, S. and Davies, C. (2007) 'For love of the word: English teaching, affect and writing', *Changing English*, vol. 14, no. 1, pp. 87–98.

Gee, J. P. (2000) *Identity as an Analytic Lens for Research in Education* (Revised November 2000). Retrieved from http://www.jamespaulgee.com/sites/default/files/pub/Identity.pdf.

Gergen, K. J. (1991) *The Saturated Self*, New York, Basic Books.

Gleeson, A. and Prain, V. (1996) 'Should teachers of writing write themselves? An Australian contribution to the debate', *The English Journal*, vol. 85, no. 6, pp. 42–49.

Goodwyn, A. and Findlay, K. (2003) 'Shaping literacy in the secondary school: Policy, practice and agency in the age of the National Literacy Strategy', *The British Journal of Educational Studies*, vol. 51, no. 1, pp. 20–35.

Graves, D. H. (1983) *Writing: Teachers and Children at Work*, London, Heinemann Educational Books.

Gubrium, J. and Holstein, J. (2000) 'The self in a world of going concerns', *Symbolic Interaction*, vol. 23, no. 2, pp. 95–115.

Hall, L. A. (2012) 'Rewriting identities: Creating spaces for students and teachers to challenge the norms of what it means to be a reader in school', *Journal of Adolescent and Adult Literacy*, vol. 55, pp. 368–373.

Hall, S. (1990) 'Cultural identity and diaspora', in Rutherford, J. (ed.) *Identity: Community, Culture, Difference*, London, Lawrence and Wishart, pp. 222–237.

Heath, S. B. (1983) *Ways with Words: Language, Life and Work in Communities and Classrooms*, Cambridge, Cambridge University Press.

Hinchman, L. P. and Hinchman, S. K. (1997) *Memory, Identity, Community: The Idea of Narrative in the Human Sciences*, Albany, State University of New York Press.

Hochschild, A. R. (1979) 'Emotion work, feeling rules and social structure', *American Journal of Sociology*, vol. 85, no. 3, pp. 551–575.

Holland, D., Lachicotte, W. and Skinner, D. (1998) *Identity and Agency in Cultural Worlds*, Cambridge, MA, Harvard University Press.

Holland, D. and Leander, K. (2004) 'Ethnographic studies of positioning and subjectivity: An introduction', *Ethos*, vol. 32, no. 2, pp. 127–139.

Ivanič, R. (1998) *Writing and Identity: The Discoursal Construction of Identity in Academic Writing*, Philadelphia, John Benjamins.

Ivanič, R. (2004) 'Discourses of writing and learning to write', *Language and Education*, vol. 18, no. 3, pp. 220–245.

Kaufman, D. (2002) 'Living a literate life, revisited', *The English Journal*, vol. 91, no. 6, pp. 51–57.

Labov, W. and Waletzky, J. (2003) 'Narrative analysis: oral versions of personal experience', in Paulston, C. B. and Tucker, G. R. (eds) *Sociolinguistics: The Essential Readings*, Oxford, Wiley Blackwell, pp. 74–104.

Lave, J. and Wenger, E. (1991) *Situated Learning: Legitimate Peripheral Participation*, Cambridge, Cambridge University Press.

Lewis, C., Enciso, P. and Moje, E. B. (2007) *Reframing Sociocultural Research on Literacy: Identity, Agency, and Power*, Mahwah, NJ, Lawrence Erlbaum Associates.

Luce-Kapler, R., Chin, J., O'Donnell, E. and Stoch, S. (2001) 'The design of writing: Unfolding systems of meaning', *Changing English*, vol. 8, no. 1, pp. 43–52.

Luke, A. and Woods, A. (2009) 'Policy and adolescent literacy', in Christenbury, L., Bomer, R. and Smagorinsky, P. (eds) *Handbook of Adolescent Literacy Research*, New York, Guilford Press, pp. 197–219.

McAdams, D. P. (2001) 'The psychology of life stories', *Review of General Psychology*, vol. 5, no. 2, p. 100.

McCarthey, S. J. (2001) 'Identity construction in elementary readers and writers', *Reading Research Quarterly*, vol. 36, no. 2, pp. 122–151.

McCarthey, S. J. and Moje, E. B. (2002) 'Identity matters', *Reading Research Quarterly*, vol. 37, no. 2, pp. 228–238.

MacCleod, F. (2004) 'Literacy identity and agency: Linking classrooms to communities', *Early Child Development and Care*, vol. 174, no. 3, pp. 243–252.

McKinney, C. and Norton, B. (2008) 'Identity in language and literacy education', in Spolsky, B. and Hult, F. M. (eds) *The Handbook of Educational Linguistics*, Chichester, West Sussex, Wiley-Blackwell, p. 192.

McKinney, M. and Giorgis, C. (2009) 'Narrating and performing identity: Literacy specialists writing identities', *Journal of Literacy Research*, vol. 41, no. 1, pp. 104–149.

McVee, M. B. (2004) 'Narrative and the exploration of culture in teachers, discussions of literacy, identity, self, and other', *Teaching and Teacher Education*, vol. 20, no. 8, pp. 881–899.

Mishler, E. G. (1999) *Storylines: Craft Artists' Narratives of Identity*, Cambridge, MA, Harvard University Press.

Moje, E. B. and Luke, A. (2009) 'Literacy and identity: Examining the metaphors in history and contemporary research', *Reading Research Quarterly*, vol. 44, no. 4, pp. 415–437.

Moje, E. B., Overby, M., Tysvaer, N. and Morris, K. (2008) 'The complex world of adolescent literacy: Myths, motivations, and mysteries', *Harvard Educational Review*, vol. 78, no. 1, pp. 107–154.

Munro, P. (1998) *Subject to Fiction*, Buckingham, Open University Press.

Peel, R., Patterson, A. H. and Gerlach, J. M. (2000) *Questions of English: Ethics, Aesthetics, Rhetoric, and the Formation of the Subject in England, Australia, and the United States*, London, Psychology Press.

Polkinghorne, D. E. (1991) 'Narrative and self-concept', *Journal of Narrative and Life History*, vol. 1, nos. 2 and 3, pp. 135–153.

Poulson, L. and Avramidis, E. (2003) 'Pathways and possibilities in professional development: Case studies of effective teachers of literacy', *British Educational Research Journal*, vol. 29, no. 4, pp. 543–560.

Redeaux, M. (2011) 'A framework for maintaining white privilege: A critique of Ruby Payne', in Ahlquist, R., Gorski, P. C. and Montano, T. (eds) *Assault on Kids: How Hyper-Accountability, Corporatization, Deficit Ideologies, and Ruby Payne are Destroying our Schools*, New York, Lang, pp. 177–198.

Richardson, P. (1998) 'Literacy, learning and teaching', *Educational Review*, vol. 50, no. 2, pp. 115–134.

Riessman, C. K. (2003) 'Analysis of personal narratives', in Holstein, J. and Gubruium, J. F. (eds) *Inside Interviewing: New Lenses, New Concerns*, London, Sage, pp. 331–346.

Rowsell, J. and Pahl, K. (2007) 'Sedimented identities in texts: Instances of practice', *Reading Research Quarterly*, vol. 42, no. 3, pp. 388–404.

Sarup, M. (1996) *Identity, Culture and the Postmodern World*, Edinburgh, Edinburgh University Press.

Satterfield, T. (2004) 'Emotional agency and contentious practice: Activist disputes in old-growth forests', *Ethos*, vol. 32, no. 2, pp. 233–256.

Schultz, K. and Fecho, B. (2000) 'Society's child: Social context and writing development', *Educational Psychologist*, vol. 35, no. 1, pp. 51–62.

Smith, F. (1988) *Joining the Literacy Club: Further Essays into Education*, Portsmouth, NH, Heinemann.

Smith, J. and Elley, W. (1998) *How Children Learn to Write: Insights from the New Zealand Experience*, London, Paul Chapman Educational Publishing.

Stanley, L. and Temple, B. (2008) 'Narrative methodologies: Subjects, silences, re-readings and analyses', *Qualitative Research*, vol. 8, no. 3, pp. 275–281.

Street, B. V. (1984) *Literacy in Theory and Practice*, Cambridge, Cambridge University Press.

Street, B. V. (2003) 'What's "new" in new literacy studies? Critical approaches to literacy in theory and practice', *Current Issues in Comparative Education*, vol. 5, no. 2, pp. 77–91.

Street, C. (2003) 'Pre-service teachers' attitudes about writing and learning to teach writing: Implications for teacher educators', *Teacher Education Quarterly*, vol. 30, no. 3, pp. 33–50.

Street, C. and Stang, K. (2008) 'Improving the teaching of writing across the curriculum: A model for teaching in-service secondary teachers to write', *Action in Teacher Education*, vol. 30, no. 1, pp. 37–49.

Thorne, A. (2004) 'Putting the person into social identity', *Human Development*, vol. 47, no. 6, pp. 361–365.

Urrieta, L. (2007) 'Figured worlds and education: An introduction to the special issue', *The Urban Review*, vol. 39, no. 2, pp. 107–116.

Van Sluys, K. (2004) 'The risk zone: Intersections of identity and literacy in a multiage, multilingual classroom', in Jeffrey, B. and Walford, G. (eds) *Ethnographies of Educational and Cultural Conflicts: Strategies and Resolutions*, Greenwich, CT, Jai Press, pp. 225–253.

Vygotsky, L. S. (1978) *Mind in Society*, Cambridge, MA, Harvard University Press.

Watson, C. (2006) 'Narratives of practice and the construction of identity', *Teachers and Teaching*, vol. 12, no. 5, pp. 509–526.

Whitney, A. (2008) 'Teacher transformation in the national writing project', *Research in the Teaching of English*, pp. 144–187.

Wood, D. R. and Lieberman, A. (2000) 'Teachers as authors: The National Writing Project's approach to professional development', *International Journal of Leadership in Education*, vol. 3, no. 3, pp. 255–273.

Wortham, S. (2001) *Narratives in Action: A Strategy for Research and Analysis*, New York, Teachers College Press.

Wortham, S. (2004) 'The interdependence of social identification and learning', *American Educational Research Journal*, vol. 41, no. 3, pp. 715–750.

Wray, D. and Medwell, J. (2006) *Progression in Writing and the Northern Ireland Levels for Writing*, A research review undertaken for the CCEA, Warwick, University of Warwick.

2

PROFESSIONAL WRITERS' IDENTITIES

The perceived influence of formal education and early reading

Teresa Cremin, Theresa Lillis, Debra Myhill and Ian Eyres

Introduction

The range and amount of writing taking place across all domains of life in the twenty-first century is expanding rapidly. At home, in school, at work and in the community, children, young people and adults write for numerous purposes and in multiple modes. Professional writers too capitalise on the multimodal diversity available and employ a range of materials and technologies. What it means to be a 'writer' in different domains and the myriad of influences upon individual writers' texts composed in different contexts is part of the focus of this book. Predominantly it explores the identities of teachers, trainee teachers and students as writers, both within and beyond school. However, this chapter focuses on the identities of professional writers. It draws upon a cross-university study which investigated the nature of twelve UK-based professional writers' identities and histories as writers and their composing practices.

There is a great deal of literature which retrospectively examines professional writers' life stories and personalities (e.g. Piirto, 2002; Kaufman, 2002; Goertzel, Goertzel and Goertzel, 1978), and a long tradition of self-reflection on the part of novelists and poets who write for children and young people, mainly considering their childhoods (e.g. Dahl, 1984; Ahlberg, 2014) and/or their compositional practices (e.g. Le Guin, 2004; Morpurgo, 2006). Additionally, there is considerable research examining academic writers' identities (e.g. Ivanič, 1998; Lea and Stierer, 2011; Lillis, 2001; Lillis and Curry, 2010) and some material produced by writers who have been or still are teachers (and vice versa), reflecting upon the challenges and interplay involved (e.g. Spiro, 2007; Vakil, 2008). Indeed, many well-known and respected writers, both novelists (e.g. David Lodge, Michael Morpurgo, Iris Murdoch, Maya Angelou, Philip Pullman) and poets (e.g. W.H. Auden, Tony Mitton, Robert Frost) have been teachers. There is, however, noticeably less research which explicitly employs an identity lens to consider the identity enactments and practices of professional writers from diverse domains. Within the current study, the perspectives of writers from three professional domains – novelists/poets, journalists/magazine columnists and academic writers – were examined. A biographical stance was adopted in the interviews conducted and on this basis the multiplicity and diversity of their voices and identity enactments were examined.

The intention of this chapter is to give voice to these professional writers' perspectives to complement those offered elsewhere in the book and to explore possible insights related to the teaching of writing and the development of young writers. To do so, it focuses upon data related to the writers' early reading practices and their reported experience of formal schooling.

The chapter commences by considering the challenge of developing young people's identities as writers in education, and then examines research into professional writers' identities. Then the research study's design and methodology are presented. Two research questions are explored:

- What significant/critical 'formal education' memories do the professional writers recall/report?
- What, if any, connections to early reading do the professional writers make?

Next the findings related to these questions are presented in turn and discussed. The chapter concludes by considering the ramifications for policy and practice.

Young writers' identities

Young people, like adults, write to communicate, to make meaning, to sustain and negotiate relationships and to get things done; in the process they portray themselves in specific ways. As Ryan (2014, p. 130) observes, 'writing is a social performance'. Research suggests that from the earliest years, young children's writing interests and identities are shaped by influential others, such as parents, peers and teachers (Dyson, 2009; Rowe, 2008). In particular, teachers' conceptions of writing and pedagogical practice frame, shape and often constrain the identity positions offered to young writers in school (Bourne, 2002; Bernstein, 2014). Drawing on a longitudinal study of adolescents' school-based writing identities, Elf highlights the danger of teachers ascribing students a fixed writer identity at a particular point in time (see Chapter 12). People's identities as writers are fluid, socially constructed and contextual. Indeed, research also reveals that the young, in seeking to exercise agency as authors, may take up or reject the roles on offer (Fisher, 2010; Ryan and Barton, 2014). As Rowe and Nietzel (2010) have shown, children's underlying interests and orientations influence the ways they seek to position themselves as writers and their writing choices.

In performative cultures in which accountability measures of young people's (and teachers') performance is closely monitored and assessed, the predominant focus is not on writers, but on writing as an assessable skill. Underpinned by autonomous, not ideological models of literacy (Street, 1984), the policy imperatives in many educational systems around the world tend to foreground writing as a decontextualised product, not as situated social practice. In contrast, the research on which this chapter draws, adopts a sociocultural approach to learning (Lave and Wenger, 1991; Vygotsky, 1978) and literacy (Barton, Hamilton and Ivanič, 2000). Such a perspective recognises that learning is an act of participation (Rogoff, 2003), and that a plurality of literacies exist across the different realms of life, home, work and school. It also recognises the significance of identity in literacy practices. As an interdisciplinary research team (encompassing educationalists and sociolinguists), we recognise the existence of multiple identities or as Burgess and Ivanič (2010, p. 232) describe it, a multifaceted identity which:

> is constructed in the interaction between a person, others, and their sociocultural context. It includes the 'self' that a person brings to the act of writing, the 'self' she constructs through the act of writing, and the way in which the writer is perceived by the reader(s) of the writing.

Nonetheless we are acutely aware that in formal schooling in the UK the prevailing emphasis remains on the production of the 'expected standard' of written text, and the requirement to 'play the game called writing' (Grainger, Goouch and Lambirth, 2003, p. 4). This shapes young people's understandings of what it means to be a writer. A recent systematic review of teachers as writers further underscores the professional challenge of developing young writers (Cremin and Oliver, 2016). It reveals that teachers lack confidence as writers and have narrow 'schooled' conceptions of writing. The kind of identity work they do appears to obscure opportunities for acknowledging identity work around writing – both their own and that of their students. This constrains how teachers approach children and young people's writing.

Furthermore, young people may have few opportunities to learn about writing through working with professional writers. School-based residencies and writing workshops can be inspiring experiences, although traditionally only novelists, poets and playwrights are involved. In England such projects are predominantly targeted at children aged 7–11 years in areas of relative affluence (The Warwick Report, Warwick Commission, 2015). For many young people, therefore, what could be viewed as a cultural entitlement to work with a professional writer is effectively denied. Even those who do access such opportunities are unlikely to encounter a diverse range of writers. This may perpetuate teachers and students' perceptions of 'writers' which tend to be dominated by romantic notions of authorship, creativity and self-expression (Wilson and Myhill, 2012; Cremin and Baker, 2010). Despite the ubiquitous nature of writing in contemporary life, public notions of what it means to be a 'writer' arguably remain tethered to notions of 'creative' writers and primarily linked to novelists and poets.

In response to this context, the study sought to investigate the identities and composing practices of professional writers from diverse domains in the hope that their perspectives might inform and widen educational understanding of the lived experience of being a writer, and support the development of young writers and the teaching of writing.

Professional writers' identities

Whilst writing is central to much contemporary leisure and work (Lillis, 2013), the significance of identity in writing has tended to be foregrounded only in relation to a particular, socially prestigious type of writing: literary writing. It has been explored in a number of ways by literary writers themselves (e.g. Heaney, 1990) and by their biographers and critics (e.g. Ben-Shir, 2007). Far less attention has been given to the significance of identity for those engaging in a considerable amount of writing as part of their professional lives. This emphasis has often been premised on particular assumptions about the relationship between identity, writing and creativity, for example that 'scientific' writing is transactional (rather than creative) and that issues of identity (either as a scientist or a writer) are not therefore significant.

Research into the discursive construction of writers' identities and the 'socially available possibilities for selfhood' (Ivanič, 1998) outside of creative or literary writing has only recently been foregrounded. Studies in adult literacy education (Burgess and Ivanič, 2010, p. 237) in the academy – of students and lecturers (e.g. Ivanič, 1998; Lea and Stierer, 2011, Lillis and Curry, 2010) – and in work-based writing (e.g. Brandt, 1999; Lillis and Rai, 2011) are the exception in this regard. These complementary bodies of work, drawing on largely sociocultural perspectives, highlight the significance of identity in writing across all domains and across stages of experience and expertise. Identity is signalled as significant in a number of ways; the importance of imagining oneself as a writer to write effectively in particular domains (for example in Brandt's work (2009) on 'workaday writers', she illustrates how a policeman's imagining of himself as a film-script writer enables him to carry out his apparently factual reporting of arrests); the tensions around self and ascribed identities in writing (for example, student-writers explicitly masking particular aspects of their writing for fear of being ascribed by readers a particular ethnic identity/sensitivity) (Lillis, 2001); and multilingual scholars' concern at being ascribed 'novice' rather than 'expert' academic identities because of particular uses of language (Lillis and Curry, 2010).

In the current study the aim was to explore the potential significance of identity as a dimension to writing across a range of domains and to explore how twelve writers from three discrete (although not completely distinct) domains of professional experience construed this significance – through their accounts of their journeys as writers and the importance attached to ascriptions of identities and how these shaped possibilities for writing. As Ben-Shir acknowledges:

> a narrator of an identity story, like a narrator of any story, maintains a central and active role as interpreter and editor, picking and choosing from among

the endless elements of his life experience while at all times endeavouring to reconcile them to a coherent and meaningful life story.

(Ben-Shir, 2007, p. 190)

In telling their stories the professional writers were choosing how to represent themselves as they responded to the university-based researchers. Connecting to Clark and Ivanič's (1997) conception of the autobiographical self as one element of writer identity, the study recognised that writing is affected by writers' life histories and that in narrating their past lives as writers, the study's participants were performing their identities in this context.

Methodology

A biographical approach was adopted and semi-structured interviews undertaken; these offered the writers an opportunity to reflect upon their histories as writers and to consider their approaches to composing. The current chapter attends to the first focus: the writers' identities as expressed and constructed in interview, and focuses upon research questions which were perceived to have potential with reference to the educational challenge of fostering positive writer identities in the young. The focus is on their memories of formal education and the influence of childhood reading. The research team sought to achieve a diverse representation of professional writers and identified three broad categories of writers: novelists and poets; journalists and magazine columnists; and academic writers. It was recognised from the outset that this was a simplistic categorisation, but in recruiting four participants from each category, diversity across the sample was ensured. It was later established that each of the writers engaged in a very wide range of writing, well beyond their initial classification.

The writers

Highly experienced writers were recruited who had published widely and whose work was well known within their given primary domain. For example, within the academic category, only professors were invited, none of whom worked in university education or English departments. Participants were recruited either via existing links between researchers and writers or through contact with publicly known writers. A combination of purposeful and convenience sampling (Merriam, 1998) was employed. It was perceived that these expert writers provided potentially rich cases from which we could 'learn the most' (Stake, 1995, p. 446). The study followed the British Educational Research Association (BERA, 2011) ethical guidelines. Informed consent was obtained and participants were apprised of their right to withdraw at any time. They could choose assured anonymity (changed names) or disclosed identity – all but two agreed to be publicly identified (see Table 2.1: * denotes pseudonyms). Assurance of secure storage of data was given.

TABLE 2.1 The twelve professional writers

Hilary Mantel, DBE, is best known for her novels; she also writes short stories and essays.

Geraldine McCaughrean is best known for her children's books, mostly novels and retold myths and legends.

Mal Peet, a former English teacher and illustrator, is best known for his young adult fiction.

Jean Sprackland, Reader in Poetry at Manchester Metropolitan University, UK, is best known for her poetry.

Jeni Harvey, Journalism tutor at Sheffield University, UK, is best known as a journalist.

Fiona Millar is best known as an educational columnist in *The Guardian* and for campaigning on educational issues.

Juliette Towhidi is best known as a screenwriter and script-editor; previously she worked in journalism.

Mathew Marder* is best known as a journalist and broadcaster; he has also written books about contemporary issues.

Tim Barraclough, Professor of Evolutionary Biology at Imperial College London, UK, is best known for his writing on species diversity.

Richard Carter, Professor Emeritus at the University of Lancaster, UK, is best known for his writing on electromagnetics and microwave engineering.

Nigel Mason, Professor of Molecular Physics at the Open University, UK, is best known for his writing on the application of molecular physics natural and technological phenomena.

William Shandlow*, Professor of Biosciences at a UK university, is best known for his writing on astrochemistry.

---

* pseudonym

Data collection

Data was collected through semi-structured interviews in contexts convenient to the writer. This encompassed university premises (5), the writer's home (3), the writer's place of work (2) and other locations (2). The in-depth interviews explored the writing practices they adopt, the choices they make whilst composing and their writer identity. Secondary data was also gathered; participants were invited to bring a piece of their writing that had been compositionally challenging in some way to the interview. These pieces provided a context for exploring participants' composing processes and their sense of self in relation to this 'problematic' writing. Interviews lasted between 45 and 110 minutes and were transcribed by a professional transcriber.

Data analysis

The process of analysing the interview data was inductive (Coffey and Atkinson, 1996). The intention was to examine the interview data for dominant or key themes across the data set, and to give voice to unique perspectives which might be present in only one interview. As four researchers were involved in the process of thematic coding, a systematic analysis process was adopted to ensure consistency. The analytic programme NVivo was used. The process involved the following steps:

1. All researchers read and discussed two interviews and their respective views of represented themes.
2. All researchers independently coded the same interview, then discussed the coding and definitions being attributed to their themes. At this point agreement was reached on common themes evident in the researchers' coding.
3. The remaining interviews were coded using the agreed themes but also generating new themes where appropriate.
4. With this initial phase of coding complete, the researchers met to discuss the themes, their definitions and the new themes. This led to a further revision of the coding and some initial re-organisation of the analysis into over-arching themes and sub-themes.
5. Each coder then reviewed their coding in the light of this revision.
6. Two of the researchers then undertook systematic checking of each theme and sub-theme, determining the appropriacy of the definition, and the accuracy of the match of segments of the interview data to each theme and sub-theme (see Table 2.2 for an example of the coding and definitions within the Writer Identity theme and the life experience sub-theme).
7. The final analytic phase involved all researchers discussing the outcome of the systematic check and agreeing changes to be made.

The analysis led to three over-arching themes: 'Purpose for Writing', 'Writing Choices' and 'Writer Identity', each with their own sub-themes. Four sub-themes were identified for Writer Identity: life experience, sense of self as a writer, manifestations of self as a writer and conceptions of writing, and being a writer. The first two each had multiple strands: the life experience sub-theme strands included: formal education, family and other adults, reading, work experience, social class and context, and the sense of self as a writer sub-theme strands included: self-doubt, critical early memories, private/public and multiple writer identities. The remaining sub-theme manifestations of self as a writer and conceptions of writing and being a writer were not divided into strands. This chapter examines two strands of the life experience sub-theme, namely formal education and reading (see Table 2.2).

Findings

This chapter draws from all twelve writers' identity stories. Examination of the life experience sub-theme highlighted that the strand 'formal education' was most frequently mentioned and by each participant. Another frequently reported influence on their early journeys as writers was reading. It is recognised this dual focus represents a partial picture of the participants' multiple writer identities; however, given the focus on the potential educational consequences of the data and the need to give voice to diverse perspectives, we confined the chapter's focus to these strands.

TABLE 2.2 Writer identity life experience sub-themes

Writer identity		Definitions	Examples
Life Experience			
	Formal education	Comments referring to how formal education influenced their identity as a writer and/or their writing	Mathew: 'I have a lot of disdain about my Catholic education . . .* but one thing it left me with . . . is this thing that you exist in the world to change and improve the world.'
	Family and other adults	Comments referring to how family/other adults influenced their identity as a writer and/or their writing	Nigel: 'I used to play libraries . . . I'd write little books and then my parents would have to come and get them out.'
	Reading	Comments referring to how reading influenced their writing	Geraldine: 'And we did Keats and I would go away and write poetry myself and things and I just loved it.'
	Work experience	Comments referring to how work experience influenced their identity as a writer and/or their writing	Fiona: 'I did a two-year training (on the *Daily Mirror*) . . . you just had to watch them and learn by experience really.'
	Social class	Comments referring to how social class influenced their identity as a writer and/or their writing	Hilary: 'I had to learn how to be middle class and this made me very observant of every detail, . . . I started really, really attending to what people said – exactly – not just the content but the form as well.'
	Context	Comments referring to how the context influenced their identity as a writer and/or their writing	Jeni: 'I used the word "inaugural" and the sub-editor said "you can't use the word inaugural in the *Rochdale Observer*".'

*The ellipsis on each occasion refers to ongoing comments by the writer

Memories of formal education

Narrating their lives and commenting upon the part played by education in shaping their interests and development as writers, the participants predominantly spoke about primary and secondary schooling. Only Tim Barraclough and Mal Peet mentioned university; Tim perceived the 'intensive' writing focus for scientists at Cambridge was challenging but supportive, and Mal recalled doing cartoons for the university paper which he saw as significant. Hilary Mantel observed that the kind of writer she became was shaped by what she described as a 'rather tortuous past with the education system'. Other challenges were also recounted:

> Well everything was set up almost to discourage me from being a writer, in that at no point during my education was imaginative writing privileged or welcome . . . I was unfortunate in having a particularly discouraging English teacher (secondary) . . . she was unenlightened and uninspired but she was also crushing. She thought it was her duty to crush you and she was just profoundly anti-original.
>
> *(Hilary Mantel)*

> When I was about ten I wrote a book of poems, a little book that I made and took to school to show to my teacher and he stuck a gold star on it, but I was very disappointed actually because I knew that he hadn't really read it properly . . . he didn't have any real comments to make on it . . . he wanted to reward it because he thought it was, you know impressive that I'd made this little book. But I actually wanted him to *read* the poems; I wanted to know what he thought of them.
>
> *(Jean Sprackland)*

> At my primary school we were expected [to have] rather neat round handwriting . . . for entry into a handwriting competition . . . I found it rather difficult. . . . I remember the experience reduced me to tears.
>
> *(Richard Carter)*

> I know it is a terrible cliché, I did have a particular English teacher who hated me for three years and gave me a wretched time.
>
> *(Mal Peet)*

All the eight writers who narrated negative school experiences also noted positive memories which they perceived had supported their journeys as writers. Mal Peet, Hilary Mantel and Jean Sprackland, for example, recalled teachers who offered encouraging, if sometimes transient, feedback. The teachers mentioned who were mainly primary professionals or secondary English or History teachers were seen as highly influential. For example, Hilary noted: 'I did have a very good History teacher and I wrote for her, it was for her I polished my style consciously'. Others also recalled encouraging individuals and incidents:

I'd come top and he actually did this amazing thing for a schoolmaster in those days, he walked to where I was sitting at the back of the class . . . and said something like 'Well Peet I seem to have misunderstood you, I apologise' . . . that was quite remarkable . . . and he was very, very encouraging and it was he who sort of started suggesting I was capable of university.

(Mal Peet)

I had encouragement in my first year . . . . When I put in my 1st (English) essay she put 'This is well written'. When I put in my 2nd essay she put 'You write well' which is a much more specific statement. I think the first might have been an accident but the second was science. So I cherished that. However, by the second term she'd taken up her red pen. I think they probably told her in the staff room, you know, that's not the way to keep control of them, tell them their mistakes.

(Hilary Mantel)

I had a fantastic English teacher in my secondary school, and I owe him an enormous debt . . . he recognised that I was very, very interested in poetry and he taught me so much just by reading me poems and giving me poems to read and actually at one point giving me *his* poems to read and comment on . . . that really sort of moved things up a gear . . . as if we were equals.

(Jean Sprackland)

Some writers, including William Shandlow, Juliette Towhidi and Geraldine McCaughrean, observed that their negative school experiences had made them more determined to succeed: through working harder, rebelling against the system and turning to writing outside school. In Geraldine's case, whilst she reported that her self-assurance as a writer was affected, she perceived her desire to write remained.

I got told off by an English teacher . . . who told me I was no good at writing . . . I thought I'm not having this, this is no good, so I spent a lot of time reading, and reading good quality articles and looking at what makes a good sentence, what makes a bad sentence . . . I reacted cussedly to it and fixed it and I think that's what you should do.

(William Shandlow)

It was kind of pretty emotionally barren . . . I did feel very trapped there and I sort of made a deal with myself that I would work incredibly hard and do very well and then never have to feel contained by anyone else's rules and regulations ever again.

(Juliette Towhidi)

The school, having decided that I wasn't clever, left me in no doubt that I was of very little use to them, it did give me a sense of the fact that, as my sister put it, 'the third one's always stupid' . . . I took their word for it . . . so I did writing as a private past-time.

(Geraldine McCaughrean)

In contrast, four writers did not narrate negative or difficult school experiences. Fiona Millar, for example, commented she did not remember doing much writing at school, although she recalled a teacher had suggested she take up journalism, that she 'loved writing stories' and had had some published in the school magazine. This passion for narrative was commonly narrated in relation to reading and writing, although Richard Carter, who reported seeing himself as a scientist from mid-secondary school onwards, observed he 'wasn't the kind of child who wrote stories much' and 'there wasn't a need for extended writing' in his chosen science subjects. The writers who reported an interest in imaginative storying at home and school engaged in this in various ways: physically (for example, Nigel Mason described playing historically based games with friends at school and 'libraries' at home, as he noted: 'I'd write little books and then my parents would have to come and get them out'); through drawing (for example, Mathew Marder recounted 'writing big long Narnia-style things with drawings and maps and things'); through a sibling story writing club (which Geraldine McCaughrean participated in); and as part of 'creative writing' in school.

We kind of created our own world, you know and it was very much that imagination, we had fairly long lunch breaks . . . we did War Games, so it was very much a creative feel . . . you immersed yourself into different worlds.

(Nigel Mason)

I used to like writing stories in my own time. I guess as a child, that's an extension of your imagination. My motivation as a child was creative writing, stories and so on.

(Tim Barraclough)

I wrote stories and diaries, what I was doing at school today, who was my best friend . . . all the ordinary comings and goings and fallings out that young girls do, all the chronicles.

(Jeni Harvey)

My teacher would say 'today I want you to write about' and I never really heard what she wanted me to write about because I was already off writing stories about horses, always horses . . . , it was one of those periods of enjoyment – of making up stories.

(Geraldine McCaughrean)

The influence of reading on writing

Whilst a focus on education was explicit in questions in the interview, no questions related to the writers' reading practices or preferences. Nonetheless these were often referred to, alongside the influence of listening to language. Most of the writers noted their pleasure in reading as a child. Mal Peet observed he was 'forever reading and taking a keen interest in how things were written', and Hilary Mantel that she had engaged in 'a really, really intensive and earnest course of reading'. Jeni Harvey perceived her pleasure had been fostered by her parents and the space for independent reading at school, and Nigel Mason, who was likewise encouraged to read at home, reported that the school reading club and a teacher's recommendations were influential. Other reading drivers and supports frequently mentioned included the library, aspirational parents and a desire to escape into imaginary worlds.

> I did become a reader from a very early age . . . not because I came from a bookish household but it was just that my father took me to the public library. My father disappeared from my life when I was ten, but by then I had thoroughly got the habit of reading and I remember some of the best times in my childhood were sitting with my father in a room, him reading silently, me reading silently.
>
> *(Hilary Mantel)*

> My dad was a miner and later a lorry driver. . . . He was not a great reader! My mum was kind of self-educated – she's from the lower middle class really and was the source of the access to education, but it was a household really in the 60s full of aspiration to be cultural! . . . My mum encouraged me to read fiction older than I could read.
>
> *(Mathew Marder)*

> When I was a child the imaginary world, through books and film, was an escape . . . it was much nicer being in the world and the story than in the [real] world I was sort of forced to be in.
>
> *(Juliette Towhidi)*

The potency of listening to the tunes and rhythms of language at home, school or church was often mentioned, for example Geraldine McCaughrean recalled the end-of-day story as 'incredibly important', as did Mathew Marder, and Jean Sprackland spoke of being 'completely mesmerised' by her teacher's reading of *The Wasteland*, and of the influence of religious language.

> Some of those old Methodist preachers were often amazing speakers . . . as a child I was usually bored sort of crawling about on the floor, I didn't think I was listening, but nevertheless you hear and I think something about speech

rhythms and the phrasing and the way that they spoke, sort of entered me like osmosis.

(Jean Sprackland)

My mum often read to us . . . and in primary school one of our teachers read one of the most dramatic end chapters of Cronin's *The Stars Look Down*, I can still remember it and he didn't just do it once – he did it day after day until it was finished. . . . It absolutely spellbound everybody!

(Mathew Marder)

Tim Barraclough reported reading factual books in his childhood more than fiction and did not refer to any perceived links between reading and writing; this was in contrast to other writers who narrated explicit connections between their reading and writing. Mal Peet expressed this succinctly by noting, '[m]aybe a reader is merely a parked writer'. Unprompted, many named childhood books that they reported influenced their later writing, and Mathew Marder and Juliette Towhidi also named other media (e.g. film, TV dramas and documentaries).

I read Frank Herbert's *Dune* in a single day when I was 12. I think I read *Lord of the Rings* not long after. I always liked big created worlds and some of the earliest things I then wrote as a kid fictionally were kind of an attempt to write soap/CS Lewis-style fictional worlds . . . I had good sources of inspiration – that time was full of culturally very rich drama and documentary: Ken Roach; *Cathy Come Home*; *Kes*.

(Mathew Marder)

It wasn't like we had the classics, the complete works of Dickens or anything like that. We had lots and lots of children's books around, Roald Dahl, Dick King Smith, all the Enid Blytons, we were a household full of children's books. I read all those, and decided to write as well.

(Juliette Towhidi)

The writers that I avidly consumed when I was young were American mainly. . . . I went sort of straight from Biggles to Raymond Chandler and John Steinbeck and . . . I'm all about the language you know (in current writing), it's not the story it's the language with me and the writers that I adore are linguistic conjurors.

(Mal Peet)

The two books that profoundly changed things for me were *Kidnapped* and *Jane Eyre* . . . and the themes that I am working away at all my life were in *Kidnapped*.

(Hilary Mantel)

Discussion

In talking about their life histories and themselves as writers, the twelve professional writers, influenced by societal values and attitudes about what writing is and who writers are (Brandt, 2009), were performing and enacting their 'master narratives' (Hammack, 2011) as writers. Reflecting upon their experience of formal education, the writers reported diverse constraints: a systemic lack of attention to and interest in imaginative writing, limited interest on the part of teachers in their writing and some difficult educational relationships. In addition, specific adverse writing memories appeared salient in the life stories narrated. Despite these recollections, most of the participants positioned themselves as having been child writers, albeit some acknowledged they did not recognise themselves fully as 'writers' at the time. Many narrated strategies they had employed to address the lack of support and active discouragement experienced. Some, such as Geraldine McCaughrean, chose to write at home – initially privately, then later forming a writing club with her brother and sister – whilst others such as William Shandlow worked assiduously to improve their writing style for school. In so doing, however temporarily, they positively shaped their sense of self-esteem as writers. This shaping of negative experiences into 'the material of positive identity' to construct coherent life stories has also been noted by Day (2002, p. 132) in his examination of writers' identities.

Affirmative educational feedback about their writing was frequently reported, occasions when teachers made them feel, as Geraldine McCaughrean observed, 'that you actually had something to say'. In offering positive vignettes from schooling when the young writers' skills were recognised (e.g. work was published in school magazines and praise was received), the professional writers primarily positioned themselves as successful school writers. The significance of childhood feedback on writing, both positive and negative, on writers' identities has been documented in studies of teachers as writers (Cremin, 2006; McKinney and Giorgis, 2009), and shown to have diverse consequences. For some of the professional writers it appeared to enhance an emerging sense of self as a writer, promoting a desire to write. This desire seemed to be influenced for some by an interest in narrative world-creation, which in turn is likely to have been shaped by the stories they reported encountering in books, television and film. All reported being avid readers, a finding noted in previous studies (Gallo, 1994), although not all read fiction. Several recalled the pleasure of being read to and listening to language. Many reported mapping out and making up stories at home and school. This marked pleasure in narrative writing has been noted in studies of primary-aged writers (Grainger et al., 2003), although teenagers tend to reflect more diversity (Myhill, 2005). It may be that the freedom to shape one's own narrative and exert authorial agency is particularly motivating for young writers.

Drawing on their conception of the autobiographical self as one aspect of writer identity, Clark and Ivanič (1997) suggest that writers' life histories and a sense of their roots influence their writing, even as they write. This was manifest with reference to the reported echoes and intersections between the writers' early reading and later writing. Many noted the sea of 'voices' on which they still draw; for example, Hilary Mantel perceived the themes and language from *Kidnapped* and *Jane Eyre* remained influential, Mal Peet made connections between his reading preferences and later attention to language, Nigel Mason connected his early passion for historical novels with his later history writing, and Mathew Marder and Juliette Towhidi noted connections between the social and cultural themes encountered in books and films and their later work in journalism and documentaries.

Conclusion

This study offers new insights about the perceived influence of formal education and early reading on the emerging identities of twelve professional writers. It reveals that writers from diverse domains recalled specific and significant memories of formal education, including constraints and challenges; particular teachers; and feedback about their writing. In narrating these they reported their self-esteem as writers had been affected. As a consequence, some had written in defiance of negative experiences, while others had written in search of receiving more positive affirmation. All persevered despite difficulties. The data indicates that their desire to write was partly influenced by a pleasure in reading and narrative world-creation (through play, drawing and writing). All but one of the writers reported a deep, early pleasure in fiction, mainly, but not exclusively, found in books. For several these remembered texts were perceived to have had a long-term impact on shaping their interests as writers – influencing their choice of themes and language regardless of the diverse domains in which they later worked. Whilst the writers commonly narrated a sense of an emerging writer identity in and through formal education, there was also considerable uniqueness and diversity; two science academics did not mention connections between early reading and later writing. This may have been due to the texts being significantly different in nature to those they now produce in contrast, say, to the novelists or poet. In addition, the influence of others on their development as writers, in school, at home and in the community, and the wider social and historical context was evident, alongside their different personal responses to circumstance.

Although as Gee (2000, p. 50) argues, the education system must avoid 'reproducing the identities and practices of experts', these writers' perspectives on their childhood experiences of schooling and their pleasure in reading raise issues for consideration. For many of them, imaginative writing was neither profiled nor valued in school. In the context of contemporary education in England, little appears to have changed; the emphasis on spelling, grammar and punctuation in national assessments effectively sidelines composition and effect. Additionally, despite reading for pleasure being mandated, studies suggest teachers struggle to profile this, in part due to its non-assessed nature (Cremin et al., 2014). Yet as this research reveals, writers need opportunities to read and write stories; narrative is a crucial way of making sense of the world and appears to motivate young writers.

The professional writers' narrated memories also reveal the uniqueness of their early journeys as writers, the socially situated nature of writing and the ways in which identities are heavily shaped by social experience. In many classrooms, however, the emphasis remains almost entirely upon 'schooled writing' with its attendant objectives and specified outcomes. Little or no attention is given to the emerging identities of young writers, to discussions about students' reading and writing preferences and practices in different domains within or beyond school, or their attitudes towards writing and being a writer. Young people's development as writers should not be measured simply by their command of writing's codes and conventions, without cognisance of their dispositions, attitudes and motivation. These are crucial to effective practice since emotion and self-esteem are key catalysts in the process of becoming a writer and believing oneself to be a writer.

Drawing on the perspectives of respected professional writers, this study suggests that both more research and more work in school is needed to explore students' (and their teachers') histories and identities as writers, to understand the shaping influence of writers' early journeys and social experiences of learning to write and becoming writers. Additionally, we suggest a wider range of professional writers should be involved in education; their voices offer lessons for us all.

Acknowledgements

The authors wish to recognise the contribution of Tatjana Dragovic to the work reported here and to thank the professional writers.

References

Ahlberg, A. (2014) *The Bucket: memories of an inattentive childhood*, London, Penguin.

Barton, D., Hamilton, M. and Ivanič, R. (2000) (eds) *Situated Literacies: Reading and Writing in Context*, London, Routledge.

Ben-Shir, D. (2007) 'The endless search: Writing as a way of being', *New Writing*, vol. 4, no. 3, pp. 188–204.

BERA (British Educational Research Association) (2011) Revised Ethical Guidelines for Educational Research. www.bera.ac.uk.

Bernstein, M. (2014) 'Three planes of practice: Examining intersections of reading identity and pedagogy', *English Teaching: Practice and Critique*, vol. 13, no. 2, pp. 110–129.

Bourne, J. (2002) '"Oh what will miss say!" Constructing texts and identities in the discursive processes of classroom writing', *Language and Education*, vol. 16, no. 4, pp. 241–259.

Brandt, D. (2009) 'When people write for pay', *Journal of Advanced Composition*, vol. 29, no. 1(2), pp. 165–197.

Britton, J. (1982) *Prospect and Retrospect: Selected Essays of James Britton* (G. Pradl, ed.), London, Heinemann.

Burgess, A. and Ivanič, R. (2010) 'Writing and being written: Issues of identity across timescales', *Written Communication*, vol. 27, no. 2, pp. 228–255.

Clark, R. and Ivanič, R. (1997) *The Politics of Writing*, New York, Routledge.

Coffey, A. and Atkinson, P. (1996) *Making Sense of Qualitative Data*, London, Sage.

Cremin, T. (2006) 'Creativity, uncertainty and discomfort: teachers as writers', *Cambridge Journal of Education*, vol. 36, no. 3, pp. 415–433.

Cremin, T. and Baker, S. (2010) 'Exploring teacher-writer identities in the classroom: Conceptualising the struggle', *English Teaching: Practice and Critique,* vol. 9, no. 3, pp. 8–25.

Cremin, T. and Oliver, L. (2016) 'Teachers as writers: A systematic review', *Research Papers in Education*. Retrieved from http://dx.doi.org/10.1080/02671522.2016.1187664.

Cremin, T., Mottram, M., Collins, F., Powell, S. and Safford, K. (2014) *Building Communities of Engaged Readers: Reading for Pleasure*, London and New York, Routledge.

Dahl, R. (1984) *Boy: Tales of Childhood*, London, Penguin.

Day, S. X. (2002) '"Make It Uglier. Make It Hurt. Make It Real": Narrative Construction of the Creative Writer's Identity', *Creativity Research Journal,* vol. 14, no. 1, pp. 127–136.

Dyson, A. H. (2009) 'Writing in childhood worlds', in Beard, R., Myhill, D., Nystrand, M. and Riley, J. (eds), *Handbook of writing development*, London, Sage, pp. 232–245.

Fisher, R. (2010) 'Young writers' construction of agency', *Journal of Early Childhood Literacy*, vol. 10, no. 4, pp. 410–429.

Gallo, D. R. (1994) 'The writing processes of professional authors', *English Journal,* vol. 83, no. 5, pp. 55–60.

Gee, J. P. (2000) *Identity as an Analytic Lens for Research in Education* (Revised November 2000). Retrieved from http://www.jamespaulgee.com/sites/default/files/pub/Identity.pdf

Goertzel, M. G., Goertzel, V. and Goertzel, T. G. (1978) *Three Hundred Eminent Personalities*, New York, Jossey-Bass.

Grainger, T., Goouch, K. and Lambirth, A. (2003) 'Playing the game called writing', *English in Education,* vol. 37, no. 2, pp. 4–15.

Hammack, P. (2011) 'Narrative and the politics of meaning', *Narrative Inquiry*, vol. 21, no. 2, pp. 311–318.

Heaney, S. (1990) *The Redress of Poetry*, Oxford, Clarendon Press.

Holland, D. and Lave, J. (2001) 'History in person: An introduction', in Holland, D. and Lave, J. (eds), *History in Person: Enduring Struggles, Contentious Practice, Intimate Identities*, Sante Fe, NM, School of American Research Press, pp. 1–32.

Ivanič, R. (1998) *Writing and Identity: The Discoursal Construction of Identity in Academic Writing*, Amsterdam, John Benjamins.

Ivanič, R. (2006) 'Language, learning and identification', in Kiely, R., Rea-Dickens, P., Woodfield, P. H. and Clibbon, G. (eds) *Language, Culture and Identity in Applied Linguistics*, London, Equinox, pp. 7–29.

Jinkins, M. (2004) 'The professor's vocations: Reflections on the teacher as writer,' *Teaching Theology and Religion,* vol. 7, no. 2, pp. 64–70.

Kaufman, D. (2002) 'Living a literate life, revisited', *The English Journal* vol. 91, no. 6, pp. 61–57.

Lave, J. and Wenger, E. (1991) *Situated learning: Legitimate peripheral participation*, Cambridge, Cambridge University Press.

Le Guin, U. K. (2004) *The Wave in the Mind: Talks and Essays on the Writer, the Reader and the Imagination*, Boston, MA, Shambhala.

Lea, M. R. and Stierer, B. (2011) 'Changing academic identities in changing academic workplaces: Learning from academics' everyday professional writing practices', *Teaching In Higher Education,* vol. 16, no. 6, pp. 605–616.

Lillis, T. (2001) *Student Writing: Access, Regulation, Desire*, London, Routledge.

Lillis, T. (2013) *The Sociolinguistics of Writing*, Edinburgh, Edinburgh University Press.

Lillis, T. and Curry, M. J. (2010) *Academic Writing in a Global Context*, London, Routledge.

Lillis, T. and Rai, L. (2011) 'A case study of a research based collaboration around writing in social work', *Across the Disciplines*, vol. 8, no. 3, ISSN: 1554–8244.

McKinney, M. and Giorgis, C. (2009) 'Narrating and performing identity: Literacy specialists' writing identities', *Journal of Literacy Research* vol. 41, no. 1, pp. 104–149.

Merriam, S. B. (1998) *Case Study Research in Education: A Qualitative Approach*, San Francisco, CA, Jossey-Bass.

Moje, E., Luke, A., Davies, B. and Street, B. (2009) 'Literacy and identity: Examining the metaphors in history and contemporary research', *Reading Research Quarterly*, vol. 44, no. 4, pp. 415–437.

Morpurgo, M. (2006) *Singing for Mrs Pettigrew: A Story-Maker's Journey*, London, Walker.

Myhill, D. A. (2005) 'Writing creatively' in Wilson. A. (ed) *Creativity in Primary Education*, Exeter, Devon, Learning Matters, pp. 58–69.

Myhill, D. A. and Wilson, A. C. (2013) 'Playing it safe: Teachers' views of creativity in poetry writing', *Thinking Skills and Creativity*, vol. 10, pp. 101–111.

Piirto, J. (2002) *"My Teeming Brain": Understanding Creative Writers*, Cresskill, NJ, Hampton.

Rogoff, B. (2003) *The Cultural Nature of Human Development*, New York, Oxford University Press.

Rosenwald, G. and Ochberg, R. (1992) (eds) *Storied Lives: Cultural Conditions of Self Understanding*, New Haven, CT, Yale University Press.

Rowe, D. W. (2003) 'The nature of young children's authoring', in Hall, N., Larson, J. and Marsh, J. (eds) *Handbook of Early Childhood Literacy*, London, Sage, pp. 258–270.

Rowe, D. W. (2008) 'The social construction of intentionality: Two-year-olds' and adults' participation at a preschool writing center', *Research in the Teaching of English*, vol. 42, no. 4, pp. 387–434.

Rowe, D. W. and Neitzel, C. (2010) 'Interest and agency in 2- and 3-year-olds' participation in emergent writing', *Reading Research Quarterly*, vol. 45, no. 2, pp. 169–195.

Ryan, M. E. (2014) 'Writers as performers: Developing reflexive and creative writing identities', *English Teaching: Practice and Critique,* vol. 13, no. 3, pp. 130–148.

Ryan, M. E. and Barton, G. (2014) 'The spatialized practices of teaching writing in elementary schools', *Research in the Teaching of English*, vol. 48, no. 3, pp. 303–328.

Spiro, J. (2007) 'Teaching poetry – writing poetry – teaching as a writer', *English in Education*, vol. 41, no. 3, pp. 78–93.

Stake, R. (1995) *The Art of Case Study Research*, Thousand Oaks, CA, Sage.

Street, B. V. (1984) *Literacy in Theory and Practice*, Cambridge, Cambridge University Press.

Vakil, A. (2008) 'Teaching Creative Writing', *Changing English*, vol. 15, no. 2, pp. 157–165.

Vygotsky, L. S. (1978) *Mind and Society: The Development of Higher Mental Processes*, Cambridge, MA, Harvard University Press.

Warwick Commission (2015) *Enriching Britain: Culture, Creativity and Growth*, Coventry, University of Warwick.

Wilson, A. C. and Myhill, D. (2012) 'Ways with words: Teachers' personal epistemologies of the role of metalanguage in the teaching of poetry writing', *Language and Education*, vol. 26, no. 6, pp. 553–568.

SECTION B

Writing identity and the development of teachers

3

"I'M NOT A GOOD WRITER"

Supporting teachers' writing identities in a university course

Denise N. Morgan

Introduction

Teachers should write so they understand the process of writing from within. They should know the territory intellectually and emotionally; how you have to think to write, how you feel when writing. "Teachers of writing do not have to be great writers, but they should have frequent and recent experience in writing. If you experience the despair, the joy, the failure, the success, the work, the fun, the drudgery, the surprise of writing, you will be able to understand the composing experiences of your students and therefore help them understand how they are learning to write" (Murray, 2004, pp. 73–74).

Many teachers who enter the classroom are not well prepared to teach writing (The National Commission on Writing, 2003). Researchers have identified the issue of teachers' limited experience and preparation in writing as an area of concern (Morgan and Pytash, 2014; Street and Stang, 2008). Writing is a subject where many teachers place themselves along a good–bad continuum, positioning themselves at one end or the other (Morgan, 2010). Teachers' notions about their writing ability are often shaped by previous experiences in school. In addition, few teacher education programs specifically address the teaching of writing, often leaving teachers ill-prepared to teach writing well (National Writing Project and Nagin, 2006; The National Commission on Writing, 2003). This lack of preparation may be contributing to the limited amount of writing occurring in K-12 classrooms (Applebee and Langer, 2006, 2009, 2011, 2013; Cutler and Graham, 2008).

When teaching writing, many teachers may be drawing upon their own apprenticeship of observation (Lortie, 1975), recreating the kinds of writing opportunities and activities they themselves experienced as learners. Past experiences can affect "the frequency and quality of the writing opportunities that teachers then offer their students" (Whitney and Friedrich, 2013, p. 24). Before teachers teach writing, it is important that they know or become reacquainted with the terrain in writing. What is missing for many teachers is "frequent and recent experience in writing", Murray (2004) advocates. Do current teachers see themselves as writers? Do they possess the identity of a writer? Can they talk about the craft of writing? The notion that teachers need to possess a writer's identity appears self-evident: A writing teacher needs to write.

This notion takes on greater importance if we hold true Parker Palmer's (1998) idea that "we teach who we are." On the simplest level, identity is highly tied to one's sense of someone who does this thing. Identity is related to our knowledge and experience, as someone who sees oneself as a doer and cultivator of that thing. Good teaching is rooted in the identity of the teacher (Palmer, 1998) so it stands to reason that if teachers do not identify as writers, then the kind and quality of teaching they provide is likely to be limited. However, identities are social constructions and can change depending on context and interactions with others (McCarthey and Moje, 2002; Moje, Luke, Davies, and Street, 2009).

The challenge for teacher education

Teacher educators are therefore challenged with helping teachers develop or broaden their identities as writers and can do so by helping them come to know the landscape of writing. There is a constructed and dynamic nature to identity (McCarthey and Moje, 2002) that teacher educators need to heed in their work with teachers. I argue that the writing identity that may be most helpful to teachers is one where they identify as a writer who understands *how* and *why* writers enact their craft. It is not enough to have teachers write and see themselves as writers; they must also be able to teach students *how* to write. The teaching of how is tied to being able to recognize and discuss craft in writing, to examine not just what the author said but how the author said it. Being a strong writer does not always translate into being an effective teacher of writers if the individual lacks the meta-cognition or the language to explain the internal decisions made when shaping a text. Writers make deliberate decisions when writing, but not all writers can articulate what they have done in a way that allows others to see these possibilities for their own writing. In teaching writing, teachers are challenged with pulling back the curtain, so to speak, on the words that appear on the page, to discuss the thinking that underpins certain choices. The goal is not to determine why the author did this exact thing – rather, why would an author choose to do this instead of something else and how does this influence the reader? In doing this work, teachers begin to "notice and name" craft to their students so they can begin to see these things for themselves (Johnston, 2004).

One way to support this development in noticing and naming is by drawing upon professional authors who provide insight into their craft through their books on writing (e.g. King, Lamott and Murray), professionals who study writing and write books for teachers (e.g. Fletcher, Ray and Kittle), and direct experiences with examining well-written passages and discussing the craft. Writers share their identities in their books on writing, naming the qualities and habits that help them persist in a challenging and daunting task. From these individuals, teachers can learn about the mindset and practices of such writers, gaining insight into the lives of those who write and broadening their knowledge and composing vocabulary. From such experiences, teachers begin to examine writing in a new way and can consider these ideas when writing themselves. These understandings can shape a teacher's identity as writer. Ray (2006) argues, "When what you know about 'people who write' becomes what you know 'as a person who writes,' what you know *changes*" (p. 32). If we hold true the notion that teachers teach who they are, unless they have had these kinds of experiences as writers, they cannot teach from this place of knowing.

Then how can teachers' identities as writers be fostered, especially since many teachers have noted their lack of or limited preparation in this area (Brimi, 2012; Smagorinsky, 2010)? While there are many ways of fostering such identities, the one open to me, as a teacher educator, is through graduate coursework. For this investigation, I posed the following research question: how do teachers describe their understandings about writing and teaching writing within a graduate writing course experience?

Method

Context of the study

Teaching Writing as a Process is a graduate-level course for in-service teachers earning their Master's degree in Reading Specialization. However, the course is also open to students earning their Masters of Teaching (M.A.T.) degrees in both Special Education (Grades K-12) and secondary English Education (Grades 7–12). Such students possess a degree in another area and seek licensure to be certified to teach. The course population was a mixture of teachers and teacher candidates. For the purpose of this chapter, I use the term "teachers" to represent both populations in the course.

Approach to the course

In my course design, I used Brian Cambourne's (1988) *Conditions of Learning*. In his theory of natural learning, learners are supported through the conditions of immersion, demonstration, expectation, responsibility, use, approximation, response, and engagement. These conditions represent both states of being (doing, creating, behaving) and circumstances that co-occur in learning situations (Cambourne, 1995). These conditions provide support on multiple levels for the learners and offer shared responsibility between instructor and learners. While this theory stems from his work with young children, I argue these conditions are applicable to adult learning as they can be identified in instances of learning of other subjects and abilities.

Specifically, the course goals were to help teachers rediscover writing while developing their understandings of principles, practices, theories, and research related to writing development and instruction. Students engaged in process writing through a unit of study approach to teaching writing. A unit of study is an organized, extended series of lessons focused on a writing product (e.g. specific genre) or process (e.g. revision) (Ray, 2006). Woven throughout the course was an emphasis on learning how to read like a writer (Smith, 1988), a stance that promotes noticing, studying, and talking about ways authors use craft. It was expected that noticing craft would influence teachers' writing but also provide them with tools to share in their classrooms. In class, teachers experienced a unit of study on flash fiction (a short fiction story between 250 and 750 words). Teachers read several mentor texts – strong examples of flash fiction – to develop a sense of the genre. We analyzed those texts, noticing and naming the craft, the way the authors used language and structured their writing. I taught mini-lessons about writing within this genre (e.g. what to include and not include when a piece is short, the work titles can do in a short piece) and teachers wrote "under the influence" of these mentor texts and lessons (Ray, 2006). Teachers then developed their own unit on a genre of choice. As the instructor, I drew from my teaching experiences, teaching from a process approach guided by the work of Atwell (1987), my participation in the University of New Hampshire Summer Writing Program, a program similar in intent and style to the National Writing Project, and my professional work in this area.

Participants

The participants in the study were 13 teachers (four males, nine females, all Caucasian) who took the course in Fall 2014 at a public university in the Midwest. Of the 13 participants, three were secondary English Education MAT students, three were Special Education MAT students, and seven were licensed teachers. Of those seven certified teachers, three held teaching positions and four were either full-time Master's students or seeking a teaching position. The course was an elective for all but the three secondary MAT students, who took the course as their writing methods. All teachers agreed to participate in the study.

Data collection and analysis

Data included all course experiences and assignments including:

- in-class unit of study of flash fiction;
- self-selected unit of study;
- use of Twitter to follow authors and other writing professionals;
- literature discussion on a book on writing by professional writers;
- use of young adult literature to study the intentional crafting of writing;
- reading responses on class wiki;

- exit slips students completed at the end of each class;
- emails; and
- self-reflection essays on the above-mentioned experiences or assignments.

All documents were collected and stored electronically. Data were analyzed using the constant comparative method (Glaser and Strauss, 1999). Using a continuous and recursive process, I initially coded using an open coding system guided by my desire to understand what teachers learned about writing and the teaching of writing. Initial codes such as "feeling nervous," "self belief as bad writer," and "breakthrough moment" emerged. Later, through more focused coding, initial codes led to more clearly defined categories such as "reflective insights about themselves as writers," which subsumed the initial categories mentioned above. The quotes included within each theme are the ones that seemed to best represent ideas identified by participants collectively or ones that illuminated the process of developing awareness for writing and teaching writing.

Findings

In the findings, lines between what teachers learned as writers and as teachers of writing were often blurred. In some cases, teachers identified their new understandings about writing and sense of self as writer in the context of what they wanted to do as a teacher or how their teaching needed to better reflect their own experiences as writers. Hence, I document both aspects of these findings.

New understandings about and experiences with writing

Within this finding, teachers identified instances where their past understandings about writing were tested, often resulting in a deeper or expanded understanding of a particular concept.

The value of time and new experiences with writing

The teachers indicated that in-class writing experiences contrasted with past experiences. Many said they were one-draft writers, submitting pieces composed the night before the due date. In addition, they were solo writers, writing on their own, not sharing or discussing their pieces with others. However, in this case, teachers had weekly writing and conferring time in class. That time provided them with opportunities not previously experienced, as Rebecca explained:

> I was able to dedicate much time to the process instead of moving to new writing. Not only do you have more time, but you are able to explore mentor texts, experiment with drafts, and work collaboratively with others.

Several teachers identified "feeling like a student" while composing in a genre of their choice. Veronica described her experience:

> This was the first time in a long, long time where I experienced what a student might experience with writing. I'm usually among the first to say, 'Yupp. Writing? No problem. Got it. Next!'

However, her "next" came with indecisions and uncertainty when writing commentary, her self-selected unit of study genre. In her reflection, she shared:

> Well, I learned that I'm human. Never before have I struggled so much to write a piece, mostly because I don't typically struggle with writing. At all. Sure, I might have the occasional stall, but I have NEVER struggled in the way I struggled with this.

Instead of "just writing" a piece from previous knowledge, Veronica knew she needed and wanted to include craft and genre knowledge she learned from her genre inquiry.

Teachers articulated their belief that writing in the same genre as their students was important. This provided them, they felt, with first-hand knowledge of the potential challenges and difficulties students would face and which they could share with them. For Rachel, it provided her with a sense of what she needed to do. She reflected:

> I have read and read about units of study used in the classroom, but to do one made me have enough confidence to teach a unit in own classroom. By doing each of the steps I now have a clear understanding of what it takes, what I need to do, and how to best support children.

Ally, who was teaching at that time, said that she had "way more empathy for my students now and am becoming a lot more patient and giving them more time to think" as result of her own writing experiences.

Search for and importance of topic

The teachers frequently attributed personal investment in writing to choice of topic. At the same time, the openness of choice provided anxiety. Mary Kate realized that changing "your original idea (many times) is perfectly fine." A few teachers disposed of their first drafts completely; others changed course mid-stream. Some teachers expressed surprise at the topic they ultimately explored. Initially, Kate wanted to write about animal rescue but changed her topic to focus on the aftermath of drunk driving in her flash fiction piece. She wrote, "I was very surprised by that [change] because this is a topic very sensitive to me and I am very reserved about this and sharing alone." Since this topic mattered deeply to her, she cared how she crafted her piece. She commented:

> I began writing and incorporating strategies I learned in class. I went back to my writer's notebook and played a lot with my words to decide how I can

get the most out of the strategy. I thought it made my writing strong and added much personality. It was nice to take something we learned in class and be able to apply it to our real life writing.

This initial struggle gave way to feeling a sense of accomplishment. When Ally commented on her journey, she wrote:

I truly dreaded this at first. As time went on, and I found myself feeling somewhat proud of my work, I enjoyed going back and revising again and again. After reading it aloud, I felt some sort of vindication from my fears and self doubt that I struggled with when starting my piece.

The teachers expressed a sense of wanting to do justice to the topic they selected, because the topic mattered to them.

Uncovering "truths" about teaching writing

Within this finding, teachers' began to question or outgrew their prior beliefs about teaching writing. Their previously held notions of what it means to write and the processes that writers go through were tested against what they experienced or read in class.

Living a process

The teachers identified the difficulty of articulating what you most wanted to say in the way you wanted to say it, of "getting it right," on paper. Rachel realized that writing will not be "perfect the first or second time." After revising "15 or more times," Alex learned that "even the slightest change to a word or sentence can really help improve the piece." Kate expressed seeing how "each step you take to get there [final product] is just as important." Teachers discussed their learning about aspects of the process, such as multiple drafts and constant revision of ideas, but also examined and named the inherent process within a unit of study.

From his experience with the unit of study, Cody said, "I'm learning that you don't just have to teach from an expensive program to deliver quality instruction. This process just seems to scream quality." He found this process supports student "growth and success. Every day learning a new technique and creating their own spin and examples gives students' growth they can touch. I don't get why I didn't do this as a kid!" The process of studying mentor texts, selecting a topic of choice, and drawing ideas and possibilities from these texts provided many teachers with a working process they did not previously possess.

Reflective insights about themselves as writers

Clark identified that what his professional reading of Kittle (2008) and Lamott (1994) had done was "dispel the feeling that it [writing] comes naturally to others, just not me." Others realized that they did not have to be an amazing writer to teach writing well, understanding they could rely upon well-written examples from various authors.

Cody spoke of his avoidance behaviors when writing, stepping away from the computer thinking he would return when he got something "really good." At the end of the semester, he reported, "I've learned that it's not about being the best. It's not about having this perfect piece. It's just about doing it." Clark, who publicly declared in the first class "I'm not a good writer" and met with me to discuss this issue outside of class, struggled initially in class. It seemed that everything we were doing was outside his comfort zone. Yet with his flash fiction piece he surprised himself with his use of descriptive language and "at least what I felt, the quality of [my] writing." In class, we discussed a writing technique we called "not, not, is." With this technique, something is described first by identifying what it is not before identifying what it is. Here Clark tries it in his piece:

> the leaves were stirred from the rustling of a light cool breeze. Not a breeze that will make you want to get inside out of the cold, and not a breeze that will make your eyes water, but just a light, cool, comfortable breeze that you pull your jacket tighter around yourself and keep going.

For Clark, naming the writing techniques writers used was helpful to his growing sense of self as a writer, allowing him to have in his words an "I did what I did not think I could do" experience.

Another experience that supported teachers' insights about themselves as writers was sharing writing with others. Weekly, teachers shared a snippet of their writing with the class. However, at the conclusion of the flash fiction unit, teachers read their piece aloud. All but one of the teachers specifically stated being nervous or self-conscious when sharing. After having shared, teachers reported feeling more self-confident and a sense of accomplishment from revealing a part of themselves to others. They also appreciated hearing laughs at the right places or seeing shocked looks on people's faces when their piece took a surprising turn, knowing that their piece conveyed what was intended.

Developing awareness of the craft of writing

Within this theme, teachers identified their need to find and use appropriate texts to support their growing ability to talk about the craft of writing and to help students see possibilities within their writing.

Selecting texts

Before craft can be analyzed, there must be a text worthy of examination. Teachers were expected to select mentor texts within their chosen genre. Many found this process daunting. In describing her experience, Jeanne noted:

Collecting anchor texts was a huge challenge. Not only was there plenty to consider with each selection, but I quickly found that each selection I made would not fit into my unit of study. I selected close to 30 books, only to narrow it down to eight that I could really call good anchor texts. It took a great deal of time to sift through the books, making notes on what I liked about each piece, the commonalities they shared, and the elements that made them stand out as being exceptional. The outcome, though, was fantastic.

The teachers soon realized that not any text would do. They needed texts that showcased different writing possibilities for students to illustrate what authors do in their selected genre. Tim described his frustration with his search:

I learned that finding mentor texts can be really difficult. I spent weeks trying to find the appropriate pieces . . . I got really frustrated, to the point of wanting to ditch the genre. . . . The point here is that it took a lot of persistence to find the right books – and even more to read through them, one by one, in order to find the best examples of quality writing.

Teachers described the influence of mentor texts on their writing. Kara stated that mentor texts "can shape your whole idea, and guide your thinking if you don't know which step to take next." When reflecting on his experience Cody wrote: "If I didn't learn that choosing great anchor texts is critical then I should probably fail this course." In part, his realization of how difficult the process could be was related to having to articulate why the texts were appropriate in length, writing craft, and topic for students, a finding elaborated in the next section.

Naming craft in writing

Reading like a writer (Smith, 1988) and discussing writing techniques challenged the teachers. Weekly, at the beginning of class, teachers studied a short excerpt, sometimes a single sentence or paragraph, and eventually an entire text. From that, teachers described and named what they thought the author was doing. The idea was to identify and create a name for the technique that could become part of the course vernacular and develop the skill of reading like a writer. Teachers did not create "official names" that could be found in texts on writing, but rather self-created names bestowed on the example to describe the technique to make it memorable. The teachers all regarded this noticing and naming as a new experience for them, describing having limited or no previous opportunities to see or talk about writing in this way. Initially, they were often frustrated due to a lack of background knowledge or previous experience in analyzing writing to this extent. Jeanne reflected on her process:

marking the details that make the book unique guides me to better understand what I'd be teaching and will guide my own students what to look for when they read the texts. This also helped me determine what I would include in my own piece later. Although a tedious process, and sometimes frustrating because I felt I did not have enough background knowledge, I grew not only as a writer but a reader. I formed better noticing skills, now being able to look through books and quickly pick up a few specific elements that make the books 'anchor text' worthy.

Initially, being explicit about noticing and naming the craft was daunting in that this was unfamiliar to them. In addition, teachers identified past writing advice they were given or would tell their students, such as "add sensory details" to be more descriptive, as not as helpful as working from specific examples that illustrated multiple ways to write descriptively. Teachers reported now being able to provide concrete examples and talk about the examples in ways that could help students envision doing similar things themselves.

Seeing commonalities in writing and teaching writing

The teachers identified convergence among experiences, assignments, and readings in their understanding about writing and teaching writers. The teachers learned from living the process first-hand but also from witnessing how particular lessons influenced their own and fellow classmates' writing. These observations were coupled with their reading about writing from published writers, following writers on Twitter, and reading about this process in K-12 classrooms through professional readings. For example, Clark noted that *Bird by Bird* (Lamott, 1994), written for the general public, "reiterated a lot of similar thoughts as the text from Penny Kittle (2008)," a professional text written for teachers. Mary Kate found the ideas she lived in class amplified by the educators she followed on Twitter. Teachers identified hearing a common message of unity in the multiple voices that discussed what it means to write and the challenges inherent in teaching writing.

Teachers found that instead of being outsiders looking into the process of writing, they stood within the writing circle. Through this immersion in writing, the teachers entered into writer-to-writer conversations. They noted the power of these conversations and the rethinking and revision they prompted. Brittany described how these conversations helped her:

> I learned which areas were too much, too little, told too much, showed too little, and which areas were confusing. He [my partner] showed me which areas were strong so I could take those weak areas and mimic my strong ones. I think the feedback was incredibly helpful. I also loved that the person should ask questions about specific parts and do critical investigation rather than saying 'this is wrong.'

Through multiple means, there were consistent messages about the messiness, difficulty, struggle, and doubt of writing. These repeating messages helped teachers dispel the myth that writing comes easily to a select few. As they experienced this struggle first-hand and witnessed it in others, they questioned if and how they currently allowed for the messiness of writing to occur in their own teaching or how they would allow for it when in the classroom. These multiple voices appeared to support them in embracing and believing this message.

Discussion

An important issue facing teachers today is the need for increased writing instruction in classrooms. University programs are the "foremost settings for learning how to teach" (Smagorinsky, Cook and Johnson, 2003, p. 1407). Teacher educators can help in-service and preservice teachers examine prior experiences with writing, while also helping them consider the writing instruction they will provide their students. This is important, as many teachers indicated that their teaching of writing is tied to their own experiences as a writer (Whitney and Friedrich, 2013). Teacher educators are in a position to aid teachers in developing their identities as writers so that when they teach from "who they are," their writing identity guides this instruction. In a course committed to having teachers write regularly, teachers can encounter the challenges of writing, mirroring many of the challenges their students will face. This first-hand experience coupled with engaging in an active analysis of how writing is crafted can support teachers in developing a writing identity that actively supports the work they do in the classroom.

The teachers in this study articulated their learning on both these fronts. They became more aware of their own personal process of writing, which may be a result of the "noticing and naming" of the process that was occurring within class. Teachers began to think deliberately about the use and need for time to think, draft, and revise. As a result, many came to a realization about the time students will also need when writing. Teachers began to view writing from a student perspective, articulating the benefit (and struggle) of writing something that their students will write, to learn first-hand the possible stumbling blocks students may encounter and ways to support them when they encounter such blocks.

Teachers found that being able to turn to mentor texts to help them consider ways to craft or structure their own writing, and their evolving abilities to read like writers and talk about writing, allowed them to begin to read others' writing in new ways. This developing ability supported them in their own writing; they drew upon what others had done to help them write in new and different ways, expanding their sense of possibilities. For some teachers, their relationship to writing changed as they began to view their own writing abilities in a more positive light. With these experiences came for some the emergence of seeing their relationship to writing change as they viewed their own writing abilities in a new light.

A teacher as writer identity can encompass someone who writes but who has the ability to talk about writing in a way that helps students envision making particular choices. Simply being a strong writer does not always translate into a strong teacher of writers. In the teaching of writing, there must be much talk about writing, about possibilities and choices, about the process and the craft. Teachers who "notice and name" craft for their students ensure that students begin to notice and name for themselves, thus allowing them to see their abilities as writers in new ways (Johnston, 2004).

These lived experiences helped shape how teachers thought about themselves as writers and how they came to know the intricacies of writing. The realizations highlighted in the findings are close in texture and tone to the truths that professional writers share about their own writing experiences. If identity relates to one who does this thing and knows it well, the teachers in the study strengthened this sense of identity. These findings add to prior research that advocates the need for teachers to have these first-hand writing experiences (Grossman et al., 2000; Street and Stang, 2008) and highlight the influence of supporting teachers in developing their awareness and ability to talk about writing craft.

A limitation of this study and of many course-based studies is that the teachers were not followed into the classroom. What teachers reported learning is identified but how this learning shaped subsequent teaching practices is unexamined. However, the findings illustrate a broadening of teachers' identities as writers, and these findings can serve as a window into possibilities that may speak to other teacher educators.

If teacher educators expect teachers to engage students in authentic writing instruction, then they must provide opportunities within their courses for teachers to experience the same. To teach writing well, teachers need to engage with writing first-hand and be able to talk about writing in a way that allows students to see windows of possibilities for their own writing. Supporting teachers in developing these abilities can disrupt previous notions of what it means to write and teach writing. As Veronica explained:

> Writing teachers should have to get their hands dirty before they can truly teach anything even remotely connected to a writing piece. I don't care what it is; writing teachers should immerse themselves in the genre before they can say they "know" how it should look. Finding and providing mentor texts, explicitly listing the nuts and bolts of the genre you're teaching, and writing your own are all component parts to not only understand what it is you're teaching at its very core but enables you to give an honest explanation of how you do what it is you're hoping students create, too.

Such struggles provide teachers with opportunities to transform their former version of themselves as writers. Given multiple opportunities and time to write, teachers may be better positioned to teach writing from a place of personal knowing, where their identities as writers shape the instruction they provide to their students.

References

Applebee, A.N. and Langer, J.A. 2006, *The state of writing instruction in American schools: What existing data tells us*, Center on English Learning and Achievement, University of Albany, State University of New York, Albany.

Applebee, A.N. and Langer, J.A. 2009, 'What is happening the teaching of writing?' *The English Journal*, vol. 98, no. 5, pp. 18–28.

Applebee, A.N. and Langer, J.A. 2011, 'A snapshot of writing instruction in middle schools and high schools' *English Journal*, vol. 100, no. 6, pp. 14–27.

Applebee, A.N. and Langer, J.A. 2013, *Writing instruction that works: Proven methods for middle and high school classrooms*, Teachers College Press, New York.

Atwell, N.A. 1987, *In the middle: Reading, writing and learning with adolescents*, Heinemann, Portsmouth, NH.

Brimi, H. 2012, 'Teaching writing in the shadow of standardized writing assessment: An exploratory study', *American Secondary Education*, vol. 41, no. 1, pp. 52–78.

Cambourne, B. 1988, *The whole story: Natural learning and the acquisition of literacy in the classroom*, Scholastic, Auckland.

Cambourne, B. 1995, 'Toward an educationally relevant theory of literacy learning: Twenty years of inquiry', *The Reading Teacher*, vol. 49, pp. 182–190.

Cutler, L. and Graham, S. 2008, 'Primary grade writing instruction: A national survey', *Journal of Educational Psychology*, vol. 100, pp. 907–919.

Glaser, B. and Strauss, A. 1999, *The discovery of grounded theory: Strategies for qualitative research*, Aldine Publishing Company, Hawthorne, NY.

Grossman, P., Valencia, S., Evans, K., Thompson, C., Martin, S. and Place, N. 2000, 'Transitions into teaching: Learning to teach writing in teacher education and beyond', *Journal of Literacy Research*, vol. 32, pp. 631–662.

Johnston, P.H. 2004, *Choice words: How our language affects children's learning*, Stenhouse, Portland, ME.

Kittle, P. 2008, *Write beside them: Risk, voice, and clarity in high school writing*, Heinemann, Portsmouth, NH.

Lamott, A. 1994, *Bird by bird: Some instructions on writing and life*, Doubleday, New York.

Lortie, D. 1975, *Schoolteacher: A sociological study*, University of Chicago Press, Chicago, IL.

McCarthey, S.J. and Moje, E.B. 2002, 'Identity matters', *Reading Research Quarterly*, vol. 37, no. 2, pp. 228–238.

Moje, E., Luke, A., Davies, B., and Street, B. 2009, 'Literacy and identity: Examining the metaphors in history and contemporary research', *Reading Research Quarterly*, vol. 44, no. 4, pp. 415–437.

Morgan, D.N. 2010, 'Preservice teachers as writers', *Literacy Research and Instruction*, vol. 49, pp. 357–365.

Morgan, D.N. and Pytash, K.E. 2014, 'Preparing preservice teachers to become teachers of writing: A 20-year review of the research literature', *English Education*, vol. 47, no. 1, pp. 6–32.

Murray, D.M. 2004, *A writer teaches writing* (2nd edn), Thomson/Heinle, Boston, MA.

National Commission on Writing for America's Families, Schools and Colleges (The) 2003, *The neglected "R": The need for a writing revolution*. Available from: http://www.writing commission.org.

National Writing Project and Nagin, C. 2006, *Because writing matters: Improving student writing in our schools*, Jossey-Bass, New York.

Palmer, P.J. 1998, *The courage to teach: Exploring the inner landscapes of a teacher's life*, Jossey-Bass, San Francisco, CA.

Ray, K.W. 2006, *Study driven: A framework for planning units of study in the writing workshop*, Heinemann, Portsmouth, NH.

Smagorinsky, P. 2010, 'Teaching writing in the age of accountability: Reflections from the academy', in *Putting Writing Research into Practice: Applications for teacher professional development*, eds G.A. Troia, R.K. Shankland and A. Heinz, Guilford Press, New York, pp. 276–305.

Smagorinsky, P., Cook, L.S. and Johnson, T.S. 2003, 'The twisting path of concept development in learning to teach', *Teachers College Record*, vol. 105, pp. 1399–1436.

Smith, F. 1988, *Joining the literacy club: Further essays into education*, Heinemann, Portsmouth, NH.

Street, C. and Stang, K. 2008, 'Improving the teaching of writing across the curriculum: A model for teaching in-service secondary teachers to write', *Action in Teacher Education*, vol. 30, no. 1, pp. 37–49.

Whitney, A.E. and Friedrich, L. 2013, 'Orientations for the teaching of writing: A legacy of the National Writing Project', *Teachers College Record*, vol. 115, pp. 1–37.

4

ADDRESSING RESISTANCE

Encouraging in-service teachers to think of themselves as writers

Chris Street and Kristin K. Stang

Introduction

As a response to the need for improving the state of writing in secondary schools and for improving teacher training in the area of writing, we provide the background and framework for a research-based course for in-service teachers, designed to better prepare them to meet the challenges of using writing across all secondary content areas. Years of experience have taught us that many content-area educators do not feel well prepared to teach writing. Often, these in-service teachers lack the confidence to use writing with their secondary students.

Teachers serve as a crucial link in the continued efforts to improve the literacy skills of K-12 students (Allington and Johnston 2000; Darling-Hammond 1997; Joyce and Showers 2002; National Commission on Writing 2003, 2004, 2005, 2006; National Writing Project and Nagin 2006). The need for improving the effectiveness of writing teachers is underscored in an evaluation by the National Assessment of Educational Progress (NAEP), which indicated that only half of the students in Grades 4, 8, and 12 in the United States are able to write adequate responses to informative, persuasive, or narrative writing tasks (National Commission on Writing 2003). The NAEP report revealed that students generally receive little writing instruction and suggested that the writing process was not as well established in the US as thought (Graham et al. 2014; National Commission on Writing 2003, 2006). Educators and researchers from both sides of the Atlantic have expressed similar concerns (Locke 2015).

As the pressure to have students graduate from public schools as competent writers mounts, it is vital to understand how to better prepare the teachers charged with the task of instructing these student writers. In American secondary schools, the majority of middle- and high-school teachers determine how their lessons will be designed and which resources they will draw upon while teaching. As such, these teachers serve as the primary decision-makers on whether they will use writing in the classroom. In the United States, with the recent adoption of the Common Core State Standards, there is a renewed emphasis on writing (Graham and Harris 2015), which should result in increased writing instruction and writing in American schools (Graham and Harris 2015; Kohnen 2013). In addition, it is hoped that as secondary teachers become more comfortable and confident with their own writing, they will become more effective teachers of writing (Bratcher and Stroble 1994; Locke 2015; Street and Stang 2009).

A growing body of research highlights the connections between self-identity or self-efficacy and writing motivation (Andrade et al. 2009; Boscolo and Gelati 2007). The National Writing Project (NWP) has long recognized this important connection. Following the tenets of the NWP model, this graduate-level writing course was designed to allow teachers an environment where they could engage with writing in meaningful ways within communities of practice. Research associated with the NWP professional development approach in the United States and, more recently, the United Kingdom and New Zealand suggests that teachers can experience transformative effects when the tenets of this approach are applied (Locke 2015).

Addressing resistance

In most, if not all, English-speaking countries, students' writing performance and their motivation to write are less than hoped for (Locke 2015). In the United States, the National Commission on Writing for America's Families, Schools, and Colleges (2006) specifies that writing across the curriculum programs should be well supported. They also challenge teacher preparation programs to provide opportunities for "teachers already in the classroom to upgrade their writing skills and competence as writing teachers" (p. 65). Yet many classroom teachers do not feel comfortable teaching writing, nor do they feel knowledgeable about how to use writing with students (Murphy 2003; Napoli 2001; Street 2003).

This lack of confidence may be because teachers are heavily influenced by their own biographies as writers (Mathers, Kushner-Benson and Newton 2007; Street 2003). From Lortie (1975) onwards, research has consistently reported the powerful influence that teachers' attitudes about teaching exert on their learning (Clifford and Green 1996; Florio-Ruane and Lensmire 1990; Grossman et al. 2000; Schmidt and Kennedy 1990; Shrofel 1991). Since "teachers enter their professional education already trapped in their own relationship with the subject" (Kennedy 1998, p. 14), the writing attitudes and experiences they bring with them to the university may be difficult to change.

The social nature of learning

Such research suggests that the social nature of learning should be an important consideration when designing professional development workshops or college courses for in-service teachers. This point lies at the heart of the NWP model of professional development (Andrews 2008; Lieberman and Wood 2003; National Writing Project and Nagin 2006) and has been recognized as an important consideration by recent writing reports examining models of professional development for writing teachers (National Commission on Writing 2003, 2005, 2006).

We agree with Lave and Wenger (1991) that the development of identity is central to the development of teachers as writers. If we want teachers to see themselves as members of both writing and teaching communities, teacher educators would do well to consider issues of biography, self-confidence, and proficiency with writing in undergraduate and graduate courses. As is evidenced from current research, the writing histories of teachers play an important role in their ability – or inability – to use writing with their students (Bratcher and Stroble 1994; Chambless and Bass 1995; Mathers, Kushner-Benson and Newton 2007; Street 2003; Tschannen-Moran and Hoy 2001).

When teachers are engaged in college courses or professional development experiences that allow them to take risks as writers, practice their emerging craft, and interact with peers, they often come to realize that they too have the ability to write well. Chambless and Bass (1995) remind us that "formal instruction in how to teach writing and a wide variety of successful experiences with writing positively affect one's attitudes about writing, which in turn influences one's performance as a teacher of writing" (p. 154).

The National Writing Project: a research-based model of professional development

The NWP is a group that understands this issue, and believes that teachers must be comfortable and confident with writing before they can feel competent as teachers of writing (Bratcher and Stroble 1994; National Writing Project 2010). According to the NWP, until teachers know as insiders what writing is like, they will never truly be able to teach their students to write well. Hence, every attempt is made to immerse NWP teachers in the role of authors, inviting them to experience writing from the inside out. As chronicled by Lieberman and Wood (2002a), "[c]ore activities . . . include sharing best lessons or strategies, participating in small writing groups, and receiving peer feedback" (p. 40) from colleagues.

As a response to recent calls for action in the United States and elsewhere, the NWP emerges as a successful model of professional development, offering teachers the kind of support that research suggests they require (Bratcher and Stroble 1994; Lieberman and Wood 2002a, 2003; Locke 2015; Locke, Whitehead and Dix 2013; National Writing Project and Nagin 2006; Raymond 1994; Street 2003). The NWP model of professional development addresses the major challenge outlined in this chapter: how to build teachers' self-confidence as writers in the context of offering them meaningful and sustained professional development. As a model of professional development, it is collaborative: "The university and schools work together as partners, believing that the 'top-down' tradition is no longer acceptable as a staff development model" (Raymond 1994, p. 289). Successful professional development must be "on-going and systematic"; moreover, bringing "teachers together regularly . . . to test and evaluate the best practices of other teachers" is crucial to this model of professional development (Raymond 1994, p. 289).

Another strength of the NWP model is that teacher-fellows act as a support network for one another. Research suggests that teachers benefit from the kind of extended support system modeled by such professional development (Bratcher and Stroble 1994; Lieberman and Wood 2002a, 2002b, 2003; Locke 2015; National Writing Project and Nagin 2006; Raymond 1994). As Smith (1996) contends, "[t]his model, as opposed to the traditional model of teacher as passenger, demands that teachers get behind the wheel and make informed decisions about where to go and how to get there" (p. 11). Once accepted, these teacher-fellows join a national network of exemplary teachers, who act as a support system for one another, often meeting regularly to discuss issues of practice.

As suggested by the NWP, until teachers know as insiders what writing is like, they will never truly be able to teach their students to write well (Boscolo and Gelati 2007; Cremin and Baker 2014; Locke, Whitehead and Dix 2013; Street and Stang 2008, 2009). This assertion finds support in the work of Fearn and Farnan (2001), who maintain that writing is a complex cognitive task, and that developing writers need to understand what published authors understand: that there is no "process formula" that can simply be followed (p. 180). With this consideration in mind, every attempt is made to immerse NWP teachers in the role of authors, asking them to experience writing from the inside out.

The NWP realizes that professional development needs to begin where the teachers are, acknowledging that their writing histories are a vital consideration when working with them. Research suggests that the writing histories of teachers play an important role in these educators' capacity to use writing for instructional purposes (Bratcher and Stroble 1994; Chambless and Bass 1995; Street 2003; Tschannen-Moran and Hoy 2001). Hence, the NWP's professional development tenets provided the foundation for the course described in this chapter.

Teacher education and staff development

Because of the crucial role of writing in American schools (National Commission on Writing 2003, 2006; National Writing Project and Nagin 2006), there needs to be a continued examination of how teachers are prepared to teach writing. A lack of professional training regarding how to use writing in disciplinary content areas is a concern among American researchers and scholars (National Commission on Writing, 2003, 2006; National Writing Project and Nagin 2006). A substantial body of research investigating the preparation of writing teachers suggests that many American teachers are not prepared to use writing with their students (National Commission on Writing 2003, 2006; National Writing Project and Nagin 2006).

Furthermore, as reported in *The Neglected "R"*, most preservice teachers in the United States "receive little instruction in how to teach writing. At this time, only a handful of states require courses in writing for teacher certification" (National Commission on Writing 2003, p. 23). When teachers do experience professional development in this area, it tends to be a one-off workshop devoted to writing across the curriculum or unrelated to the individual needs of the teacher (Lieberman and Wood 2003; National Writing Project and Nagin 2006). This is unfortunate, since research suggests that student achievement and student literacy levels are directly linked to the professional development of teachers (Allington and Johnston 2000; Darling-Hammond 1997; Joyce and Showers 2002; National Writing Project 2010). Students tend to perform better when expectations are high. If teachers are trained in methods that foster student access to challenging curricular material, then performance expectations will increase. This, in turn, should increase actual student performance (National Writing Project 2010).

Since most teachers receive limited training and professional development in this area (National Commission on Writing 2003, 2006; National Writing Project and Nagin 2006), some important lessons emerge from the research on how to best meet the needs of writing teachers (Bratcher and Stroble 1994; Lieberman and Wood 2002a, 2003; Locke 2015; Locke, Whitehead and Dix 2013; National Writing Project and Nagin 2006; Raymond 1994; Street 2003). These lessons are especially informative to those professionals working in teacher education and staff development. Many of those lessons are revealed in the design of the course described next.

Course background

Internationally, teacher educators, literacy experts, and researchers are currently engaged in a quest to discover how to best provide professional learning opportunities for teachers of writing (Andrews 2008; Cremin and Baker 2014; Fletcher 2015; Graham and Harris 2015; Locke 2015). On both sides of the Atlantic, there is a need for teachers who have the professional skills, dispositions, and knowledge to positively influence the writing skills of their students. This need, along with a realization that all teachers leaving our university should be equipped to use writing for instructional purposes, drove us to develop this course.

A semester-long graduate writing course was designed as a research-based model of professional preparation in a large teacher preparation program (Street and Stang 2008). The primary goals were to improve the writing attitudes, skills, and teaching practices of in-service middle- and high-school educators teaching in all content areas. This course is now a required course for the masters of secondary education degree at our university.

The course follows the basic tenets of the NWP model of professional development (Andrews 2008). At the start of the class, all students create a writing autobiography so that the instructor has a better sense of who the teachers are as writers (Street and Stang 2008). The instructor models this assignment by sharing his own writing autobiography (Street 1998). As a way to foster a sense of community in the class, we ask teachers to write and then share their writing autobiographies with the rest of the group. This exercise serves several purposes. It allows all teachers to begin with a piece of "first-person" writing. Since writing in the first person ("I") is often the easiest form, this is how many NWP leaders also open their summer institutes.

This activity also allows participants to open up and share their work within a network of other caring professionals. Such sharing enables teachers to see that they are not alone in their fears and perceived limitations as writers. In fact, once teachers share their writing histories with one another, they find many commonalities among the members of the group. This helps to cement a sense of community among members of the writing group. Finally, these writing histories provide a place for teachers to grow, for it is only by knowing who we are as writers that we are able to move forward and improve our own attitudes and skills as writers. We always open our classes and workshops with this activity, because it lays the foundation for the rest of the learning experience.

Because the work of teachers is often solitary, sharing writing with a group of trusted colleagues is a way of creating a community that extends beyond the confining barriers of classroom walls. In this course, writing groups are an effective way to bring teachers together. Teacher self-select their groups (3–4 per group), but the groups tend to naturally form based on a shared content area and/or a shared work setting. Because working in a writing group puts everyone in a student role, the teachers experience what it is like to consider writing from the other side of the desk. They experience being student writers again. Most importantly, these writing communities build confidence, inspire writing, and encourage revision within a supportive network. Peer feedback within communities of practice is a core component of the course.

Teachers also receive significant feedback from their instructor on all written assignments; these assignments can be rewritten as many times as the students like. This revision policy is both necessary and appreciated by the students, since "earning an A" in this class indicates that the instructor believes the work is "publication ready." As suggested by the NWP and others (Fearn and Farnan 2001; Graham, Harris and Hebert 2011; National Writing Project and Nagin 2006; Street 2002), it is important for teachers to realize that feedback and revision lie at the heart of writing well.

Written assignments focus on effective writing, writing across the curriculum, writing for professional audiences, and teaching writing to adolescents. Teachers are also expected to participate in numerous in-class and online discussions, write reports to administrators, and complete additional brief papers and class assignments. Through in-class and online discussions, the constant sharing of "in-process" writing, and the work of teachers within their writing groups, a sense of community develops.

A writing portfolio containing all major assignments is assessed at the end of the course. Prior to the writing portfolio, the instructor provides detailed feedback on student writing, but no grades are assigned. Students typically revise each of the final portfolio assignments 2–6 times before submitting them in their polished form for a formal grade. The ability of teachers to revise their written work after receiving extensive instructor feedback and support from peers has always served as the cornerstone of the course.

Research on the course

Research on this course suggests that, indeed, teacher beliefs and attitudes regarding writing can change (Street and Stang 2009). More specifically, teachers appreciated the opportunity to work and share their writing with their peers; they acknowledged the growth in their writing over time; and they commented on how their outlooks regarding writing had evolved.

Student self-confidence was measured through qualitative data at both the beginning and end of the course (see Table 4.1). Students were grouped according to their positive, neutral, or negative beliefs regarding their own self-confidence as writers. Of the 25 students, 5 had *positive* levels of self-confidence as writers (20 percent), 8 were *neutral* (32 percent), and 12 had *negative* feelings of self-confidence as writers (48 percent) as they entered the course. Self-confidence – or lack thereof – was not associated with any particular grade level or content area. In fact, no significant relationships between gender, years teaching, subject matter or grade level taught, and group membership were identified.

On course completion, a total of seven students had *positive* levels of self-confidence as writers (28 percent), 15 students held *neutral* views (60 percent), and three students held *negative* views (12 percent). No significant relationships between gender, years teaching, subject matter or grade level taught, and group membership post course were identified.

It is important to note that before the class, 48 percent ($n = 12$) of the students held negative self-beliefs about their ability as writers, whereas after completion of the course only 12 percent ($n = 3$) held negative self-beliefs. Of the seven students holding positive beliefs following the course, one student had moved from an originally negative self-belief, one student had moved from a neutral self-belief and the remaining five students were in the original positive group.

TABLE 4.1 Participants grouped according to post-course self-confidence as writers ($n = 25$)

Group gender	JH/HS	Yrs tching	Ethnicity	Subject	Pre-class
Positive ($n = 7$)					
Female	JH	2–5	Other	Social Sciences	Negative
Female	HS	11–15	Cauc	Social Sciences	Neutral
Male	HS	11–15	Cauc	Math	Positive
Female	HS	2–5	Cauc	Science	Positive
Male	HS	2–5	As Am	Science	Positive
Male	HS	2–5	As Am	Math	Positive
Female	JH	2–5	Cauc	Arts	Positive

(continued)

TABLE 4.1 *(continued)*

Neutral (*n* = 15)					
Female	JH	2–5	AsAm	Language Arts	Neutral
Female	HS	2–5	Hispanic	Math	Negative
Female	HS	2–5	Hispanic	Language Arts	Neutral
Male	HS	2–5	Other	Social Sciences	Negative
Female	HS	11–15	Cauc	Science	Neutral
Male	JH	2–5	Cauc	Math	Negative
Female	JH	16–20	Cauc	Physical Ed.	Negative
Female	HS	2–5	Cauc	Foreign Lang.	Negative
Female	HS	1	As.Am.	Math	Negative
Female	HS	11–15	Cauc	Math	Negative
Female	JH	11–15	Cauc	Voc. Ed.	Negative
Male	HS	11–15	Cauc	Math	Negative
Male	JH	2–5	Hispanic	Language Arts	Neutral
Male	JH	2–5	As. Am	Science	Neutral
Female	HS	1	Cauc	Language Arts	Negative
Negative (*n* = 3)					
Female	HS	2–5	Cauc	Science	Negative
Female	JH	2–5	As Am	Math	Neutral
Male	JH	2–5	As Am	Language Arts	Neutral

Of the 15 students in the neutral writing group, five were originally in the neutral group and ten had held negative beliefs. Of the three students who remained in the negative group following completion of the course, two moved from the neutral group to the negative group and one student's negative self-beliefs about herself as a writer remained unchanged. A significant difference existed between student writing, self-confidence, and group membership pre- and post-intervention of the writing course.

In the follow-up questionnaire, students were asked to describe their levels of self-confidence in the class and comment on whether they thought those self-confidence levels had changed as a result of the class. Students also responded to discussion topics that dealt with their evolving identities as writers. Finally, their writing history essays were used to gauge how the course influenced their identities as writers.

The teachers from all three confidence groups reported that the course significantly improved their self-confidence as writers. Representative comments from those teachers who moved out of the negative self-confidence group help illustrate just why these changes in group membership occurred. Dana, a teacher who experienced "panic" whenever she was asked to write before the class, remarked that her

> perceptions of writing [had] definitely changed. Before this class writing was a dreadful task that needed to be done. Writing is still a task that I continue to put off, but instead of being dreadful there is some pleasure that comes from a finished product. I have gained some respect for writers. A quality

piece of writing takes alot [sic] of work. I thought that writing was easy for some and a chore for others. Ultimately, there is no sense of anxiety when I have to write and that's a great feeling.

Other teachers who moved out of the negative self-confidence group mentioned that they now felt "refreshed" as writers, that they were "making progress," and that they had a better sense of writing as a process. As stated by Jennie:

I found [writing] to be much more challenging than I ever believed. Throwing thoughts and ideas onto paper as they flow out of my head is not very good writing. The way in which I order my thoughts and ideas needs to be consistent and precise. My sentences need to follow along with the topic and support each other so the reader can understand the message. According to Zinsser (2001) I have too much junk in my writing. Writing is a process of rewrites and change to reach the final product.

Kamie, one of the most fearful writers when the class began, came to see the fun side of writing again, something she "had not felt in years." In fact, she acknowledged that her

level of self-confidence changed immensely. When I entered this class I know I wrote poorly . . . the task of writing for a graduate class frightened me. I feared turning in the first draft of my writing history paper. I knew it would come back full of suggestions, remarks, and criticism. However, I recognize that my writing improved significantly over the course of this class. I feel more comfortable asking my peers and colleagues to read my writing. I realize it will most likely need changes throughout. I can live with the fact that I will never perfect my writing; I can only better it with each revision.

Thomas, a math teacher and reluctant writer, came to realize that his

self-confidence was definitely in the poor category at the beginning of the course. But as each assignment was completed and feedback was received, I gained more confidence as a writer.

What is notable is that so many teachers' views of themselves as writers improved. However, these improvements in self-confidence, though compelling, should not be accepted without qualification. Some teachers, like Amber, still would "avoid writing if given the chance," though now she felt "more confident as a writer."

It was the process of constant revision that seemed most compelling to these writers. They appreciated the instructor and peer feedback that they received. They benefited from the unlimited revision policy and were able to make real gains as writers over the course of the semester. Catalina, another writer whose views changed significantly as a result of this course, stated that her "portfolio really represented some solid writing" and that through "constantly revising her papers" she came to realize that writing was a "time-intensive but rewarding experience."

Many of these teachers were genuinely surprised by their changing perceptions of their own levels of self-confidence as writers. Gabby, a math teacher, said that she "never expected that a single class could help her to see writing as a writer would see it." Alisa, the one teacher who changed from the negative to the positive group, commented on the "positive group support" as really contributing to her changing sense of self as a writer. She had experienced many "brutal attacks" on her writing as a student, so she really appreciated the comfortable, professional atmosphere that was established in this course.

It is interesting to note that of the 25 teachers in the study, two actually declined in self-confidence, reporting that the class hindered rather than helped their self-confidence as writers. In one case, Tobias, an English teacher who was in the neutral group when the class started, stated that:

> My level of self-confidence as a writer has lowered since I came into the class. I don't think I reacted well to the level of feedback I received on the first draft of my writing history paper. I felt fairly demoralized, feeling that there was more wrong than right with my paper. I thought that perhaps it wasn't salvageable and should be scrapped. Faced with this possibility scared me immensely. I couldn't see the end of the process or the possibility of making it there. I wasn't sure that I understood or had the ability to produce what my audience was looking for.

He stated that his "eyes have been opened to just how important revision and meaningful feedback is to the writing process," yet he did not seem to find the copious amounts of instructor feedback helpful. Rather, he seemed overwhelmed by the feedback, coming to state that his earlier writing, which he described as "chaotic," needed to be more tightly focused.

The second writer who moved into the negative group after the course was also overwhelmed with the feedback she received on her writing. Ivy, a math teacher, stated that, "My perceptions of writing have changed dramatically in that a once difficult task has become more challenging." Ivy's honest response is enlightening:

> I think my self-confidence has diminished because I used to think of myself as an average writer. Recently, the more I read my own work, the more dissatisfied I become with what I produce. I think it will take some time to gain confidence as a writer, and perhaps I need to become a more avid reader before I can write with confidence.

Surrounded by their peers, many of whom were more proficient writers than they were, Ivy and Tobias realized how much they still needed to learn about writing. The class seemed to engage them in the writing process to the point where they began to see the weaknesses in their own writing that may not have been pointed out to them by previous instructors. Both had had previous instructors who "told them they were pretty good writers," but neither had experienced an intensively focused writing course where they were expected to produce writing that was "publication ready."

Implications for teacher educators

The writing histories of the students in this course played a key role in their ability – or inability – to escape their own biographies as writers. Teacher preparation and staff development programs must begin with where the teachers are, acknowledging that the writing histories of teachers are a vital consideration when working with educators. Since research suggests that many practicing teachers possess poor writing attitudes (Florio-Ruane and Lensmire 1990; Shrofel 1991; Street 2003), it is often a challenge for university faculty and staff development professionals to overcome these negative attitudes. Chambless and Bass (1995) suggest that if teacher educators want to influence teachers' writing attitudes, they must stress process writing pedagogy in their courses. A significant body of research demonstrates that indeed, writing attitudes and skills can be changed by effective university courses and professional learning experiences (Andrews 2008; Chambless and Bass 1995; Franklin 1992; Lapp and Flood 1985; Locke 2015; Stover 1986; Street and Stang 2009). The graduate writing course described here led these teachers to both reflect on themselves as writers and look forward as teachers of writing.

Years of experience teaching this course have highlighted for us the importance of preparing teachers within "communities of practice" (Lave and Wenger 1991). This course was successful partly because of the constant sharing of "in-process" writing. Through this constant sharing, a sense of community developed. This sense of a community is vital to the success of the NWP model of professional development, and to courses such as this one. Considerable research (Bratcher and Stroble 1994; Lieberman and Wood 2002, 2003; National Writing Project and Nagin 2006; Pella 2011; Raymond 1994; Street 2003; Street and Stang 2009) supports the notion that teachers learn and grow within these kinds of "communities of practice" (Lave and Wenger 1991).

Lastly, professional development opportunities should support teachers' identities as writers (Locke 2015). Clifford and Green (1996) suggest that how teachers feel about their own effectiveness as teachers becomes a significant factor when looking at how they develop professional identities. Since a history of unaccomplished writing may diminish a writer's confidence (Bratcher and Stroble 1994; Mayher 1990), many teachers are in need of professional development opportunities that support their identities as writers. As such, this social model of learning in communities of practice provides a foundation for the kind of learning experiences that the NWP and this course supports: namely, that teachers learn to teach writing by writing in the company of supportive and committed colleagues. From this perspective, the ways in which teachers enter a community of practice is tied to their evolving identities as writers. They are acquiring the ways of being writers and teachers of writing (National Writing Project 2010).

Meeting the needs of all our students

As teacher educators, we can often sense teachers' anxieties and their desire to better support their student writers. It is important to remember that teachers first need to feel comfortable with their own writing abilities before we ask them to use writing with their own students. It is vital that all students are able to write well; yet this will not happen unless the professional development of teachers across the content areas is improved. Unless teachers feel confident, comfortable, and competent as writers – and as teachers of writing – they will likely not feel equipped to develop their students' writing skills (Bratcher and Stroble 1994). Therefore, experts should design meaningful professional development opportunities that not only cover the pedagogical aspects of using writing for instructional purposes, but must begin the professional learning with where the teachers are, taking the time to ask teachers to reflect upon their own histories as writers.

Final thoughts

In our graduate-level writing classes, we have helped many teachers – some who complain that they hate writing and are not good at it at the beginning of the semester – come to see themselves as capable writers with unique and impressive styles. Our decades of experience have confirmed that teachers must first feel comfortable and confident with writing before they are ready to use writing well with students. They also need to feel that writing will benefit their students. Otherwise, teachers will avoid using writing with students. This teacher knowledge will need to be fostered if we hope to honor the important role that writing must play in our schools.

References

Allington, R. and Johnston, P. 2000, *What do we know about effective fourth grade teachers and their classrooms?*, Report Series 13010. The National Research Center on English Learning & Achievement, University at Albany, State University of New York.

Andrade, H., Wang, X., Du, Y., and Akawi, R. 2009, 'Rubric referenced self-assessment and self-efficacy for writing', *The Journal of Educational Research*, vol. 102, no. 4, pp. 287–301.

Andrews, R. 2008, *The case for a National Writing Project for teachers*. Available from: http://cdn.cfbt.com.

Boscolo, P. and Gelati, C. 2007, 'Best practices in promoting motivation for writing', in *Best practices in writing instruction*, eds S. Graham, C. MacArthur and J. Fitzgerald, Guilford Press, New York, pp. 202–221.

Bratcher, S. and Stroble E.J. 1994, 'Determining the progression from comfort to confidence: A longitudinal evaluation of a National Writing Project site based on multiple data sources', *Research in the Teaching of English*, vol. 28, no. 1, pp. 66–88.

Chambless, M.S. and Bass, J.A. 1995, 'Effecting changes in student teachers' attitudes toward writing', *Reading Research and Instruction*, vol. 35, no. 2, pp. 153–160.

Clifford, E.F. and Green, V.P. 1996, 'The mentor-protégé relationship as a factor in pre-service education: A review of the literature', *Early Child Development and Care*, vol. 125, pp. 73–83.

Cremin, T. and Baker, S. 2014, 'Exploring the discursively constructed identities of a teacher-writer teaching writing', *English Teaching Practice and Critique*, vol. 13, no. 3, pp. 30–55.

Darling-Hammond, L. 1997, *The right to learn: A blueprint for creating schools that work*, Jossey-Bass, San Francisco, California.

Fearn, L. and Farnan, N. 2001, *Interactions: Teaching, writing and the language arts*, Houghton Mifflin, Boston, Massachusetts.

Fletcher, J. 2015, *Teaching arguments: Rhetorical comprehension, critique, and response*, Stenhouse, Portland, Maine.

Florio-Ruane, S. and Lensmire, T.J. 1990, 'Transforming future teachers' ideas about writing instruction', *Curriculum Studies*, vol. 22, no. 3, pp. 277–289.

Franklin, M.R. 1992, 'Learning the writing process in teacher education classes', *Action in Teacher Education*, vol. 14, no. 2, pp. 60–66.

Graham, S., Harris, K., and Hebert, M.A. 2011, *Informing writing: The benefits of formative assessment, A Report from the Carnegie Corporation*, Carnegie Corporation, New York. Available from: https://www.carnegie.org.

Graham, S., Capizzi, A., Harris, K., Hebert, M., and Morphy, P. 2014, 'Teaching writing to middle school students: A national survey', *Reading and Writing*, vol. 27, no. 6, pp. 1015–1042.

Graham, S. and Harris, K. 2015, 'Common core state standards and writing: Introduction to the special issue', *The Elementary School Journal*, vol. 115, no. 4, pp. 457–463.

Grossman, P.L., Valencia, S.W., Evans, K., Thompson, C., Martin, S., and Place, N. 2000, 'Transitions into teaching: Learning to teach writing in teacher education and beyond' *Journal of Literacy Research*, vol. 32, pp. 631–662.

Joyce, B. and Showers, B. 2002, *Student achievement through staff development*, 3rd edn, Association of Supervision and Curriculum Development, Alexandria, Virginia.

Kennedy, M. 1998, *Learning to teach writing: Does teacher education make a difference?*, Teachers College Press, New York.

Kohnen, A. 2013, 'Content-area teachers as teachers of writing', *Teaching/Writing: The Journal of Writing Teacher Education*, vol. 2, no. 1, pp. 29–33.

Lapp, D. and Flood J. 1985, 'The impact of writing instruction on teachers' attitudes and practices', *Proceedings of the thirty-fourth national reading conference on issues in literacy: A research perspective*, pp. 375–380, ed. J.A. Niles, National Reading Conference, Inc., Chicago, Illinois.

Lave, J. and Wenger, E. 1991, *Situated learning: Legitimate peripheral participation*, Cambridge University Press, New York.

Lieberman, A. and Wood, D. 2002a, 'The National Writing Project', *Educational Leadership*, vol. 59, no. 6, pp. 40–43.

Lieberman, A. and Wood, D. 2002b, 'Untangling the threads: Networks, community and teacher learning in the National Writing Project', *Teachers and teaching: theory and practice*, vol. 8, no. 4, pp. 295–302.

Lieberman, A. and Wood, D. 2003, *Inside the National Writing Project: Connecting network learning and classroom teaching*, Teachers College, New York.

Locke, T. 2015, *Developing writing teachers: Practical ways for teacher-writers to transform their classroom practice*, Routledge, New York.

Locke, T., Whitehead, D. and Dix, S. 2013, 'The impact of 'Writing Project' professional development on teachers' self-efficacy as writers and teachers of writing', *English in Australia*, vol. 48, no. 2, pp. 55–69.

Lortie, D.C. 1975, *Schoolteacher*, University of Chicago Press, Chicago, Illnois.

Mathers, B.G., Kushner-Benson, S. and Newton, E. 2007, '"The teacher said my story was excellent." Preservice teachers reflect on the role of the "external" in writing', *Journal of Adolescent and Adult Literacy*, vol. 50, no. 4, pp. 290–297.

Mayher, J. 1990, *Uncommon sense*, Heinemann, Portsmouth, New Hampshire.

Murphy, P. 2003, 'Discovering the ending in the beginning', *Language Arts*, vol. 80, no. 6, pp. 461–469.

Napoli, M. 2001, 'Preservice teachers' reflections about learning to teach writing', Ph.D. thesis, Pennsylvania State University.

National Commission on Writing for America's Families, Schools, and Colleges 2003, *The neglected "R": The need for a writing revolution*, College Board. Available from: http://www.collegeboard.com.

National Commission on Writing for America's Families, Schools, and Colleges, September 2004, *Writing: A ticket to work . . . or a ticket out: A survey of business leaders*, College Board. Available from: http://www.collegeboard.com.

National Commission on Writing for America's Families, Schools, and Colleges 2005, *Writing: A powerful message from state government*, College Board. Available from: http://www.collegeboard.com.

National Commission on Writing for America's Families, Schools, and Colleges 2006, *Writing and school reform including, the neglected "R": The need for a writing revolution*, College Board. Available from: http://www.collegeboard.org.

National Writing Project 2010, *Writing Project professional development continues to yield gains in student writing achievement*. National Writing Project. Available from: www.nwp.org.

National Writing Project and Nagin, C 2006, *Because writing matters: Improving student writing in our schools*, Jossey-Bass, San Francisco, California.

Pella, S. 2011, 'Teaching in politically, socially-situated contexts', *Teacher Education Quarterly*, vol. 38, no. 1, pp. 107–125.

Raymond, R.C. 1994, 'Southeastern writing projects and the two-year college teacher', *Teaching English at the Two-Year College*, vol. 21, pp. 288–296.

Schmidt, W.H. and Kennedy, M.M. 1990, *Teachers' and teacher candidates' beliefs about subject matter and about teaching responsibilities*, National Center for Research on Teacher Education, East Lansing, Michigan.

Shrofel, S. 1991, 'Developing writing teachers', *English Journal*, vol. 23, no. 3, pp. 160–177.

Smith, M.A. 1996, 'The National Writing Project after 22 years', *Delta Kappan*, vol. 77, pp. 688–703.

Stover, L. 1986, 'Writing to learn in teacher education', *Journal of Teacher Education*, vol. 37, no. 4, pp. 20–23.

Street, C. 1998, 'Rivers and writing: A teacher's reflection on the writing process', *California English*, vol. 4, pp. 18–19.

Street, C. 2002, 'The P.O.W.E.R. of process writing in content area classrooms', *Journal of Content Area Reading*, vol. 1, no. 1, pp. 43–54.

Street, C. 2003, 'Pre-service teachers' attitudes about writing and learning to teach writing: Implications for teacher educators', *Teacher Education Quarterly*, vol. 30, no. 3, pp. 33–50.

Street, C. and Stang, K.K. 2008, 'Improving the teaching of writing across the curriculum: A model for teaching in-service secondary teachers to write', *Action in Teacher Education*, vol. 30, no. 1, pp. 37–49.

Street, C. and Stang, K. 2009, 'In what ways do teacher education courses change teachers' self-confidence as writers?', *Teacher Education Quarterly*, vol. 36, no. 1, pp. 75–94.

Tschannen-Moran, M. and Hoy, A.W. 2001, 'Teacher efficacy: Capturing an elusive construct', *Teaching and Teacher Education*, vol. 17, pp. 783–805.

5

DEVELOPING THE TEACHER-WRITER IN PROFESSIONAL DEVELOPMENT

Anne Whitney

Introduction

While the exhortation that "the teacher of writing should also write" is now a commonplace, the action and identity it denotes is not. The teacher-as-writer ethic has been generally shared among educators since at least 1974 (the inception of the National Writing Project) and has shown to be helpful not only to teachers but also to their students (Brooks 2007; Whitney et al. 2012; Whitney 2008; Smiles and Short 2006; Whyte 2011; Frager 1994). Yet even in 2016, many children have never seen their teacher in the act of writing. Many teachers dread and avoid writing, and some by extension dread and avoid *teaching* writing. Many of those teachers who do write tend to do it privately. Some keep it solely in the context of teaching a lesson (crafting a model on their own to show students in class, for example, but never finishing a text or sharing it with another adult). Others write only in the personal and private domain of a journal, which can certainly be beneficial but which excludes the many ways in which writing is actually also a public and interactive activity. Under these conditions, both teachers and students are deprived of the benefits of a writing pedagogy in which the teacher is positioned as a writer among writers.

While the above describes the general state of primary and secondary school teachers' practices with respect to writing, there is also a long-standing and growing movement of teacher-writers. These are teachers who claim the title of "writer" deliberately, write frequently, and consider writing to be a professional activity. As such, they often write in class when the children are writing. They model writing strategies live, in front of the children, using real writing of their own rather than pre-made models. They write in the context of teacher inquiry, and/or to add to the professional knowledge base in the form of educational journals, books, and other texts for their colleagues. And, increasingly, they write for the public, advocating for the profession and for children in the face of a neoliberal reform movement that undermines the autonomy of teachers and interrupts their relationships with children through the imposition of external assessment and accountability schemes. These "teacher-writers" (Whitney, Zuidema and Fredricksen 2014) enact identities as teachers who write, with powerful implications for their students and for their own trajectories as teachers.

Although it is beneficial to teachers and their students that teachers write, and although it is beneficial to teachers and the profession at large that they become "teacher-writers," only rarely do scholars and teacher educators deliberately support teachers in developing teacher-writer identities. By and large, the formal structures by which we attempt to shape teachers' identities—programs of initial teacher education, continued study, and professional development—only rarely attend directly to the formation of teacher-writer identities. Instead, we share structures and strategies for teaching writing (which are certainly important for teachers to learn), and simply reiterate the exhortation "teachers of writing should write!" without seeing to it that they actually do. We can do better.

Other chapters in this volume explain how teacher-writer identity might be better inculcated in initial teacher education. In this chapter, I turn to the context of ongoing professional development. First, I will advance one framework (Whitney, Zuidema and Fredricksen 2014) for conceptualizing the teacher-writer that is helpful for supporting the growth of teacher-writers as well as understanding them in their historical context. Next, I will briefly discuss the benefits of teacher-writer identity both to a teacher's students and to their own professional existence, while mindful that others in this volume further elaborate those benefits from different angles. I will discuss implications for professional development, recommending specific activities and experiences that research has shown are conducive to the development of teacher-writer identity (Smiles and Short 2006; Whitney 2009a, 2012; Whitney and Badiali 2010; Whitney et al. 2012). Finally, I will offer an argument about why the exhortation that "teachers should write" remains relatively unheeded (Whitney et al. 2012; Whitney, Zuidema and Fredricksen 2014). At the heart of the difficulty is the problem of teacher agency in the wider educational discourse.

Conceptualizing the teacher-writer

All teachers are writers in the sense that all teaching requires at least some writing. On a cave wall somewhere we can probably find the first formal lesson plans written by some early hunter-gatherer-teacher. Teachers of writing write, in sheer volume of words, more in the margins of student work than many published authors write in a lifetime. The first *English Journal* in 1912 was written by teachers; teachers wrote and reflected together in the days of John Dewey's laboratory school; teachers write reports, assessments, and books.

But apart from the writing that permeates our job, we also have a solid history of teachers *naming* themselves writers, engaging in writing deliberately as an identity. This history has unfolded in three major phases. In a trajectory of years, we have moved from an occasional exhortation that teachers should write to a clear conception of the *teacher-writer* (Whitney, Zuidema and Fredricksen 2014) as an available and beneficial identity option for working teachers.

Initially, in the 1970s and 1980s, the discussion focused on the "teacher as writer." This grew out of concerns about students' perceived failings as writers (Sheils 1975; Andrews 2008; Elgin 1976; Simmons 2009). It was popularized among educators by the writing process movement, which constructed writing as a process and not just a product, and which viewed that process as something we might share with students and help them navigate (Britton 1972; Britton 1975; Atwell 1986; Murray 1968; Murray 1972; Emig 1969). It followed that teachers themselves should try writing, so that they could speak from experience when instructing students. This rationale for teachers writing remains pertinent.

Second, in the 1990s and 2000s, there was a focus on the "teacher-researcher." A revolution in teacher knowledge was under way, in which teachers undertook classroom inquiry projects and, sometimes, wrote about them for the benefit of other teachers. Teacher-research groups sprang up (and many still thrive) in schools, colleges of education, and National Writing Project sites. Writing was integral to that inquiry, and sometimes writing for publication was also a goal. Teacher research also remains important; many wrongheaded policies in education today follow from a stance of ignoring both teacher knowledge and education research and relying instead on market ideology and "common sense" originating outside the classroom.

The third and most recent development is the shift to the "teacher-writer" (Whitney, Zuidema and Fredricksen 2014). This teacher writes to advocate for themselves, for students, and for the profession. Contesting the absence of teachers' voices in the local and national discourse on education, the teacher-writer as advocate finds ways to raise his/her voice, writing op-eds, speaking to parents, organizing alliances with other teachers sharing similar concerns, and otherwise finding large and small ways to speak truth—classroom truth—as an exercise of power (Fleischer 2014; Fleischer 2000; Fleischer and Buchsbaum 2006; Smagorinsky 2015).

This last kind of teacher-writer is important if teachers are to free themselves from the managerial structures now in place around the world, which undermine the authority of teachers and displace them as the primary thinkers about instruction. Teacher writing is disruptive in a context that is being reverse-engineered to restrict the teaching role to that of the obedient deliverer of a pre-packaged curriculum product. When teachers write, they find they have things to say—things we *need* them to say for the sake of the profession and our students at large.

But we also need the teacher-writer in the classroom, for the sake of specific teachers and specific children in the local sense. What's critical is that the teacher-writer doesn't just write, and doesn't just teach, but teaches *and* writes, allowing those two things to feed and complicate one another in whatever ways they will. The teacher-writer has moved from writing as something she occasionally *does* to something that helps constitute her professional identity.

Being a teacher-writer

So, what is a teacher-writer? A teacher-writer is:

A teacher who writes. Sometimes this is writing outside of the school day. It's also writing alongside students, when students are writing, and sometimes even writing "cold" in front of them. And sometimes it's writing *about* teaching, either to reflect privately on what is happening or maybe to share with a colleague.

A teacher who draws on their own writing experiences to teach. Sometimes this is direct, in the sense of showing students something learned from experience. Other times it has to do with empathizing with students from experience, simply being alongside them in solidarity as they learn to write.

A teacher whose writing lives and teaching lives feed one another. A teacher-writer lives the teaching life more fully because it is infused with writing. As Anais Nin put it in her diary: "We write to taste life twice, in the moment, and in retrospection. . . . We write to be able to transcend our life, to reach beyond it. We write to teach ourselves to speak with others, to record the journey into the labyrinth" (as cited in Webber and Grunman 1978, p. 38). The writing renders teachers more attentive to themselves and others, noticing the journeys both are on as they work.

A teacher who writes as a teacher. That is, a teacher-writer speaks to and for the profession through writing. Sometimes this means writing to or for one's local colleagues; other times it means writing to influence the public or policy. Always it means bearing witness to that which can best be seen from inside the classroom.

A teacher-writer is a teacher who has incorporated writing not just as an extra activity but as an integral part of teaching. A teacher-writer is a teacher who uses writing to understand and experience their teaching. And a teacher-writer is a writer who brings the writer's awareness, the writer's struggles, and the writer's humility into the classroom.

The teacher-writer for the students

A primary benefit to students of learning from a teacher-writer is the teacher's awareness of the emotional components of writing; in particular, the struggles associated with it. This in turn improves instruction in specific writing processes.

Empathy: sharing the problems of writing

Writing is hard. Sometimes it's staring at the blank page or screen, not knowing how to begin. Other times it's sitting stuck in the middle of a sentence or a paragraph, reaching for a word that doesn't come. Or it's writing oneself halfway into an argument that suddenly, somewhere in the middle, breaks down. Or it's sharing writing with a reader and finding, painfully, that you have not made yourself clear, or hesitating fearfully before sharing with a reader, or before writing at all, for fear of criticism.

Writing is filled with hard moments. Even the best writers find it hard. But the best and most prolific writers have something that many others don't: the hard moments don't stop them. They know that if they can face the hard moments, the moments will pass, and the bad feelings of those moments, the shame and fear and worry, will pass too. They also have a repertoire of strategies for getting through those hard moments productively: routines for settling down and getting to work; strategies for drafting and revising; and skills for eliciting helpful feedback from others and for processing the feedback they receive.

In school, however, we often pretend that writing is straightforward, or that it should be. "OK, write for ten minutes," we say, and we expect people simply to begin. Or we hand out prompts, writers write someplace else, and days or weeks later, we collect pieces of writing. These practices hide the difficulty of writing in ways that writers take personally. When writers struggle, they end up feeling they are doing so alone. They look around, see other students seemingly doing fine, and then they take their own difficulty as a sign that they're doing it wrong—or worse, that they simply aren't good writers.

It is better to acknowledge the difficulty of writing, to name its hard moments and explicitly teach how to get through these. Teacher-writers have an advantage in this. Having experienced writing's difficulty repeatedly, and recently, they are apt to remember it when planning for writing instruction, when inviting students to write, when conferring with struggling writers, and in providing feedback (Anderson 2011; Whitney 2009b; Norman and Spencer 2005; Whitney and Friedrich 2013; Whitney et al. 2008; Cremin 2006). Teacher-writers can respond to student writers—to both their writing and the *person* writing—from an empathetic stance.

Process: solving shared problems

This empathy promotes a more focused attention to the writing process than might otherwise occur. Rather than thinking about process in the abstract, as a set of steps a student might follow or as "chapters" in the life of a piece of writing, a teacher-writer can look at specific writing problems of specific writers and ask, "how might we work through them?"

As a result, specific strategies can be modeled and taught in the context of specific challenges in a piece of writing. This, for example, has been a legacy of National Writing Project involvement in the classrooms of teachers who took part in that professional development network in its first twenty years of existence. Teachers more explicitly supported students through the entire process of writing, with instruction occurring frequently along the way of drafting a product rather than only at the outset (Whitney and Friedrich 2013). Further, the processes and strategies taught by such teachers became more responsive to what students were actually experiencing, with processes modeled for students and practiced by students directly in situations where they were needed. This stood in contrast to other classrooms where instruction about processes tended to occur before students began writing anything, and where finished products were offered as models without teachers actively modeling processes themselves (Whitney et al. 2008).

The teacher-writer for the teacher themself

Teacher-writers are thus good for students directly, in terms of their practice as teachers of writing. However, much of the impact of being a teacher-writer is on the teacher themself, in terms of professional identity and professional development.

Significant experiences in my own past as a one-time secondary school teacher of English helps to make this point. In the first few years of my teaching career, I attended a Summer Institute of the National Writing Project, in which I found myself writing daily for an hour or more alongside twenty experienced teachers. Two years later, a group of colleagues and I formed an online writing group for the following school year (Elrod 2003).

These experiences had important aspects in common: they let me be the same person on the page, whether I wrote about school or the other parts of my life. Both were important, since personal and professional growth are far more tightly connected than we tend to acknowledge (Whitney 2009b; Dawson et al. 2013; Kissling 2014). When I wrote about life, I better understood what I was asking of students, and I also fed and nurtured those parts of me that had sometimes begun to shut down under the overwhelming pressure and pace of the school year. When I wrote about school, time temporarily stopped, allowing space to actually think about what was happening in school without the immediacy of needing to do something right then.

I wrote along with students almost every time they wrote in class; then when it was time to share, I could share my own writing or even simply what it was *like* to write. Sometimes this was sharing the words themselves, but other times it was sharing a problem I had had: I had struggled to get started; I had struggled to find the right word; I had struggled to organize something; I felt stuck. I became a writer among writers, a writer who struggled, as students did, and I could share how I worked through those struggles. This made me an experimenter. It made it OK that a plan hadn't worked. It made it OK that deadlines changed, or that a conversation led somewhere totally unexpected, or that different kids wrote different kinds of products in different ways. It made it OK, even helpful, that I never knew quite what would help a particular writer in my class; all I could do was invite the writer to experiment with something that had worked for me or for another student. The student would have to do the writing him/herself.

As a teacher-writer, my business was no longer primarily to convey information, or to plan and then execute plans; it was to guide people as they wrote, using my experience and theirs as guides. What were once anxieties and failures became wonderings, experiments, shared ventures. Slowly, over years of being a teacher-writer, my relationships with students changed. Over time, my lessons changed, starting with shared problems more often than with stern instructions.

While this is a story of one blessed set of circumstances in one teaching career, research suggests that these experiences are in fact typical experiences of teacher-writers. Writing benefits the teacher as a professional and person. First, writing, including writing for publication, provides a means of engaging with professional communities beyond the walls of the local school or region (Ballenger et al. 2006; McEntee 2003; Smiles and Short 2006; Whitney 2012; Rathert and Okan 2015; Whitney et al. 2012; Perrillo 2010; Whitney 2009a). These publications also provide vital knowledge for teaching. Through writing, a teacher can enrich their own teaching but also that of colleagues near and far. It follows that such writing is a form of teacher leadership (Whitney and Badiali 2010; Lieberman and Friedrich 2007).

But such benefits include a broader kind of development: the development of ways of being in the classroom that are rewarding and sustainable. Robert Yagelski (2011) calls writing "a way of being." Schools have conventionally treated writing as a set of skills one learns, or as a set of procedures one follows to create vessels into which ideas are then put. Yagelski, in contrast, views writing as an experience in which the writer is present, simultaneously and reflexively, to the ideas in play; to the text being developed; to the social network of others whose ideas and texts are touched by the work and to which the work responds; to readers present and future, living and imagined. Because of all this, Yagelski says, the writer is fully present to him/herself, and thus *fully alive* when writing. Thus the experience of writing is the experience of being *fully alive*: present, engaged, reflective, and connected, at once in relationship to oneself and to the world of others around oneself. Writing provides a means of remaining in the stressful and sometimes life-depleting context of the classroom while remaining "fully alive" to the work and the people in it. Writing provides "breathing space" (Dawson et al. 2013) for identity work through which teachers work out how they shall position themselves amidst the multiple and sometimes conflicting identity options for teaching (Dawson 2009; Whitney et al. 2014; Cremin and Baker 2014; Whitney 2006).

Professional development for the teacher-writer

How might we might develop and support teacher-writers in ongoing professional development? I elect to describe two approaches that are, for the most part, small in scale and teacher-directed in their implementation. While contexts surely must exist in which these ideas might grow into programs that support and respect teachers, too often the opposite happens. Particularly in the measurement-oriented, neoliberally grounded policy context for education in most Western countries right now, professional development is often top-down in origin, mandated in participation, narrowly defined in purpose, and tightly connected to particular curricular products. These are inappropriate for the development of teacher-writers. If, as Donald Graves (1994) wrote, writers need time, choice, response, demonstration from experienced writers, expectation that they can learn to write, predictable conditions in which to take chances, and evaluation by real audiences (pp. 103–12), then, for now at least, much of the best professional development for teacher-writers will occur outside of the authority structures governing teaching.

The National Writing Project model

The first and most long-standing and effective model for developing teacher-writers among practicing teachers is the National Writing Project (NWP). Begun in 1974 at the University of California, the NWP brings groups of experienced, practicing teachers from varying grade levels and subjects together in groups of twenty or so for multi-week, intensive Summer Institutes. Over three to five weeks of full-day sessions, these Summer Institutes involve daily writing, ranging from informal jottings to finished products and ranging from personal to professional. Teachers share slices of classroom practice, inquiry about these, and other specific lessons, while reading current research and theory about writing. They share close community, food, feedback on writing, authority for knowledge creation, a rigorous atmosphere of questioning and inquiry stance, and an ethic of safety and acceptance (Whitney 2008; Wood and Lieberman 2000; Goldberg 1998; Lieberman and Wood 2003; Gray 2000). After the Summer Institute, teachers go on to join a network of former participants, engaging in a wide range of network activities such as leading professional development workshops for other teachers in the area, forming writing groups (some of which go on for many years), gathering for continuity programs and advanced institutes on topics of teachers' choosing, and looking together at student work.

Participation in the NWP produces "orientations" to teaching writing that last: (1) seeing the purpose of writing as being a tool for learning and developing ideas; (2) seeing writing processes as a way to scaffold students' writing practices; and (3) linking the teaching of writing to their own experience as writers (Whitney and Friedrich 2013). From these orientations follow ways of evaluating and organizing practices that endure, even as specific curricula, students, and teaching contexts change. For the teacher her/himself, participation in the NWP has frequently been called "transformative," and research shows that transformative learning emerges specifically from the writing in which teachers engage and from the frequent sharing and responding to such writing, where teachers are able to experiment with voice and teacher-writer identity options (Whitney 2008; Whitney 2009b; Whitney 2006).

While the NWP itself is based in the United States, its ideas and organization have been picked up in other parts of the world. The NWP has participated in pilot programs, affiliated international sites, demonstration projects, or other dissemination activities in locations as diverse as US territories such as the US Virgin Islands and Puerto Rico, and in Malta, Norway, Hong Kong, and New Zealand. The case has been well made for a NWP-like network in the UK (Andrews 2008), and a New Zealand Writing Project was successful in the 1980s and has been recently resurrected (Locke et al. 2011; Carruthers and Scanlan 1990).

Teacher writing groups

Another well-documented mechanism for developing teachers as writers is the teacher writing group. While these vary significantly in form and focus, they involve teachers gathering (in person or virtually), writing, and sharing feedback on writing. These writing groups typically form out of existing networks such as schools, NWP sites, or university courses. For example, Robbins, Seaman, Yancey, and Yow (2006) offer portraits of three different groups emerging from a NWP site along with narratives from group members. These vary in focus and goals, but all offer examples of how the culture and support of a NWP experience was then extended over time as teachers returned to their various classrooms. Meeting with teachers working in different schools, and focusing together on writing, made it possible to experience writing in the light of different perspectives, enriching reflection. Dawson also describes a group formed of people from a shared prior context; they had been classmates and instructor in a university teacher preparation program, who continued their relationship as an online writing group as they all moved on to teaching jobs in remote locations (Dawson et al. 2013; Dawson 2009).

Some groups focus specifically on personal writing, some on specific genres such as fiction or poetry, some on producing professional texts. The Centre Teacher-Writers (CTW) (Whitney and Badiali 2010), a local writing group I facilitate, provides insight into these varying aims. The CTW welcomes teachers from preschool to Grade 12 in the local county; a typical meeting attracts between five and twelve teachers. We began in 2008 with a focus on professional writing. While all professional writing was welcomed, at the time of our initiation two of us were guest editing an issue of a small journal focused on "the voices of teachers." Using the special issue as an impetus, members drafted articles at our monthly meetings and planned a special two-day retreat to share feedback and revise. In later years, a member who said she "needs deadlines" suggested we ask the local newspaper for a regular column, which we would then have to write. Our town is small enough that this was possible, and the newspaper agreed, even though we had no samples to show them and no prior experience with op-ed writing. The column became our focus for a year or two; while we still have it, we have also pursued other projects. With grant support from one of the teacher labor unions, we spent a year writing our own assignments and producing a booklet of exemplars and reflections on our experience. Another grant funded a year-long consideration of conferencing, in which the group read and practiced conferring, while still meeting for monthly writing meetings. At the moment, there is no one central project; the column is still an option, but members are also blogging, writing for graduate programs, writing fiction, journaling, and responding to calls for papers that I bring to their attention. Some months we talk explicitly about teaching, but more often we don't, focusing instead on the people in the room and what they are trying to do as writers.

Writing groups help teachers develop writer identity. Two studies of the CTW itself make the case for its benefit to the teachers who participate. Anderson (2011) found that teachers benefitted from writing in the community, where they might otherwise have worked alone. Benefits included (a) networking with other teachers from different school settings in the local area and (b) accountability for getting writing done. Particularly helpful were opportunities to think in new ways about audiences, which arose through supported experiences with writing for publication that helped the teacher-writers to consider themselves as writers at large rather than simply as members of a class or school group. Fallon (Fallon and Whitney n.d.) has shown how offering feedback to colleagues, in particular, is helpful to teacher-writers in the group, both in terms of their specific skills in writing and their identities as writers. To encounter one another in the CTW is to be positioned as a writer among writers. The group's name highlights the identity focus, and the activities of the group necessitate stepping into the role of a writer, whether a teacher really feels ready to claim the name or not. Consequently, in acting as a writer acts (writing, sharing feedback, and publishing), the identity becomes familiar and useful. These shifts become possible in part through the development of and play with what Godbee (2012) calls "affiliative relationships" for collaborative writing talk. All of this is to say that it's not so much the writing as it is the relationships around writing and the talk about writing that activates teacher writing groups' potential for developing writer identity.

Conclusion: teacher-writer as trouble

Woodard has shown that being a teacher-writer is more complicated than writing texts outside school and then bringing them into class. The connection between the writing practices of teachers and the writing practices they share with students is not so direct (Woodard 2015; Woodard 2013a; Woodard 2013b). The link is writer identity—that a teacher names, claims, and then draws upon an identity as a writer when thinking about and enacting writing instruction in the context of relationships with student writers.

It is this development of writer identity among teachers that has been missed in so much professional development connected to writing. Sometimes classroom instructional practices have been taught (prescribing writing practices for students) without the teachers engaging in those practices themselves. Other times, writing has been incorporated as a component of professional development schemes, having teachers write about inquiry projects or journal about experiences in the classroom, for instance. In this instance, teachers have acquired writing practices and skills of their own but have not always integrated these in their writing instruction. And this suggests why, given the long history of the notion that "teachers should write," the teacher-writer is not yet a commonplace. Many have asked teachers to write, but fewer have explicitly targeted the development of writing identity. The NWP and teacher writing groups such as the CTW, spaces in which teachers write *and* name and reflect on what they are doing *and* call themselves writers *and* speak and act from that role, are exceptions to the rule.

Given the evidence that teacher-writers thrive as teachers and bring valuable resources to their teaching, why is writing identity not an explicit goal of initial teacher education programs, induction schemes, or ongoing professional development requirements? And more to the point, why is the teacher-writer still so rare "in the wild," after university preparation? After all, the message that "teachers of writing must write" has been sounded since the 1970s. Why has it not been heeded at the level of institutional preparation and ongoing teacher development? Why does this news remain so new?

One reason is that being a teacher-writer, by its nature, means being a kind of teacher not anticipated or supported by a top-down, managerial, educational environment. At the heart of the difficulty is the problem of teacher agency in the wider educational discourse: it is difficult for teachers to position students as "real" writers having ideas worthy of development, when powerful cultural and political forces conspire against such positioning. Yet I hope this chapter makes clear that adopting such a stance is worth the trouble—and worth the potential for trouble in the current managerial, neoliberally informed, and tightly controlled context for education. After all, if teachers write, *they might say something*. And that is precisely what today's policy context demands.

References

Anderson, K. (2011) *Teacher-as-writer and Writer-as-teacher: An Inquiry Into a Community of Teacher-writers*, Pennsylvania State University. Available at https://etda.libraries.psu.edu/paper/11920/7184 (Accessed September 1, 2015).

Andrews, R. (2008) *The Case for a National Writing Project for Teachers*, Reading. Available at http://cdn.cfbt.com/~/media/cfbtcorporate/files/research/2008/r-the-case-for-a-national-writing-project-for-teachers-2008.pdf (Accessed August 10, 2010).

Atwell, N. (1986) *In the Middle: Writing, Reading, and Learning with Adolescents*, Heinemann. Available at http://eric.ed.gov/?id=ED315790 (Accessed December 22, 2015).

Ballenger, R. et al. (2006) 'Our reflections on writing for publication', *Language Arts*, vol. 83, no. 6, p. 534.

Britton, J. (1972) 'Writing to learn and learning to write', in National Council of Teachers of English (ed.) *The Humanity of English: NCTE distinguished lectures*, Urbana, IL, National Council of Teachers of English.

Britton, J. (1975) *The Development of Writing Abilities*, London, pp. 11–18. Available at http://eric.ed.gov/?id=ED144049 (Accessed December 22, 2015).

Brooks, G.W. (2007) 'Teachers as Readers and Writers and as Teachers of Reading and Writing', *The Journal of Educational Research*, vol. 100, no. 3, pp. 177–191.

Carruthers, A. and Scanlan, P. (1990) 'Report on the New Zealand Writing Project: An informal evaluation', *English in Aotearoa*, vol. 11, pp. 14–18.

Cremin, T. (2006) 'Creativity, uncertainty and discomfort: teachers as writers', *Cambridge Journal of Education*, vol. 36, no. 3, pp. 415–433.

Cremin, T. and Baker, S. (2014) 'Exploring the discursively constructed identities of a teacher-writer teaching writing', *English Teaching Practice and Critique*, vol. 13, no. 3, pp. 30–55.

Dawson, C.M. (2009) *Inventing Teacher-Writers*, East Lansing, MI, Michigan State University Press.

Dawson, C.M. et al. (2013) 'Creating a breathing space: An online teachers' writing group', *English Journal*, vol. 3, pp. 93–99.

Elgin, S. (1976) 'Why "Newsweek" Can't Tell Us Why Johnny Can't Write', *English Journal*. Available at: http://www.jstor.org/stable/815562 (Accessed August 7, 2015).

Elrod, A. (2003) 'Reflections on an Online Teachers Writing Group', *Quarterly of the National Writing Project*, vol. 25, no. 1 (Winter), pp. 21–28.

Emig, J. (1969) *Components of the Composing Process Among Twelfth-Grade Writers*, Harvard University. Available at https://scholar.google.com/scholar?hl=en&q=janet+emig+process&btnG=&as_sdt=1%2C39&as_sdtp=#8 (Accessed December 22, 2015).

Fallon, L. and Whitney, A.E. '"It's a two-way street": Giving feedback in teacher writing groups.' Unpublished manuscript under review.

Fleischer, C. (2000) *Teachers Organizing for Change: Making Literacy Learning Everybody's Business*. Available at: http://eric.ed.gov/?id=ED442103 (Accessed September 8, 2015).

Fleischer, C. (2014) 'English educators as agents of change', in Goodwyn, A., Reid, L., and Durrant, C. (eds) *International Perspectives on Teaching English in a Globalised World*, Abingdon, Routledge.

Fleischer, C. and Buchsbaum, A. (2006) 'When talking makes a difference: Teachers as organizers', *Language Arts Journal of Michigan*, vol. 22, no. 1, p. 6.

Frager, A. (1994) 'Teaching, writing, and identity', *Language Arts*, vol. 71, no. 4, pp. 278–287.

Godbee, B. (2012) 'Toward explaining the transformative power of talk about, around, and for writing', *Research in the Teaching of English*, vol. 47, no. 2, pp. 171–197.

Goldberg, M.F. (1998) 'The National Writing Project: It's about the intellectual integrity of teachers', *Phi Delta Kappan* (January), pp. 394–396.

Graves, D. (1994) *A Fresh Look at Writing*, Portsmouth, NH, Heinemann.

Gray, J. (2000) *Teachers at the Center: A Memoir of the Early Years of the National Writing Project*, Berkeley, CA, National Writing Project.

Kissling, M.T. (2014) 'Now and then, in and out of the classroom: Teachers learning to teach through the experiences of their living curricula', *Teaching and Teacher Education*, vol. 44, pp. 81–91.

Lieberman, A. and Friedrich, L. (2007) 'Teachers, writers, leaders', *Educational Leadership*, vol. 65, no. 1, pp. 42–47.

Lieberman, A. and Wood, D. (2003) *Inside the National Writing Project: Connecting network learning and classroom teaching*, New York, Teachers College Press.

Locke, T. et al. (2011) 'New Zealand teachers respond to the "National Writing Project" experience', *Teacher Development*. Available at http://www.tandfonline.com/doi/abs/10.1080/13664530.2011.608509 (Accessed September 1, 2015).

McEntee, G.H. (2003) 'Diving with whales: Five reasons for practitioners to write for publication', *Quarterly of the National Writing Project*, pp. 21–26.

Murray, D. (1968) *A Writer Teaches Writing: A Practical Method of Teaching Composition*, Boston, MA, Houghton.

Murray, D. (1972) 'Teach writing as a process not product', *The Leaflet*. Available at http://www.fredonia.edu/faculty/english/spangler/Renewal2009-10/12_f_Murray--Teach_Writing_as_a_Process.pdf (Accessed December 22, 2015).

Norman, K.A. and Spencer, B.H. (2005) 'Our lives as writers: Examining preservice teachers' experiences and beliefs about the nature of writing and writing instruction', *Teacher Education Quarterly*, vol. 32, no. 1, pp. 25–40.

Perrillo, J. (2010) 'Writing for the public: Teacher editorializing as a pathway to professional development', *English Education*, vol. 43, no. 1, pp. 10–32.

Rathert, S. and Okan, Z. (2015) 'Writing for publication as a tool in teacher development', *ELT Journal*. Available at http://eltj.oxfordjournals.org/content/early/2015/05/26/elt.ccv029.abstract (Accessed September 1, 2015).

Robbins, S. et al. (2006) *Teachers' Writing Groups: Collaborative Inquiry and Reflection for Professional Growth*, Kennesaw, GA, Kennesaw State University Press.

Sheils, M. (1975) 'Why Johnny can't write', *Newsweek*. Available at https://scholar.google. com/scholar?hl=en&q=why+johnny+can%27t+write+1975+newsweek&btnG=&as_ sdt=1%2C39&as_sdtp=#0 (Accessed August 7, 2015).

Simmons, J.S. (2009) 'A conflict revisited', *The High School Journal*, vol. 93, no. 1, pp. 38–42.

Smagorinsky, P. (2015) 'Speaking out in the public sphere: Why, what, where, and how teachers can enter the fray', *English Journal*, vol. 104, no. 3, pp. 92–97.

Smiles, T.L. and Short, K.G. (2006) 'Transforming teacher voice through writing for publication transforming teacher voice through writing for publication', *Teacher Education Quarterly*, vol. 33, no. 3, pp. 133–147.

Webber, J.L. and Grumman, J. (1978) Woman as writer. Boston, MA, Houghton Mifflin.

Whitney, A.E. (2006) *The Transformative Power of Writing: Teachers Writing in a National Writing Project Summer Institute*, Santa Barbara, University of California Press.

Whitney, A.E. (2008) 'Teacher transformation in the National Writing Project', *Research in the Teaching of English*, vol. 43, no. 2, pp. 144–187.

Whitney, A.E. (2009a) 'NCTE journals and the teacher-author: Who and what gets published', *English Education*, vol. 41, no. 2, pp. 95–107.

Whitney, A.E. (2009b) 'Writer, teacher, person: Tensions between personal and professional writing in a National Writing Project Summer Institute', *English Education*, vol. 41, no. 3, pp. 235–258.

Whitney, A.E. (2012) 'Lawnmowers, parties, and writing groups: What teacher-authors have to teach us about writing for publication', *English Journal*, vol. 101.5, pp. 51–56.

Whitney, A.E. and Badiali, B. (2010) 'Writing as teacher leadership', *English Leadership Quarterly* (October), pp. 2–3.

Whitney, A.E. and Friedrich, L. (2013) 'Orientations for the teaching of writing: A legacy of the National Writing Project', *Teachers College Record*, vol. 115, no. 7, pp. 1–37.

Whitney, A.E., Zuidema, L.A. and Fredricksen, J.E. (2014) 'Understanding teachers' writing: Authority in talk and texts', *Teachers and Teaching*, vol. 20, no. 1, pp. 59–73.

Whitney, A.E. et al. (2008) 'Beyond strategies: Teacher practice, writing process, and the influence of inquiry', *English Education*, vol. 40, no. 3, pp. 201–230.

Whitney, A.E. et al. (2012) 'Audience and authority in the professional writing of teacher-authors', *Research in the Teaching of English*, vol. 46, no. 4, pp. 390–419.

Whyte, A. (2011) *Alabama Secondary School English Teachers' National Writing Project Participation and Own Writing in Relation to Their Organization of the Classroom and to Student Achievement in Writing*, Alabama Secondary School English Teachers' National Writing Project. Available at http://www.nwp.org/cs/public/download/nwp_file/15428/auburn.pdf? x-r=pcfile_d (Accessed August 13, 2016).

Wood, D.R. and Lieberman, A. (2000) 'Teachers as authors: The National Writing Project's approach to professional development', *International Journal of Leadership in Education*, vol. 3, no. 3, pp. 255–273.

Woodard, R. (2013a) '"Writing teachers must write": Tracing trajectories of teacher participation across professional and everyday practices'. Available at https://www.ideals. illinois.edu/handle/2142/45332 (Accessed September 1, 2015).

Woodard, R. (2013b) 'Complicating "writing teachers must write": Tensions between teachers' literate and instructional practices', *Literacy Research Association Yearbook*, vol. 62, p. 378.

Woodard, R. (2015) 'The dialogic interplay of writing and teaching writing: Teacher-writers' talk and textual practices across contexts', *Research in the Teaching of English*, vol. 50, no. 1, pp. 35–59.

Yagelski, R.P. (2011) *Writing As a Way of Being: Writing Instruction, Nonduality, and the Crisis of Sustainability*, New York, Hampton Press.

SECTION C

Teachers as writers

Shifting practices and positions in the classroom

6

BEING A WRITER AND TEACHING WRITING ON THE 'RACKETY BRIDGE'

Through the lens of new teachers

Marilyn McKinney

Introduction

Imagine a bridge. Not just any bridge; it's what performance art theorist (Phelan, 1993) describes as a 'rackety bridge'. On this bridge appear six middle and high school teachers. They are engaged in 'a performance suspended in the space between self and other' (p. 174) where 'neither of us ever fully meets our selves or the other'; where 'the who to whom we address our teaching is never the who who replies' (Ellsworth, 1997, p. 158) because meanings shift with time and context. But who is the other? Who is the self? As teachers of writing, who are we really?

In the study reported in this chapter, I explore intersections between novice teachers' identities as writers and performances of their roles as teachers within a large urban school district in the US that has mandated the use of a commercial literacy curriculum as part of a school reform package aimed at improving student achievement. While the research literature suggests that teachers respond to mandates along a continuum ranging from compliance to active resistance, novice teachers tend to rely on commercial materials in spite of teacher preparation programmes that emphasise the importance of adapting materials to meet the needs of diverse learners (Cobb, Sargent and Patchen, 2012; Valencia, Place, Martin and Grossman 2006). A host of reasons influence this practice – buying into the narrative that scripted curriculum is necessary to scaffold teaching during the first few years; fear of losing jobs for noncompliance; school culture that enforces 'fidelity' to a programme; power relationships that invisibly or not so invisibly structure educational spaces and relationships with students. Whatever the reason, as Valencia et al. (2006, p. 95) note: 'Teachers' interactions with these curriculum materials influence their sense of efficacy and identity as well as their vision of instruction'. Researchers such as Apple (1982) argue that scripted programmes lead to the 'deskilling' of teachers. Crucially, for children living in poverty and educators teaching in schools located in economically under-resourced areas, opportunities for authentic and culturally relevant literacy practices are severely constrained.

The teaching of writing is particularly ripe for this kind of influence because teachers traditionally feel unprepared to teach writing (National Commission on Writing, 2003). While many English language arts (ELA) teachers have clearly established identities as readers, most see writing as laborious (Yancey, 2009) and feel they lack necessary knowledge to make informed decisions about why they teach writing the way they do (O'Donnell-Allen, 2007) or to model being a writer, in part because they do not identify as writers. Because scripted curriculum coupled with teachers' diminished potential to actively engage as writers and teachers of writing ultimately impacts relationships with students and students' engagement with curriculum, there are implications for exploring writing identity from an equity perspective. Writing can be an important tool for creating change, as argued by Garcia and O'Donnell-Allen (2015, p. 81): 'Making writing something that is acceptable, encouraged, *expected* of historically marginalized youth is about affecting youth identity and social transformation'.

Given this context, I now invite you into the metaphorical space of the 'rackety bridge' where teaching is viewed as 'a suspended performance between the self and other' as a way of framing both conundrums and possibilities associated with the teaching of writing that grew out of a recent study of six middle and high school novice teachers from my graduate Teaching Writing class. These novice teachers do see themselves as writers as exemplified by their descriptions of writing of novels, as well as writing and performing poetry, plays and speeches. They entered the teaching profession through Teach for America (TFA), a national teacher preparation programme that recruits 'remarkable and diverse individuals to become teachers in low-income communities. They commit to teach for two years and are hired by . . . partner schools across the country' where they 'dramatically increase the opportunities available to their students in school and in life' (TFA website). Guided by my own experiences, beliefs and connections with National Writing Project work for over two decades, I believe that the best teachers of writing are those who write themselves, who see themselves as writers. Thus, I was fascinated by this group of teacher-writers who were required to follow a scripted commercial programme. How were they reconciling the seeming disparity between a writing identity that by definition included authorial rights of choice, authenticity and ownership, with varying levels of requirements to teach by following the content and pacing of the mandated curriculum? How were this group of teacher-writers, committed to issues of educational equity and social justice, dealing with pressures of high-stakes testing, regimes of accountability and lack of engagement by both students and teachers who were part of the system they hoped to change?

Theoretical perspectives

In this section, I draw on theoretical perspectives related to performance and identity that intertwine around pedagogical connections to the teaching of writing.

In particular, performance theorist Elizabeth Ellsworth's (1997) work related to a central concept in film theory – mode of address – offers fertile ground for exploring what she calls *pedagogical* mode of address in education. Pedagogical mode of address refers to how students and teachers are positioned in relation to each other and can be a useful lens 'to make visible and problematic the ways that all curricula and pedagogies invite their users to take up particular positions within relations of knowledge, power and desire' (Ellsworth, 1997, p. 2). In film, address can be thought of as the relationship between the intended, imagined or desired audience and film makers.

> In order for a film to work for an audience, in order for it to simply make sense to a viewer, or make her laugh, root for a character, suspend her disbelief, cry, scream, feel satisfied at the end – the viewer must enter into a particular relationship with the film's story and image system.
>
> *(Ellsworth, 1997, p. 23)*

In schools, curriculum, like film, is 'pitched' at an imagined audience, and for it to work, it is necessary for that audience to enter into that world. Ellsworth (1997) suggests,

> the terms of an address are aimed precisely at shaping, anticipating, meeting, or changing who a student thinks she is. She invites us to think with her about the question of how teachers make a difference in power, knowledge and desire not only by *what* they teach, but by *how they address* students.
>
> *(Ellsworth, 1997, p. 8)*

Writing identity was at the heart of my inquiry. In conceptualising identity I drew from current perspectives, recognising that identities are always in process, socially situated, constructed across contexts and over time; that who we are is shaped both by contexts and our perceptions of self within those contexts and by how we are perceived or positioned by 'others' (McCarthey and Moje, 2002). Of relevance for this chapter is the *identity as position* metaphor discussed in Moje, Luke, Davies and Street's (2009) article on literacy and identity metaphors. According to this perspective, identities

> are produced in and through not only activity and movement in and across spaces but also in the ways people are cast in or called to particular positions in interaction, time and spaces and how they take up or resist those positions.
>
> *(McCarthey et al., 2009, p. 430)*

The authors suggest, 'positioning metaphors allow for the doing of identity – or identity in activity – to be as powerful a means of self-construction and representation as the narrativising of identity' (Moje et al., 2009, p. 431). They suggest that literacy (including writing) can play different roles, including as 'an enabling tool, a device for making meaning of and speaking back to or resisting the call to certain positions' (Moje et al., 2009, p. 431). In the current study we see teachers positioned and positioning themselves as capable or not capable, and agentive in some spaces but not in others, depending on contexts, time and space, resources, mentors and a host of other factors. Concomitantly positioning occurs within classrooms and school sites in terms of relationships with and positioning of students by their teachers, and in relationship to mandated curricula, to the curriculum novice teachers had opportunities to develop and enact, and to engagement in an after-school writing club. (See also Cremin and Baker, 2010, 2014, Woodard, 2013 and Chapters 7 and 8 in this volume for other studies of teacher-writers that use this identity as positioning metaphor.)

Methodology: participants and context

In the spring following the Teaching Writing class, I recruited TFA Corps members via email, whom I believed had identified themselves as writers through various assignments and activities of the course. From 11 invitations, five agreed to participate. The sixth, Riya, was in the second section of this class (sections were co-planned, meeting together for guest speakers and other events) and a participant in our local writing project's summer institute. I recruited her during the institute, believing that as a Latina high school teacher, her participation would enrich the study and expand the diversity of the participant pool. Of the six participants (all participant and school names are pseudonyms), two are women. Riya is Latina, grew up locally and attended our local school district prior to college; Breanna is Caucasian and the only one who did not complete the two-year TFA commitment. Of the four male teachers, Wendom and Peter are Caucasian while Rashad is African American and Josh is Asian-American. Rashad had just completed his second year.

Five teachers were placed in middle schools and one in high school, all in low-income communities with high Latino/a/Hispanic populations (ranging from 65 per cent to 90 per cent) and 10–15 per cent African American students (in three schools). Breanna and Wendom taught at Roosevelt Middle School, Peter and Josh at Oracle Middle School, Riya at McDermott High School and Rashad at Carter Middle School. Oracle and McDermott were labelled 'turnaround schools'. All schools had large numbers of students receiving Free and Reduced Lunch; all teachers reported low reading and writing achievement levels.

For five participants, our first class was their first day of teaching as a contract teacher following an intensive five-week institute as part of TFA training. I was immediately struck by how many seemed to identify as writers in contrast to previous years. The issue of commercial curriculum was an ever-present topic threading its way into our discussions about pedagogy, curriculum and work with students. Every secondary-level teacher in the class was required to teach reading and/or writing via the ubiquitous SpringBoard curriculum (The College Board, 2016). According to the website: 'SpringBoard is the College Board's print and online programme for *all* students in Grades 6–12. It provides a customizable pathway integrating rigorous instruction, performance-based assessment, and exemplary professional learning.' In the US, the effectiveness of commercial programmes in raising academic achievement is often questioned. Critics claim that programme designers assume a student body very different from the students in most classrooms, thereby failing to engage both students and teachers and contributing to declining test scores.

Data collection and analysis

The data sources for this qualitative study included interviews, a 16-question writing survey and reflective writing from two course assignments. The semi-structured *interview protocol* included seven questions aimed at gathering information regarding teaching context; what about their teaching of writing they were most excited about/proud of; challenges; how they described themselves as writers (how, when, where and why they wrote); their writing identity/ies (influencing factors, how/ if it has changed or evolved); students as writers (in general and specific examples); intersections between their identities as writers inside and outside the classroom and possible connections with their teaching practice; and future plans as a writer and teacher. After scheduling interviews, I provided teachers with electronic copies of the interview protocol, their completed writing survey, and their reflective assignment writing to review to spark memories and connections.

The *Writing Survey* provided a way for instructors to get to know class members and for individuals to reflect on themselves as writers and teachers of writing. For the *Process Piece assignment* teachers chose to develop a piece of writing that we began in class where there were subsequent opportunities for peer response and sharing revision strategies. Final projects incorporated evidence of process and a structured reflection and were intended as an instructional resource to share with their own students. The *Synthesis Paper* asked teachers to review all materials, identify five important insights and write a two to three-page description of that learning including intentions for classroom practice.

Data analysis involved several phases and used methods recommended by Miles and Huberman (1994). After transcribing all interviews, I read through each several times, using a process of open coding, notating and developing a first level of possible codes (e.g. writing identity, specific genres of writing, challenges, teaching practices or student work they were most proud of, and intersections) while also creating theoretical notes. Next I developed matrices to compile notes across the data of each individual related to: contextual information such as demographics, teaching assignments and challenges; constructions of writing identity; and performances of roles as teachers. I then developed narrative profiles of each teacher, first from the interview data and matrices and then incorporating quotes and insights from assignment and survey responses. This connected prose generated additional insights and associations, aided in constructing axial themes, and helped me theorise from a performance theory lens. For example, I realised that in forming categories/constructions I had initially considered performance in terms of associations with genres of writing (e.g. performances of written scripts, performing poetry as spoken word) or in terms of teachers' classroom performances (practices). I then returned to Ellsworth's book in which she explored the concept of pedagogical mode of address as well as Phelan's (1993) book on the politics of performance, which Ellsworth (1997) had also incorporated into her theorising. My purpose was to conduct my own exploration of these ideas within the context of writing, in part through focusing on intersections between writing identity and classroom performance, especially in terms of pedagogical relationships.

Writing identities

Teachers constructed their identities as writers during interviews and through parts of the course assignments. As a researcher I interpreted these identities based on an analysis of the interview transcripts and written assignment reflections/writing, and the narrative profiles and matrices. Given the focus of teachers' writing identity for this chapter and to give voice to the individual teachers, I begin by describing categories of identity construction to serve as a reference for framing an exploration of how these identities played out in the classroom (intersections) and laying the groundwork for further analysis through a performativity lens. Teachers constructed their writing identities to reflect: being a writer, what I write, the intellectual/academic side, and the creative side.

Being a writer

Riya, Wendom and Peter clearly conveyed that being a writer was in essence a part of them. Riya (without knowing the title of the book!) stated, 'I honestly do not think there was a point where I decided to become a writer, but rather a moment where I discovered that I was. I write, therefore I am.' Wendom succinctly said, 'I do consider myself to be a writer. I think that's been true for a long time.' Peter commented, 'I've written pretty much as long as I can remember. It's always been a pretty huge part of my life and my personal ambition has always been to be an author.' The others were less direct. Breanna wrote in her writing survey:

> I am the writer who writes out my challenges, my pains, and my frustrations . . . I am the writer who primarily picks up my pen when I am baffled, something has gone wrong, or I feel alienated. . . . Seeking an answer is why I write and to this day is the purpose that my writing fulfills.

Josh connected writing and learning, constructing a case for being a writer: 'Because I think writing is inexorably tied to learning and I view myself as a learner, I guess I would consider myself a writer.' Finally, Rashad had come to define writing speeches as the foremost part of his writing identity: 'OK, so me, definitely I write speeches. I love to speak.'

The academic/intellectual side

Not surprisingly, as recent graduates, academic writing was a major focus. Rashad remarked, 'I love to write intellectually' and presented me with a copy of a short excerpt from the undergraduate thesis he had written in French and translated into English; it had been highlighted in his college alumni magazine. Wendom, who explained, 'I like academic writing or I aspire to be published academically', has a 'literary critical article' related to a Harlem Renaissance writer under revision. In her master's programme in Communication Studies that immediately followed college, Breanna produced a thesis, an auto-ethnography which she described as 'a lot of creative writing but . . . a lot of research. It was really hard to get started and then it ended up being my favorite form of writing'. Josh commented, 'If I were to give myself an identity as a writer [it would be] more of a rational writer, and I see writing as the best medium to articulate my ideas.' Riya said, 'I also do like . . . I guess it's like research type writing.' Inspired in college rhetoric classes with Victor Villanueva, she focused on 'languages of oppression and racism and just language and how it's used and misused'. She described her writing as 'very polemical . . . very informative at times, but it's very connected to identity'.

The creative side

Each teacher mentioned or elaborated on the creative side of their writing identities, manifested most frequently through poetry and performative genres such as play writing, spoken word and speech writing. Riya realised in college that she liked poetry. Describing her process, she said, 'I love writing poetry and it comes to me whenever. Half the time it's when I'm sleeping.' She described her writing as 'flowery or melodic' and her poetry as 'very textury'. Connecting back to Villanueva (1993), she identified herself as an 'organic intellectual', described as 'people who are aware of the struggle and they are a part of that struggle and [as a result] they can best represent the group that they are a part of'. She further explained, 'So for example, Latinos. I focus a lot on Latino voices. A lot of my poetry is like a mashing of Spanish and English.' Wendom said, 'I do consider myself a poet but a bad poet but I enjoy it. I do regularly aspire to poetry, like I've submitted my stuff to journals a handful of times. It's been rejected every time but I still feel fulfilled through poetry.' He also has a blog: 'It's a little dusty but I have put up I think maybe two poems in the last couple months which isn't horrible I guess.' Peter remembers writing his first book, a fantasy, which he described as 'pretty terrible' between the ages of 13 and 15. He worked on a science fiction book for about a year and at age 16 began writing a young adult novel that he is still revising, noting 'I wrote that probably five times over the course of the past eight years.'

Creativity and voice animated the allure of performative genres. When he was in first or second grade, Wendom's story was selected to be performed by 'a play acting troupe'; he remembered, 'it was a big deal for me to see my play in front of the whole school'. Peter discovered play writing in college where he wrote 'three full-length plays, one . . . was actually produced . . . at the Virginia Repertory Theatre'. 'It was just cool to see it staged' and learn from 'veteran writers . . . who coached me through the process'. Breanna conveyed the power of working in a community of writers and performers in college and later as part of a performance ensemble where 'there was so much creative writing and so much outlet to perform my writing. [It was] a huge part of my writing identity'. She explained that seeing her work performed 'was a huge thing for me because you can always write things but okay, now people are *hearing* what I'm saying'.

Performing spoken word poetry had recently become an important part of Riya's writing identity. She explained, 'I really like spoken word. It's different. I kind of tripped on it. I didn't find it on purpose; it just kind of happened.' Coaxed by a college friend to accompany him to a coffee house, she read but didn't perform her poem. Following the reading he told her, 'This piece, it wasn't mean to be on paper. It was meant to be spoken.'

Writing and giving speeches had become tied to Rashad's identity as a writer and connected to a multitude of events and experiences, including community organising; he had also received coaching on the process and explained the three elements: 'you tell the story of self, you tell the story of us and then you tell the story of now.' During college he typed a short story on his iPhone about his struggle to pass a course in microeconomics which he then turned into speech:

> [It] was about someone who was . . . well, an urbanite coming to rural Colorado, well urban sprawl Colorado and thinking he was the best when in actuality he was behind because in reality there was an academic gap between myself and my peers who had gone to private schools and boarding schools on the east coast. And there it was, the achievement gap first hand for me.

He delivered the speech to a class of freshmen whom he said 'felt validated in a sense because so many of them had failed in life and they were like terrified to fail in college'. He had come to realise through failure that there were other avenues that could be opened: 'And pushing away from being an economist, I found French, literature, and then speaking'. Embracing the performance aspect of speaking, Rashad described other examples of the speech-writing side of his identity, including plans to develop and leverage his talent in the political arena, eventually running for state office.

Intersections: writing identity and performativity in the classroom

In this section I focus on intersections between constructed identities as writers and teachers of writing. In this phase of the analysis, I move into the classroom, further exploring positioning aspects of writing identity through a juxtaposition of what teachers and students do as viewed through a performance theory lens. In particular, I draw from the element of pedagogical mode of address (Ellsworth, 1997).

The themes that evolved from this analysis have to do with pedagogical relationships and an exploration of Ellsworth's question, '[h]ow do teachers make a
difference in power, knowledge and desire, not only by what they teach but by
how they address students?' (Ellsworth, 1997, p. 7).

As noted, in addition to gathering information about school contexts/cultures,
demographics, teaching assignments and curriculum, I asked about challenges and
posed questions aimed at understanding how they saw their role as teachers of
writing by asking them to talk about specific students and/or assignments and what
they were most proud of/excited about. Finally, I asked directly about possible
intersections between their identities as teachers of writing and their identities as
writers. These questions revealed insights into relationships between teachers and
their students as well as their take on connections between curriculum, students
and themselves. I have clustered these insights into two themes: creativity, agency
and voice; and building community through response and advocacy.

Creativity, agency and voice

Without exception, when asked about what they were most proud of/excited
about, each teacher described writing lessons, units or experiences that fostered a
sense of creativity, a sense of agency and the power of voice.

Breanna taught a two-hour block of '7th grade accelerated reading/writing'
with 43 students and three 52-minute sections of 8th grade reading/writing. These
classes, ranging from '30–42 students on average', 'comprised primarily . . . students with special needs'. Because the school was short-staffed, the promised
co-teacher never materialised and she described her placement as 'really challenging'. However, she was still able to enact what she referred to as her *personal* writing
identity which 'tends to be more creative and more free-flowing'. For example, Breanna mentioned that she most liked 'all the freewrites and all the creative
writing', which helped her to know 'what they're thinking about, what they're
learning'. Noting that while SpringBoard had 'many really good ideas . . . the kids
were not engaged'; when the books were used they would say, 'here we go again'.
By using SpringBoard prompts in different ways such as projecting 'visuals to get
them thinking' via freewrites, they would get 'more excited'. When asked what
she liked about that process, she explained, 'a lot of the kids would think that their
opinions didn't matter or they had to put a right answer and I'd always tell them,
it doesn't matter if it's right or wrong as long as you can justify that you're right.'
She encouraged students who were having trouble getting started: 'just try, even if
you write I'm hungry, I didn't eat . . . and then they'd write.'

At the same school, in addition to two 100-minute block periods of SpringBoard
7th grade reading/writing with approximately 37 students per class, Wendom was
assigned to design an Enrichment class with only 10 students. Reflecting on his
role and sense of agency as a teacher to have the opportunity to meet standards through his own knowledge and creativity while addressing the needs of his
students, Wendom observed:

> My Enrichment classroom I think is just through and through Wendom. But my SpringBoard classroom, although I try and there's been a handful of times when it really feels like my stuff, most of the time it's a struggle . . . [to] put some garnishings that are like of my personality on top of something that's already baked.

Wendom developed the Enrichment class as an ethics course, where they examined 'issues of right and wrong' through units on race, animals and conservation, wealth and income inequality. The two units he chose to talk about came from this class. The first was focused around gender stereotypes in video games (he shared one girl's 'really cool analysis . . . of the damsel in distress trope', explaining she had 'deconstructed it in a really cool way'). The second example was from a poetry unit that incorporated a workshop by a local Slam Poetry group he brought in. Students composed their own poems about personally meaningful topics. He read one student's poem that revolved around her parents' divorce written in reverse chronological order. The small class size meant more one-on-one time for conferring 'with [his] poets' who were able to create '3 or 4 drafts'.

Rashad and I talked during his last day of school, also his last day of teaching, having fulfilled the two-year commitment. During his second year he had the opportunity to teach an elective Explorations class that was not based on the mandated curriculum and grew out of his efforts to address an equity issue: 'Some of my young African American males and some of my young Hispanic boy students were being suspended for some of the most minute things . . . for example, plucking a key off of a keyboard.' As a result of out-of-school suspensions lasting over a week 'until a parent came up and had a conversation . . . they were missing time in the classroom and . . . their writing skills were falling farther and farther behind'. He described the encounter with his principal that eventually led to creating the class:

> I was terrified! But I couldn't stand it anymore. I felt as if my little brothers and sisters were getting kicked out of school and once they come back, it's my job as their English teacher to catch them up but they've missed so much. And as a result, students failed. And so this year I actually stood up for them – well my third month as a first year teacher I stood up for them and this year I have an all boys class where . . . I have the agency to work with the dean's office or work with other teachers if a student acts up – before he even goes there . . . we remedy the situation by having a restorative justice conversation and then they don't have to get suspended or expelled.

Deeply committed to advocacy, Rashad summarised, 'And so the point of that small anecdote is to illuminate the fact that if teachers begin to advocate for students, administrators would begin to invest in teachers as the stewards of the students' education.'

Riya taught all 9th grade English using the SpringBoard curriculum in what she referred to as a 'transformational school' in the district's Turn Around Zone. Part of the challenge with the strict pacing of the curriculum was that:

they have a hard time until they experience the whole writing process so their writing isn't growing because they're just cranking out like the same material. They're never able to revise it or look at it again or get feedback on it.

Her teaching was rooted in her identity as a poet and as a writer of research which had spilled over to some of her students whom she described as 'all about research and they weren't before . . . like you can just see . . . their analytical wheels turning! It's like bread for them'. A powerful example emerged from her crafting of the SpringBoard assignment to 'pick a poet, write an analysis paper on that poet'. Bringing in poetry books for browsing, she told students 'to pick one that speaks to you'. One student was particularly enthralled with Chilean poet Pablo Neruda, winner of the 1971 Nobel Prize for Literature.

> It was just funny to see him work through all the meanings in his poems and make it like this analytical piece of work. . . . Yep, he read about him, he read his poetry, he looked at videos about him. Like he read Spanish poetry, he talked to me about it because I love Neruda. He was just trying to find as much information as possible.

She also told him about Chile, and Neruda's near exile, noting, 'if you give them a story behind what they're learning, it really connects with them'.

Riya mentioned that a few years ago she would never have said aloud that she was a poet or writer. 'But [now] with my students I can make it very clear that I am a writer, I'm a poet. But more importantly I think it's like having them see that you can become comfortable calling yourself whatever it is you want to call yourself.' She also consistently shared her writing, 'maybe a poem that I'm in the process of drafting and like I'm not sure where the lines should go and I'll show it to them as an example'. She explained:

> It almost gives you like some type of credibility, your authenticity with the kids. Because if you're constantly saying, I'm a writer, I'm a teacher of writing or I'm a poet but they never get to see how that plays out for you, how can you expect them to see that for themselves?

Although she had felt comfortable making the claim that she was a writer in front of her students, she said that recently 'I think I've owned that identity a little bit more.'

Building community through response and advocacy

All teachers were committed to building classroom community which was enacted through ways they structured components of the writing process to honour relationships with students and provided opportunities for peer interaction. These practices speak to intersections of their writing and teaching identities – how they managed to position themselves within their contexts and how their performances positioned students.

Peter discussed ways his teaching had evolved to incorporate reciprocal kinds of intersections between his identities as a teacher and writer, thereby helping to foster community and greater investment. He believed that doing all the assignments himself and the act of sharing his writing 'makes visible the fact that writing can be a form of expression because I choose to express myself a lot in those assignments'. Incorporating writing groups had resulted in 'a lot of them bounc[ing] ideas off each other and giv[ing] each other honest feedback'. The social nature of the groups reinforced that writing wasn't 'like this solitary activity that you just sort of sit down and do'. The performance aspect of the class 'like coming up and reading your work, and not just reading it but acting it out and adding elements of performance . . . has made the processes a lot more engaging and fun'. Because of 'pressure to succeed in front of their peers, a lot more students that didn't usually get invested in the assignments were . . . a lot more invested'.

Making explicit connections between himself as a writer and teacher, Peter noted:

> Particularly as a young adult writer I feel like I just have a lot better luck connecting with these kids because I've been trying to do it for . . . for so long! . . . I'm primarily a writer but I also did some acting so that made the performance aspect [of the assignment] . . . more interesting and allowed me to give more feedback . . . on their performances and I think that verbal communication has also strengthened their writing in a lot of ways.

Peter's teaching also informed his writing. By simplifying his language to make 'sometimes complex concepts more accessible to children, especially when many . . . do not speak English as their first language . . . has made [his] writing adopt a more simple prose to it'.

Breanna and Rashad each shared examples of how they strove to communicate with individual students to help them find their voice. Breanna's 8th grade student with autism learned to use an iPad to create comics and insert dialogue, a technique she felt allowed her to see 'exactly what he was thinking' in spite of the fact that 'his writing was very choppy and he was naturally kind of all over the place'. She felt that 'his writing identity was very creative'. She explained:

> He had a very hard time vocalising so I could see him come to life in his writing and then when he'd talk to me about it, he was all over the place, but he was the sweetest kid, and to see that sort of develop – he took ownership over his writing. Now it wasn't grammatically correct at all but that was his voice.

As a teacher who considers himself bilingual, Rashad was armed with experiences of learning to read and write in another language and a strong belief in the importance of student–teacher partnerships. These components of his identity were important resources when addressing his relationship with an 'emerging bilingual girl'. Rashad explained that they didn't start speaking with one another until late in the third quarter, commenting, 'I couldn't really gauge whether or not she understood what I was teaching or if she just didn't like me.' He did notice she grew more engaged when he changed SpringBoard prompts to more student-relevant topics. He also tried initiating conversations about editing and having a peer read her work, yet felt he still 'didn't know how to reach her'. Finally, he explained,

> I used one of my stronger writers in the classroom and then she made a friend and her writing improved even more . . . . [It] is much more coherent, it flows, it's pretty good. She got the highest grade in our class . . . . She still hasn't talked to me but she's writing! . . . To see her laughing and giggling in class shows me that she's exercising her voice in that writing partner. . . . But as long as she's doing it but not with me, I'm ok. And it shows in the writing.

Riya established an afterschool writing club during the second semester, enabling her to resist the constraints of SpringBoard and disrupt the 'nightmare' created by several highly critical teachers in her department. '[E]very time we met with them it was like they were peeling away at every layer of confidence that was ever built.' Both her classroom and the writing club offered relational spaces for her and her students. She emphasised, 'if it weren't for my kids, I wouldn't be doing this'. In responding to my request for student stories, Riya told me about one of the boys who had

> written about some really hard things like as a teacher I was forced to report to a counselor. Like real bad. But at the same token though, writing has been very therapeutic for him. So instead of telling him, 'No, you can't write about those things', I've told him to keep writing . . . because clearly that's something he needs to say and there's never been anybody that's listened to what he is saying. And so he's actually come into the writing club before and read some of these really difficult pieces. And they're not . . . I mean some people might not consider them the best written pieces in the world because his writing level is pretty low for a 9th grader but sometimes you just have to write things for yourself.

Back to the rackety bridge

Writing identity matters. In a system that promotes sameness through narrowing opportunities for engagement with students and curriculum, teachers in this study found ways to draw on their identities as writers to forge connections and navigate through challenges they encountered as novice teachers. By using their experiences as writers, they developed relationships with students and engaged with them as learners in ways that allowed all voices to matter, thus providing a reason to engage. The creative aspect of writing and teachers' performance of that role nurtured them and generated a sense of agency in adapting curriculum and knowing they were connecting with students and impacting learning.

Pedagogical mode of address is important. These teachers genuinely respected their students and were excited to share their love of literature and writing even within the structure and pacing of the mandated programme. Contrasting the mode of address offered by SpringBoard with what teachers on the rackety bridge constructed offers possibilities for living and working on that bridge. Ellsworth (1997, p. 8) suggests that although the messy and inconclusive nature of pedagogy and pedagogical relationships 'poses problems and dilemmas that can never be settled or resolved once and for all', considering pedagogical mode of address may offer one way through:

> Maybe some pedagogies and curriculums work with their students not because of the 'what' they are teaching or how they are teaching it. Maybe they are hits because of the who that they are offering students to image themselves as being and enacting.
>
> *(Ellsworth, 1997, p. 40)*

Phelan (1993) and Ellsworth (1997) each pose the question – what if we acknowledge the messiness of our work of walking and living on the bridge (of teaching and learning) *as the work*? This view contrasts with one that lures us to cross the bridge from one side to the other, perhaps fleeing out of fear or simply crossing from habit or because we follow a narrative constructed by others who have something to gain. Perhaps one of those narratives is about writing curriculum and what we are asked to do with it in relationship to students.

References

Apple, M. (1982) *Education and Power*, London, Routledge.

Cobb, J., Sargent, S. and Patchen, C. (2012) 'Navigating mandates: Teachers face "troubled waters"', *Language and Literacy*, vol. 14, no. 3, pp. 112–132.

Cremin, T. and Baker, S. (2010) 'Exploring teacher-writer identities in the classroom: Conceptualising the struggle', *English Teaching: Practice and Critique*, vol. 9, no. 3, pp. 8–24.

Cremin, T. and Baker, S. (2014) 'Exploring the discursively constructed identities of a teacher-writer teaching writing', *English Teaching: Practice and Critique*, vol. 13, no. 3, pp. 30–55.

Ellsworth, E. (1997) *Teaching Positions: Difference, Pedagogy, and the Power of Address*, New York, Teachers College Press.

Garcia, A. and O'Donnell-Allen, C. (2015) *Pose, Wobble, Flow: A Culturally Proactive Approach to Literacy Instruction*, Berkeley, CA, National Writing Program and New York, Teachers College Press.

McCarthey, S. and Moje, E. (2002) 'Identity matters', *Reading Research Quarterly*, vol. 37, pp. 228–238.

Miles, M. B. and Huberman, M. (1994) *Qualitative Data Analysis: An Expanded Sourcebook*, Thousand Oaks, CA, Sage.

Moje, E. B., Luke, A., Davies, B. and Street, B. (2009) 'Literacy and identity: Examining the metaphors in history and contemporary research', *Reading Research Quarterly*, vol. 44, no. 4, pp. 415–437.

National Commission on Writing (2003) *The Neglected 'R': The Need for a Writing Revolution*, New York, College Entrance Examination Board.

O'Donnell-Allen, C. (2007) 'Research that makes a difference', *English Journal*, vol. 97, no. 2, pp. 89–90.

Phelan, P. (1993) *Unmarked: The Politics of Performance*, New York, Routledge.

Teach for America (nd) Available at: https://www.teachforamerica.org/about-us/our-mission (Accessed 17 October 2016).

The College Board (2016) SpringBoard. Available at: http://springboardprogram.college board.org/ (Accessed 17 October 2016).

Valencia, S. W., Place, N. A., Martin, S. D. and Grossman, P. L. (2006) 'Curriculum materials for elementary reading: Shackles and scaffolds for four beginning teachers', *Elementary School Journal*, vol. 107, no. 1, pp. 93–120.

Villanueva, V. (1993) *Bootstraps: From an American Academic of Color*, Urbana, IL, National Council of Teachers of English.

Woodard, R. L. (2013) 'Complicating "writing teachers must write": Tensions between teachers' literate and instructional practices', in Dunstonet, P. J. et al. (eds) *62nd yearbook of the Literacy Research Association*, Oak Creek, WI, Literacy Research Association, pp. 377–390.

Yancey, K. B. (2009) *Writing in the 21st Century*, Urbana, IL, National Council of Teachers of English.

7

TEACHERS' IDENTITIES AS WRITERS

Teacher, support staff and pupil accounts of the role of emotion in the writing classroom

Sally Baker and Teresa Cremin

This chapter sits at the intersection between three established bodies of work: teachers' identities as writers, the 'emotional labour' of teaching (Hochschild, 1983) and teaching writing. There is a broad body of literature that attends to these three areas, yet the emotional experience of teaching and learning to write is an underexplored dimension within these fields of interest. The chapter seeks to contribute a multi-agent account of the emotional experiences of participating in a UK primary writing classroom, exploring the experiences of the teacher, the teaching/support staff sitting amongst the pupils, and the pupils themselves. These accounts are reflected through the shared experience of a particular instance of teaching-writing/writing-teaching, and the interactions within this pedagogical moment which are analysed through the conceptual and sensory lens of emotion. The intention to explore the perspectives of these three groups of stakeholders is a novel approach, and as such adds a fresh perspective to understandings of the role of emotions in the teaching and learning of writing.

In this chapter, we expand upon our previous work on teachers' writing identities (Cremin and Baker, 2010; Cremin and Baker, 2014). We have chosen to focus the lens on emotion specifically because this emerged as a salient intrapersonal force on how teachers position themselves, and are positioned, in their roles as teacher-writers/writer-teachers in the primary classroom. In Cremin and Baker (2010), a continuum of teachers' writing identities was offered (see Figure 7.1); a conceptualisation of the available positions and positionings that a teacher can (attempt to) inhabit as they teach writing, influenced by various institutional, intrapersonal and interpersonal factors.

The continuum was intended to demonstrate the struggle that is experienced for some writing teachers as 'an ongoing oscillation between more conforming identities: teacher-writers writing for the system and more liberating identities: writer-teachers writing more for themselves' (Cremin and Baker, 2010, p. 32). We

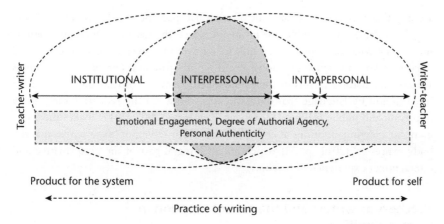

INSTITUTIONAL   INTERPERSONAL   INTRAPERSONAL

Teacher-writer

Writer-teacher

Emotional Engagement, Degree of Authorial Agency,
Personal Authenticity

Product for the system   Product for self

Practice of writing

FIGURE 7.1 A diagram to represent a teacher-writer, writer-teacher continuum
(Cremin and Baker, 2010, p. 20)

added a further layer of detail to this work, when, through multimodal analysis, we unpacked the teachers' embodied discursive practices that opened and closed particular subject positions for others in the classroom (Cremin and Baker, 2014).

Emotions in the teaching context

There is a body of work that explores the role of emotions in education; indeed, as Hargreaves succinctly observed, 'emotions are at the heart of teaching' (1998, p. 835). Widening recognition of this is reflected in a recent literature review of emotions in the teaching context in which Uitto, Jokikokko and Estola (2015) highlight an increase in related publications in *Teaching and Teacher Education*, from three articles in 1991–1996 to 38 between 2009 and 2014. In this literature, emotions and 'the affective dimension' of teaching have been explored through many lenses such as care (O'Connor, 2008); passion (Hargreaves, 1998; Grainger, Barnes and Scoffham, 2004); investment (Nias, 1996); subjectivity (Zembylas, 2003); teacher training (Timoštšik and Ugaste, 2012); change (Saunders, 2012); and emotional identity (Shapiro, 2010). Indeed it is argued that 'emotional identity is fundamental to our understanding of professional identity and the interactions it may generate or preclude' (Shapiro, 2010, p. 616).

This body of literature differs according to the ontological perspective of emotion adopted, and these distinctions align closely with how identity is viewed: from a broad psychological perspective, emotions/identity originate and are located within the individual as an internal entity/set of entities. An alternative and oppositional perspective takes the view that emotions and identities are sociocultural constructions, situated in the sociocultural world, and both produce and are the products of interactions. In his extensive writings on emotions in teaching, Zembylas (e.g. 2003, 2007, 2011) makes the case for a poststructuralist position, arguing that this view operates out of a liminal space between psychological and social constructivist worldviews. From this space the gaze can encompass attention to the roles of language, culture, ideology and power in shaping emotional discourses and discursive positions. From a post-structural perspective, emotions are not understood as private or experienced passively; instead they are constituted in and by language that blurs the edges between the reductive dichotomy of private and public feelings. Moreover, Zembylas (2007, 2011) makes the argument for viewing emotions as embodiments of our selves; of 'experiences that the body expresses' (2011, p. 34) which are an integral part of the performative and interactional experience of teaching.

Teachers as writers and the role of emotion in teaching writing

Early cognitive models of the composing process tended not to recognise or foreground emotions or other contextual factors, although as Brand (1985/6) acknowledges, in the work of Britton et al. (1975) and Emig (1971), feeling is implied. A sense of the personal is also evident in Graves' (1983) pedagogical approach which foregrounds writing workshops, although his work has been critiqued for being overly anecdotal and individualistic, 'abstracting writers and their texts from social context' (Lensmire, 2000, p. 17). Since Graves' (1983) assertion that 'teachers of writing must write' remains the focus of considerable professional and academic attention, it is surprising there is not more literature which addresses the affective dimension of their involvement as writers, within or beyond the classroom. In a recent systematic review on teachers as writers in which attention was paid to teachers' attitudes to writing, it is clear that whilst the picture is complex, there is a tendency towards negativity, evidenced in a discourse of self-doubt and self-criticism (Cremin and Oliver, 2016). Additionally this review found that teachers' past experiences of school/university writing, (both positive and negative) were recalled with considerable emotional intensity, and that such experiences had long-term consequences for their personal and professional identities and potentially for their pedagogic practice (e.g. Cremin, 2006; Gardner, 2014; Gannon and Davies, 2007; Norman and Spencer, 2005). Drawing on 21 studies from five countries, the review underscores the potency of affect and observes that 'there are more unresolved tensions than positive connections between teachers' personal attitudes and writing practices and their teaching of writing' (Cremin and Oliver, 2016).

Psychological studies of emotions *during* the act of writing suggest that feelings often come to the fore and that whilst positive affect such as relief and satisfaction increase during writing, negative emotions such as fear and anxiety are more resistant to change. This has been shown with both novice (Brand and Leckie, 1988) and professional writers (Brand and Powell, 1986). In another study with undergraduates and members of the public, D'Mello and Mills (2014) undertook two experiments to track the affective states that arose during writing. Connecting to the 'motivating cues' in the task environment of Flower and Hayes' (1981) cognitive model of the writing process, these researchers found that boredom, confusion, frustration, anxiety and engagement/flow were the major self-reported affective states. Happiness was also commonly reported, although its occurrence was tied to the topic of the writing. On the basis of this work, they claim that there is a distinction between 'topic affective states' and those more closely related to the cognitive processes involved ('process affective states'), although they acknowledge these states are not mutually exclusive. The sense of emotional angst during composing that is evident in these psychological studies has also been documented in studies of a more broadly sociocultural nature which focus on teachers who are invited to write and to share their writing as part of preservice or professional development programmes (Cremin, 2006; Gardner, 2014; Morgan, 2006; Whitney, 2008). (See also this volume, Chapters 3 and 4.) These collectively reveal considerable insecurity, anxiety and discomfort on the part of teachers; predominantly this appears to relate to a lack of self-confidence, disquiet about having nothing significant to say and the possible value judgements of others.

Notwithstanding these concerns, in two studies that examined teachers' participation in writing groups from an emic perspective, creative risks were taken and 'bravery' was shown (Cremin, 2006; Woodard, 2015). In Cremin's (2006) case study of three teachers, she notes that, in common with their colleagues in the writing group (n = 16), the teachers experienced the compositional process as uncertain and unsettling. This may have been compounded by their role-shift from apparently expert teachers to relatively novice, artistically engaged writers. Nonetheless, the tension and emotional unease generated when composing short stories for publication appeared to mobilise a kind of creative energy that involved the teachers in taking risks as writers. This allowed the unconscious and the intuitive to come into play and unexpected routes were travelled. In Woodard's study (2015), in which three teachers from a cohort of 16 who participated in writing groups acted as case studies, the concept of being a 'brave writer' is explored. The three case-studied teachers each experienced this differently: for one it meant acknowledging that sharing personal writing was difficult but worthwhile; for another it involved 'intentionally becoming vulnerable' (p. 307) with peers and students; for the last, bravery encompassed taking the risk to make substantial revisions to a composition she had already worked hard to polish. In both studies, themes of vulnerability and risk-taking came to the fore as the teachers talked about and documented their composing processes and the experience of sharing their writing with others.

In another study in which teachers' emotions were explored through their participation in workshops, data sources included ongoing surveys (n = 50) and interviews (n = 16) (Scott and Sutton, 2009). The data told different stories; the quantitative data suggested that the teachers' emotions towards writing became more positive over time, but returned to pre-training levels when the workshops ended. The qualitative data suggested that the teachers had mixed emotions about engaging in the writing process, and developed increased empathy for their students as writers as a consequence. An enhanced awareness of students' affective engagement in writing is also noted by Cremin (2006) who found that teachers reported working towards the creation of more secure writing environments in which students could share their apprehensions and were supported to take authorial risks. Woodard (2015) too emphasises the potential pedagogical value of teachers developing as 'brave writers', and includes the comments of one pedagogue who planned to design writing experiences over time to support students' comfort, confidence and risk-taking.

While these various teacher-focused studies shine a much-needed light on the emotional work of writing and draw on data from writing workshops, in relation to pedagogic practice they rely entirely on self-report; no observation of teaching writing in classrooms is included. As such they cannot capture the lived and situated experience of what it is to teach writing to young people, or examine the interplay between teachers' identity positioning and their emotions in this context. It is in this niche that the current chapter sits. Our earlier work, which we revisit here for this purpose, revealed that whilst institutional and interpersonal factors influenced the writer-teacher, teacher-writer identity positions adopted in the classroom, intrapersonal factors were also significant (Cremin and Baker, 2010). The teachers' relationships with their unfolding compositions and their emotional engagement/ disengagement with their writing appeared highly salient in influencing their situated sense of self as writers in this context. It contributed to the emotional struggle experienced by the teachers as they sought to adopt the dual identity positions of teacher and writer. In our work we conceive of identity as relational, positional and enacted in interaction (Holland and Lave, 2001). This notion of relational identity positioning is important when considering the ways in which teachers engage emotionally as writers in the public forum of the classroom. As we document later, Jeff, our case study teacher, was composing in front of 33 pupils, a teaching assistant and the class teacher. He was neither a lone writer nor a lone teacher and this had consequences for his identity positioning and emotional involvement.

Methodology

As noted, this chapter draws from a broader ethnographic study which explored the concept of teachers-as-writers. Two teachers were recruited to take part from two primary schools in the south of England. They were purposefully selected (Patton, 2015) on the basis of their previous participation in a professional development (PD) programme where practitioners were encouraged to adopt the position of 'writer' in their teaching, and which involved authentic composition and engaging with the processes, practices and products of being a 'writer' (Ings, 2009). One teacher, Elaine, worked at a Catholic primary school in a fairly affluent area; the other, Jeff, worked in a secular primary school in an area characterised as being of low socioeconomic status.

A researcher was assigned to each teacher and three sessions were observed on consecutive weeks and extensive field notes written; classroom interactions were also videoed for follow-up viewing, with consent given by all participants (from the parents in the case of the children). The subject of each observed session was the 'literacy hour' of the day, and both teachers modelled spontaneously produced compositions (hereafter referred to as 'demonstration writing') in front of the class before continuing their writing while sitting alongside pupils. Copies of the participants' written texts from both demonstration and writing alongside contexts were collected after each session.

In addition to the classroom observations, both participants participated in weekly post-session reflective interviews. In addition to interviewing the teachers, other staff (teaching assistants and a class teacher in Jeff's case), and an opportunistically selected sample of pupils, also took part in a one-to-one interview (staff) and a focus group (pupils). Furthermore, the two participants kept reflective journals of the period of data collection and beyond and participated in individual pre-observation extended 'literacy history' interviews and a collective post-observation plenary interview. In the latter they responded to the video footage and reflected on their actions and feelings at key points variously selected by the teachers and researchers.

From this engagement, albeit relatively brief, a large body of data were collected. In what follows, we create a case study from one set of data pertaining to Jeff – including interview data with Jeff, two other members of staff and a group of children, textual data, field notes and Jeff's reflective diary – to craft an analytic narrative about the emotional labour involved in the teaching and learning experiences of writing in this primary classroom. We acknowledge that the case of Jeff – as a literacy teacher without whole-class responsibility – is unique and recognise this case is not generalisable; rather we intend to offer a rich picture based on the 'thick description' (Geertz, 1973) that such ethnographic inquiries provide. We hope that other teachers and researchers reading this chapter will find resonance with the description offered of Jeff's teaching, and the emotional toil involved.

Findings

Jeff, who was in his mid-thirties at the time of the data collection, had been employed as a teacher for over 12 years and was working in a large school in a socioeconomically deprived area. Jeff was the Deputy Head and Literacy Coordinator; he did not have a class responsibility, but taught literacy to four classes (9–11-year-olds), with class teachers working alongside him.

The observed session

In the session from which the data presented in this chapter are drawn, Jeff was teaching a class of 10–11-year-olds as part of a six-week topic, 'All About Me'. Also present were the class teacher (Clare) and a teaching assistant (Debbie). The session took place at the beginning of the school year, so Clare was not well known to the children, although they were familiar with Jeff through his Deputy

Head role. Jeff started the observed interaction by sharing postmodern visuals from the book *Clarice Bean, That's Me* (by Lauren Child) with the children via the interactive whiteboard. They noted the members of Clarice's family and the often-ironic asides made about each other and then for 10 minutes drew their own families, with actions and bracketed asides. All staff joined in this activity, which was followed by sharing time when those present talked to a partner about one of their 'special people'. Jeff chose his gran who had died. Following this he stood to demonstrate how to move from the drawing/talk to writing. Initially Jeff's emotional engagement is considered, then the experiences of his audience/co-writers: both staff and children. All participants have been given pseudonyms to protect their anonymity.

Jeff's demonstration writing

Analysis of three key moments during Jeff's demonstration writing is offered. He began by talking through the session's aims and what he was doing.

Here Jeff pointedly refers to writing as something that is 'really, really, really tough', evidencing his anxiety, and arguably offering reassurance to any of the children (and teaching staff) who felt similarly. Moreover, Jeff's acknowledgement of his procrastination adds to the evidence of his nervousness that he shares with

EXTRACT 7.1 The beginning of Jeff's demonstration writing

Jeff's talk	*Contextual information*
Can I ask you now to do the hardest thing that I'm going to ask you to do probably all year? This is going to be a really, really, really tough thing to do . . . * I hope you've had a chance to talk to someone about somebody in your family, and it really helped me when I was talking. What I'm going to try and do for you now is to show you the sorts of writing that we could be doing . . . Also the other part of what we said at the start was try and engage the reader, so I'm going to try and write something on here about someone in my family. Now I'm talking a lot now because I'm trying to avoid doing it. We talked about this last week. This is going to be really hard because I don't know what to put on first of all.	Jeff uses his hands to explain himself, walking backwards and forwards and gesturing to the whiteboard

*' . . . ' is used as an ellipsis to signify when parts of Jeff's speech have been omitted from the transcript reproduced here. We acknowledge that we have made particular choices in terms of Jeff's talk and that this flavours the representation of him.

EXTRACT 7.2 Midway through Jeff's demonstration writing

Jeff's talk	Contextual information
I had a chat with the guys here; do you know who I'm going to write about? I'm going to write about my Gran . . . Whilst I write, I'm going to talk about what I'm thinking, and just to see whether that helps you when you come to write as well to show that it's not an easy thing, I'm going to struggle with this. . . . The hardest part what I say to you guys as well is starting. This is going to be really hard because I don't know what to put on first of all. For some reason straightaway I've gone into like a story mode. What I'm trying to do is I want to see if I can imagine my Gran. The problem is that because she's dead it's hard to remember so much now, so I'm trying to think back and think about what she was like, so in a dream sometimes you can remember things more.	Picks up his drawing. Goes to whiteboard Writes 'Granny' on the board, and writes his start, 'The gentle rhythm of the car and the sound of the engine slowly rocked me to sleep' . . . Points to these words . . . continues writing on whiteboard . . .

regard to starting his writing. In this way he commenced his demonstration writing with a display of authenticity: for him, starting to write on a blank page is difficult.

As Jeff begins his composition, he continues his meta-narrative of what he is doing to show the children that he was genuinely engaged in his writing, and to demonstrate his moment-by-moment authorial choices, selecting words to commit to the whiteboard. While Jeff was writing, the children were sitting quietly and watching intently.

EXTRACT 7.3 Nearing the end of Jeff's demonstration writing

Jeff's talk	Contextual information
I've got this feeling inside me at the moment which isn't good. Because I said it about my picture. I drew this picture of my Gran and it was awful, it's naff. My Gran I loved her so, so much and the picture's awful. She looks like this flat, sandy sort of thing, and just there. I've got this same sort of feeling at the moment. Whilst I'm writing it's not completely right.	Looks downcast as he looks back at the whiteboard and forward towards the children

Here, Jeff shares his negative feelings about his composition so far. The experience of writing about his gran – clearly a topic that is emotionally laden – resonated with his experience of attempting to draw her. He expressed the negative feelings he had felt (frustration, guilt, inadequacy) and then went on to finish this demonstration and moved to write alongside the children, joining a table and continuing to work on his text. Jeff's writing is reproduced as Figure 7.2.

Jeff's initial evaluation of the lesson was that it 'didn't feel good' to him, which connects with his appraisal of his writing. Hesitantly he explained how difficult he had found it to write publicly about his gran:

> I found it really, really hard [pause], because I had purposefully as we'd like said – I had not planned anything, so it wasn't [pause], in my mind I knew it'd be gran because we were talking about families and things and I thought it would be her, but when I stood there it was that whole, 'I don't know'; 'I don't know what to do' and I went straight into story mode. I felt I was trying to [pause], I didn't want to do my gran down [she] means a lot to me.

It is clear that Jeff's choice of his gran as the topic of his writing had led to tension: he was torn; his pedagogic desire was to compose spontaneously but he also had to deal with the writerly affective consequences of his chosen topic. This tension

FIGURE 7.2 Jeff engaged in demonstration writing

manifested itself as a sense of guilt as well as frustration with the children in the class, whose attention started to wain once they began themselves to write. When their talking became disruptive, Jeff, who had been diligently continuing his composition sitting alongside pupils, stood up, expressed an authorial desire for space and asked for quiet, saying, 'then we can keep our thinking going – okay? I can't do justice to my Gran with all this noise'. From his interjection into the chatter in the room, it is evident that he perceived the children were both an inhibitor and a 'nuisance' to his composition. He was left feeling 'upset' by the children's interruptions as they wrote alongside him, explaining that, 'I didn't do justice to my Gran through what I wrote and I suppose that upset me as well and in a way I thought what right have these children got to stop me?' As we have commented before (Cremin and Baker, 2010), Jeff's full engagement in his writing at that point positioned him firmly at the 'writer-teacher' end of the continuum (Figure 7.1), which resulted in conflicting desires between being the 'teacher' and wanting to be 'a writer'.

Jeff's intention to produce writing without prior rehearsal also caused a layer of anxiety. While engaged in demonstration writing, he spelt the word 'precious' incorrectly ('precius') and pondered aloud if he had made a mistake. The class teacher, Clare, counselled him 'Don't worry about the spelling now, it's not important, just underline it and come back to it later', and a child shouted out the correct spelling. At this point, Jeff appeared momentarily sidetracked and looked somewhat awkward. His genuine challenge with the spelling of this word revealed a sense of unease. He later reflected that the session 'showed the struggle of ideas, the struggle of what . . . how to move from what you've spoken about and what you shared and what you put on paper'. The pedagogy of spontaneously composing texts as a teacher in front of a class may support children to develop their nascent authorial confidence, but Jeff's reflections suggest it also poses an open risk for teachers who are emotionally invested in their role as writer/teachers and teacher/writers.

However, there was also mention of positive elements; reflecting on the experience of physically situating himself amongst his pupils and continuing to craft his text there, Jeff observed that it 'really felt we all felt we were writers in that class, all experiencing something together'. Jeff is describing the development of a space for communal writing; indeed, this notion of a writing community was reinforced by his stated intention to produce a publication where 'every child will have a piece of work in the book, teachers as well'. The idea of a community of writers is potentially transformative as it connects with a Freirean sense of the horizontal classroom, where the status of the teacher-as-expert is eroded through the sharing of knowledges and the understanding that everyone is a learner. As recent research into classroom reading communities found, when teachers reposition themselves as adult readers alongside learners, new relationships of a less hierarchical nature may develop (Cremin and Baker, 2014).

The class teacher's experience

Unlike Jeff, Clare had not participated in the PD programme on becoming a 'writer' and did not engage in authentic and spontaneous composition when she taught literacy. Like many teachers she composed her writing at home (Cremin, 2006), and during demonstration writing 'pretended' to compose what had already been written and rehearsed. Rather than the intense emotional labour that Jeff reflected upon from a writerly perspective, Clare's view of the pedagogical approaches of demonstration writing and writing alongside suggested a more teacherly view of writing:

Researcher: Does it [these approaches] make any difference to the quality of their writing do you think?

Clare: It does in some respects as they like it when it's quiet and they appreciate that we all need to focus – I can't write when all I can hear is 'it's a special locket' then you end up writing what they've said to you! It also helps the more independent kids who know they can rely upon self-help strategies. They need to know that you don't need to worry about the spelling when you are getting your ideas down or you will lose the flow.

Clare's appraisal of these approaches as facilitating 'focus' and 'quiet' suggests a set of understandings and assumptions about writing that are both personal to Clare, and commonly considered to be key tenets of teaching writing. Nonetheless, research indicates that for some children the chance to talk and share ideas is an integral part of writing, especially creative writing (Vass, 2007; Davidson, 2007). However, Clare did imply divergence from traditionally taught models of writing when dismissing the need to spell correctly if that risks 'losing the flow' of ideas.

Like Jeff, Clare spoke of the sense of a burgeoning community within the classroom:

Clare: I often feel a real urge to put my hand up and share my writing when I am writing as one of the class with Jeff.

Researcher: Do you ever?

Clare: Not often. When I'm writing in there I'm somehow invisible – one of the writers if you know what I mean.

Researcher: Not a teacher?

Clare: Well not unless a boy throws a rubber or something . . . But the rest of the time they can see I'm a writer and it's catching – we're all writers, me, Jeff, Debbie and the children.

Clare's desire to 'put her hand up' and her sense of being 'invisible' both stand in marked contrast with her normal role as teacher of the class. These suggest that as a consequence of Jeff's particular pedagogical approach, she is enabled at times to position herself as a writer-teacher and become 'one of the writers'. However, she does comment that she is pulled back to her teacher role (the teacher-writer on the continuum) by disruptive behaviour or children's requests for help. This resonates with the analysis offered in our earlier work (Cremin and Baker, 2010), suggesting that the institutional force of the teacher's role as helper/disciplinarian is strong, drawing teachers away from an authentic engagement with their compositions. Indeed, as discussed above, when Jeff sat amongst the children to continue his writing on his gran, his intent focus meant that he occasionally ignored requests for help from his 'fellow' writers and Clare was pushed to support those children.

The teaching assistant's experience

As Clare's teaching assistant, Debbie was involved in offering one-to-one learning support to pupils with particular needs beside whom she sat. Nonetheless, during Jeff's lessons and as a member of this 'community of writers', she also engaged in writing alongside the pupils. She perceived that the experience of doing so was not only helpful for developing children's writing, but that it also helped to foster closer relationships between pupils and staff:

> I think it helps us all writing and talking, as I didn't realise Charlie had four brothers and sisters like me and I told him I come from a big family too . . . Also I felt I learnt quite a bit about the two girls and they did about me – I told them my favourite place would be the Bahamas and that my daughter's at university and they seemed to like that – you know knowing about me.

The experience of sitting with the children and, significantly, behaving as a co-writer in this session prompted Debbie and her focus children to share personal information with one another, exchange contextual and relational knowledge and comment on each other's writing. However, while such sharing may prompt connections and help to build relationships, it is important to recognise that some teaching assistants, like some teachers, may be uncomfortable in situations that call for a reduction in professional distance and the positioning of the adult as co-learner. As research indicates, not all teachers are confident writers (e.g. Morgan, 2006), and teaching assistants too may find such re-positioning problematic. Debbie did not, although she acknowledged, 'I found it hard to start today, but then I adapted his ideas and I enjoyed it then'.

The children's experience

Following the third observed session, a table of five children were asked to participate in a focus group interview and give their thoughts on Jeff's literacy teaching, which they perceived as somewhat different compared with their other teachers. They brought their writing books to this session, and unprompted, shared some of Jeff's responses to their writing. When asked about the kinds of responses Jeff gave, the children indexed his investment in their writing – and themselves as writers. The notion that a 'community of writers' was developing as a result of the pedagogical approaches and related identity positions adopted by Jeff was echoed in their responses. They perceived that Jeff was genuinely interested in them, both as individuals and in what they wrote. For example, Will typically noted: 'I think he's interested in, like what you write about because of you, he wants to know what has gone on in your life before like you've come to like Year Six and that' and Ben observed, 'He kind of writes like, nice comments and like says if you don't like the comment, or agree with him, he'll like say yeah that's fine and he will like say something else and see if you agree with that'. These descriptions of Jeff's feedback suggest that he is attentive to individuals and open to contestation, to discussion, to detail and context.

On being asked what they thought was the most important thing about writing, several children mentioned the significance of expressing their feelings in and through writing. For example, Jack observed: 'How do you say it? Like your emotions and that, like how you feel and everything'. This was reinforced in part through Jeff's use of 'traffic lights' as a tool for reflection at the end of literacy sessions. At the time in England these were used for self-evaluation. Children would draw a set of traffic lights at the end of their writing and colour in one light to denote the extent to which they believed they had achieved the lesson's set objective. Somewhat counter-culturally, Jeff invited the children to use the traffic lights to reflect upon how their writing made them feel; how pleased or proud they were with their draft thus far.

Jeff's pedagogic intention to support the children as writers, his respect for their feelings, and investment in their lives and experiences was mirrored in his written responses to their writing. He not only commented upon each piece of writing, but eschewed the common practice in England at the time of giving each piece of writing a 'level'. Instead he offered personal comments, including, for example:

> Well done Ben, you, your writing reminds me about how important it is to have someone in our family who we can look up to, and want to be like. It sounds like your Grandad was a great role model to you.

> Jack, thank you for writing about Jed [his dog]. I totally understand the part where you say he's like a brother to you. Dogs are so great and no matter how you are feeling they always greet you with a waggling tail and a lick! Does Jed jump up too?

The children expressed considerable satisfaction and interest in their teacher's responses; Jeff focused on their chosen topics and often made connections to his own views and life. In several cases in the writing books the children shared, there was evidence of sustained written interchanges between Jeff and the child writer; some of these written conversations involved three turns each. In these, the adult and the child writer conversed about an issue in the written text, connected to the child's life. For example:

> Jeff: Well done Brad, Great writing. I really liked finding out about Callum's birthday. Do you all still enjoy the Xbox?
>
> Brad: Yeah but it's funny because one day it didn't work and he [Callum] shouted downstairs, Brad!!! What have you done?

Jeff: Oh Brad – you nearly got blamed for it! That happened a lot to me when I was younger.

Brad: My dad came up and plugged in a wire. That day I called him [Callum] a nutter!

Jeff's comments to the children illustrate his engagement, his empathy and his attempts to understand and validate their experiences. At this early stage in the year he had written very little in their books that focused on the pupils' writing skills; indeed, he observed he was consciously 'reading and responding to what they have to say – that's what's important just now'. Jeff's desire to connect and demonstrate his understanding of the children's 'special people' and the written dialogues affirms his emotional investment and intention to develop a community of writers in the classroom.

Discussion

The themes of vulnerability and risk-taking identified by Cremin (2006) and Woodard (2015) in their case studies of teachers' writing certainly appear to resonate with Jeff's experience presented here. Although he moves across the teacher-writer continuum throughout the observed session (see Figure 7.1), and experiences a not dissimilar continuum of positive and negative feelings about his writing, Jeff is above all a 'brave writer'. In choosing to compose an unrehearsed text in the public forum of the classroom, Jeff engaged in a 'performance of authenticity': attempting to demonstrate how writing is often iterative and disjointed, and on this occasion, was tense, joyful, sad and frustrating. As a consequence of this performance, Jeff exposed his emotional self to the class and the other adults present. In seeking to model how to move from his drawing to composing in the 'writing community' he was trying to establish, Jeff experienced conflict in both the process and the topic affective states suggested by D'Mello and Mills (2014). Jeff's frustration with his demonstrated composition, and his later irritation at the children's disruptive chatter, was likely a result of his process affective state; indeed D'Mello and Mills (2014) assert that frustration is one of four emotions that emerge from the composition process (along with engagement/flow, boredom and confusion). It was clear too that Jeff was at moments also deeply engaged with the flow of his writing and was at other points confused and unsure. Unlike the other teacher who took part in this study (Elaine; see Cremin and Baker, 2010, 2014), Jeff did not appear bored with his writing – at least not in the interaction described here.

Moreover, while Jeff wanted to offer his fellow writers an honest example of what it is like to write, he simultaneously wanted to protect the integrity of his chosen 'special' person and this also contributed to his frustration, especially when writing alongside. Jeff's investment in the topic of his gran seems to have heightened his topic affective state; a predictable consequence, according to D'Mello and Mills, as engaging in descriptive writing 'activate[s] emotional memories related to those topics' (2014, p. 153). Jeff's identification with children through his pedagogical actions – in terms of the content of their writing and in the processes and practices of writing – positions him as a human teacher in the classroom: a knowing, experiencing, feeling person. This intentional positioning supports and is supported by the actions of demonstration writing, writing along-side and offering personal responses to the content of the children's writing. As Van De Weghe (2004) observes: 'responding well calls for not only identifiable skills, but also intra- and interpersonal skills, along with such crucial emotional and cognitive dispositions as empathy and reader-based anticipation' (p. 96). There is evidence that, through his use of traffic lights focused on children's feelings about their writing and his written feedback, Jeff is cognisant of the emotional demands of composing and seeks to offer responsive support.

Interestingly, Jeff's sense of vulnerability and exposure that emerged out of his demonstration writing was not echoed in the reflections of Clare, Debbie or the children. Instead, it appears that they both recognised and celebrated the results of his intention to create a community of writers – a deepened sense of familiarity, a common sense of purpose and shared experience of composition – as long as it did not diverge from the rules of teaching, such as using correct spelling or controlling the noise level.

Conclusion

The data presented in this chapter offer a much-needed empirical account of the emotional work that is an integral part of teaching writing. What teachers of writing need to understand, Yeo (2007, p. 127) asserts, 'is the relationship between teaching, composition and life'; this, our analysis suggests, is underpinned by an awareness of affect. The exploration of the interactions within Jeff's teaching of writing, which include observations of him demonstrating writing and then writing alongside, as well as his post-teaching reflections and those of the class teacher, the teaching assistant and pupils, clearly illustrate how much is at stake emotionally for the teacher-writer. The process of spontaneous composition at the front of the class offers little in the way of protection from the emotional exposure that writing in this public context brings. In Jeff's case, the exposure was multi-layered: disclosing his experience of writing, his competence as a writer, his spelling, his humanity and his sense of self and life experiences.

In emotionally investing in spontaneous demonstration writing to support the children as writers, Jeff allowed himself to be both human and humane in the class-room, two subject positions that may have been relatively unusual to the children, particularly given the prevailing culture of performativity (Ball, 1998) in the UK school context. The audit-driven environment evident in primary schools tends to position teachers as technicians whose job is merely to raise 'standards'; this has the potential, as Fielding (2006) asserts, to create an increasingly dehumanised context for learning. Nonetheless, as this analysis of Jeff's positioning shows, if teachers choose to position themselves as fellow writers, then whilst they will be submitting themselves to the emotional risks involved in public composition (which need to be recognised and supported), they will also be working towards building communities of writers that are attentive to the social and affective nature of writing and being a writer.

References

Ball, S. J. (1998) 'Performativity and fragmentation in "postmodern schooling"', in Carter, J. (ed.) *Postmodernity and Fragmentation of Welfare*, London, Routledge, pp. 187–203.

Brand, A. G. and Powell, J. L. (1986) 'Emotions and the writing process: A description of apprentice writers', *Journal of Educational Research*, vol. 79, no. 5, pp. 280–285.

Brand, A. G. and Leckie, P. A. (1988) 'The emotions of professional writers', *Journal of Psychology*, vol. 122, pp. 421–439.

Britton, J., Burgess, T., Martin, N., Macloed, A. and Rosen, H. (1975) *The Development of Writing Abilities*, London, Macmillan.

Cremin, T. (2006) 'Creativity, uncertainty and discomfort: Teachers as writers', *Cambridge Journal of Education*, vol. 36, no. 3, pp. 415–433.

Cremin, T. and Baker, S. (2010) 'Exploring teacher-writer identities in the classroom: Conceptualising the struggle', *English Teaching: Practice and Critique*, vol. 9, no. 3, pp. 8–25.

Cremin, T. and Baker, S. (2014) 'Exploring the discursively constructed identities of a teacher-writer teaching writing', *English Teaching: Practice and Critique*, vol. 13, no. 3, pp. 30–55.

Cremin, T. and Oliver, L. (2016) 'Teachers as writers: A systematic review', *Research Papers in Education*. Retrieved from http://dx.doi.org/10.1080/02671522.2016.1187664.

Davidson, C. (2007) 'Independent writing in current approaches to writing instruction: What have we overlooked?' *English Teaching: Practice and Critique*, vol. 6, no. 1, pp. 11–24.

D'Mello, S. and Mills, C. (2014) 'Emotions while writing about emotional and non-emotional topics', *Motivation and Emotion*, vol. 38, no. 1, pp. 140–156.

Emig, J. (1971) *The Composing Processes of Twelfth Graders*, Urbana, IL, The National Council of Teachers of English.

Fielding, M. (2006) 'Leadership, radical student engagement and the necessity of person-centred education', *International Journal of Leadership in Education*, vol. 9, no. 4, pp. 299–313.

Flower, L. A. and Hayes, J. R. (1981) 'A cognitive process theory of writing', *College Composition and Communication*, vol. 32, pp. 365–387.

Gannon, S. and Davies, C. (2007) 'For love of the word: English teaching, affect and writing', *Changing English*, vol. 14, no. 1, pp. 87–98.

Gardner, P. (2014) 'Becoming a teacher of writing: Primary student teachers reviewing their relationship with writing', *English in Education*, vol. 48, no. 2, pp. 128–148.

Geertz, C. (1973) *The Interpretation of Cultures: Selected Essays*, New York, Basic Books.

Grainger, T., Barnes, J. and Scoffham, S. (2004) 'A creative cocktail: Creative teaching in initial teacher education', *Journal of Education and Teaching*, vol. 38, no. 3, pp. 243–253.

Graves, D. (1983) *Writing: Teachers and Children at Work*, Portsmouth, NH, Heinemann.

Hargreaves, A. (1998) 'The emotional practice of teaching', *Teaching and Teacher Education*, vol. 14, no. 8, pp. 835–854.

Hochschild, A. (1983) *The Managed Heart: Commercialization of Human Feeling*, Berkeley, CA, University of California Press.

Holland, D. and Lave, J. (2001) 'History in person: An introduction', in Holland, D. and Lave, J. (eds), *History in Person: Enduring Struggles, Contentious Practice, Intimate Identities*, Sante Fe, NM, School of American Research, pp. 1–32.

Ings, T. (2009) *Writing is Primary: Action Research on the Teaching of Writing in Primary Schools*, London, Esmee Fairbairn.

Lensmire, T. J. (2000) *Powerful Writing: Responsible Teaching*, New York, Teachers College Press.

Morgan, W. (2006) '"Poetry makes nothing happen": Creative writing and the English classroom', *English Teaching: Practice and Critique*, vol. 5, no. 2, pp. 17–33.

Nias, J. (1996) 'Thinking about feeling: The emotions in teaching', *Cambridge Journal of Education*, vol. 26, no. 3, pp. 293–306.

Norman, K. A. and Spencer, B. H. (2005) 'Our lives as writers: examining preservice teachers' experiences and beliefs about the nature of writing and writing instruction', *Teacher Education Quarterly*, Winter, pp. 25–40.

O'Connor, K. (2008) '"You choose to care": Teachers, emotions and professional identity', *Teaching and Teacher Education*, vol. 24, no. 1, pp. 17–126.

Patton, M. Q. (2015) *Qualitative Research and Evaluation Methods: Integrating Theory and Practice*, 4th edn, Los Angeles, CA, Sage.

Saunders, R. (2012) 'The role of teacher emotions in change: Experiences, patterns and implications for professional development', *Journal of Educational Change*, vol. 14, no. 3, pp. 303–333.

Scott, C. and Sutton, R. (2009) 'Emotions and change during professional development for teachers', *Journal of Mixed Methods Research*, vol. 3, no. 2, pp. 151–171.

Shapiro, S. (2010) 'Revisiting the teachers' lounge: Reflections on emotional experience and teacher identity', *Teaching and Teacher Education*, vol. 26, no. 3, pp. 616–621.

Timoštšik, I. and Ugaste, A. (2012) 'The role of emotions in student teachers' professional identity', *European Journal of Teacher Education*, vol. 35, no. 4, pp. 421–433.

Uitto, M., Jokikokko, K. and Estola, E. (2015) 'Virtual special issue on teachers and emotions in "Teaching and Teacher Education (TATE)" 1985–2014', *Teaching and Teacher Education*, vol. 50, pp. 124–135.

Van De Weghe, R. (2004) '"Awesome, dude!" Responding helpfully to peer writing', *The English Journal*, vol. 94, no. 1, pp. 95–99.

Vass, E. (2007) 'Exploring processes of collaborative creativity – The role of emotions in children's joint creative writing', *Thinking Skills and Creativity,* vol. 2, no. 2, pp. 107–117.

Whitney, A. (2008) 'Teacher transformation in the National Writing Project', *Research in the Teaching of English*, vol. 43, no. 2, pp. 144–187.

Woodard, R. (2015) 'Becoming brave writers and writing teachers: Teachers recognizing the affective dimensions of writing and transforming their classroom instruction', in Betrancourt, M., Ortoleva, G., Tynjala, P. and Billet, S. (eds) *Writing for Professional Development*, Brill, Studies in Writing Series.

Yeo, M. (2007) 'New literacies, alternative texts: teachers' conceptualisations of composition and literacy', *English Teaching: Practice and Critique*, vol. 6, no. 1, 113–131.

Zembylas, M. (2003) 'Interrogating "teacher identity": Emotion, resistance, and self-formation', *Educational Theory*, vol. 53, no. 1, pp. 107–127.

Zembylas, M. (2007) 'Emotional ecology: The intersection of emotional knowledge and pedagogical content knowledge in teaching', *Teaching and Teacher Education*, vol. 23, no. 4, pp. 355–367.

Zembylas, M. (2011) 'Teaching and teacher emotions: A post-structural perspective', in Day, C. and Lee, J. (eds) *New Understandings of Teacher's Work: Emotions and Educational Change*, Dordrecht, Holland, Springer, pp. 31–43.

8

WORKING TOWARDS 'I'M A WRITER AND A PRETTY GOOD WRITER'

An elementary teacher legitimizing students' writerly identities while authenticating her own

Rebecca Woodard

Introduction

In the United States, teacher writing has been advocated by the National Writing Project (a network of sites across the country anchored at universities and committed to improving the teaching and learning of writing in K-12 schools; see National Writing Project and Nagin, 2006), the Writing Across the Curriculum movement (programs centred at universities to incorporate and teach writing in disciplines beyond composition; see Shea, Balkun, Nolan, Saccoman, and Wright, 2006), and both process writing (a pedagogical focus on writing processes over writing products; see Murray, 1968) and teacher research (a movement to empower practitioners to engage in research and enter into conversations about policy, research, and practice; see Cochran-Smith and Lytle, 1992) and educators/researchers for over forty years. Advocates focus on teacher writing as: a way to concentrate on writing activities rather than evaluation, an instructional strategy, reflection, participation in the profession, and personal experience (see Dawson, 2011). Inherent in many of these approaches is the idea that teachers who identify as writers teach writing better. However, many studies have documented that both seeing oneself as a writer and capitalizing on writerly identities in instruction are complicated (Brooks, 2007; Cremin and Baker, 2010, 2014; McKinney and Giorgis, 2009; Robbins, 1996). The study reported upon in this chapter explores how an elementary English as a Second Language (ESL) teacher in the United States, Hannah (all teacher, student, and school names are pseudonyms) narrated and performed writing and teaching identities across contexts. I share data from a case study of her voluntary participation at a four-week National Writing Project Summer Institute and subsequent observations of her classroom instruction over the course of seven months to explore Hannah's complex positionings of herself and her students as writers.

Teacher-writer identities

For quite some time, researchers have been interested in documenting if and how teachers identify as writers, and what that means for their instructional practices with students. Historically, we have been interested in categorizing teachers into binary categories of writer or nonwriter. Twenty-five years ago, Robbins' (1990) case studies of twelve high school English teachers found that most teachers who engaged in personally meaningful writing considered themselves nonwriters. In 2007, Brooks completed a case study of four fourth-grade teachers who *did* consider themselves to be 'competent readers and writers' and found that the teachers in his study read and wrote different materials for different purposes, but their interests and responsibilities often guided or dictated the types of readers and writers they were. He suggested that the categorization of 'teachers who read and write' is tied to certain, privileged types of readings (e.g., children's literature above magazines) and compositions (e.g., children's articles above emails). Thus, he challenged what counts as writing and who counts as writers in common conceptions of a teacher-writer.

Current researchers are presenting more complex views of multiple identities that are differentially enacted in particular, situated contexts. For example, rather than positioning a binary view of teachers who see themselves as writers or teachers who don't, McKinney and Giorgis (2009) explored how eleven literacy specialists constructed and negotiated their identities as writers and writing teachers over two years. They identified four categories of writer-teacher identities: writers who teach writing, sometimes writers who teach writing, nonwriters who teach writing, and nonwriters who don't teach writing. Within each of these categories, they further documented how participants narrated multiple writerly identities. For example, Myra, a literacy specialist at an urban elementary school with almost forty years of teaching experience across the world, who was in the 'writer who teaches writing' category, positioned herself multiply—as 'the not so good, messy writer; the successful school writer; the world traveler letter and postcard writer; and the solitary writer' (p. 127). Teachers' writerly identities, then, are complex, complicated and sometimes contradictory.

Similarly, Cremin and Baker (2010) document how two teachers of young writers are positioned and position themselves as teacher-writers *and* writer-teachers, explicitly documenting their classroom performances of identities as sites of struggle and tension. My own research documents the tensions between writing and teaching writing identified or enacted by a middle-grade writing teacher and college composition instructor in writing purposes, identities, and authority (Woodard, 2013). This growing research base on the identity work of teachers as writers shows how 'identities as teacher-writers and writer-teachers constantly shift and are emotional, relational and conflictual, a complex and interwoven mix of jostling interpersonal, institutional and intrapersonal influences' (Cremin and Baker, 2010, p. 26).

Situational identities: tactics of intersubjectivity

This documentation of shifting identities makes sense if you take the stance that identities are attributed to situations, rather than to individuals or groups. Bucholtz and Hall (2004) developed 'tactics of intersubjectivity' as an analytic framework to 'examine the relational dimensions of identity categories, practices, and ideologies' (p. 383). Their theory names specific relational processes through which identity is carried out in social interactions over time. They argue that through language and semiotic systems we can look at ways identity is used in interaction—to establish relations of similarity and difference (*adequation* and *distinction*), of genuineness and artifice (*authentication* and *denaturalization*), and of legitimacy and disempowerment (*authorization* and *illegitimation*). Each of the six relations is defined more specifically below:

adequation is 'the pursuit of socially recognized sameness' (p. 383);

distinction is 'the mechanism whereby salient difference is produced' (p. 384);

authentication is 'the construction of a credible or genuine identity . . . [which] often involves the rewriting of linguistic and cultural history' (p. 385);

denaturalization is 'the process whereby identities come to be severed from claims to 'realness' (p. 386);

authorization is the 'attempt to legitimate an identity through an institutional or other authority' (p. 386); and

illegitimation is 'the process of removing or denying power' (p. 387).

For Bucholtz and Hall (2004), as with current teacher-writer identity researchers like McKinney and Giorgis (2009) and Cremin and Baker (2010, 2014), identity is not a stable concept; rather, it is 'crucial to attend closely to speakers' own understandings of identities, as revealed through ethnographic analysis of their pragmatic and metapragmatic actions' (Bucholtz and Hall, p. 371). Thus, when taking up teacher-writers' identities as an analytic construct, it is important to use a variety of data sources—including both interviews and observations—to document different positionings (such as how, why and when teachers distinguish themselves as writers) over time and across spaces.

I use this 'tactics of intersubjectivity' frame to showcase how an elementary ESL teacher in the United States narrated and performed writing and teaching identities across contexts.

Methods

Sites and participants

This case is drawn from a larger study of embedded case studies situated at a National Writing Project (NWP) Summer Institute. I observed an elementary teacher,

Hannah, participating and writing at the four-week NWP Summer Institute and subsequently teaching over the course of a semester. I also interviewed her extensively, and collected her writing and her students' writing.

National Writing Project Summer Institute

The NWP Summer Institute has a rich history of developing a community of teacher-writers (Gray, 2000). NWP's network of sites, anchored at colleges and universities, provides a variety of professional development opportunities for teachers, generates research, and develops resources based on these principles. Each local site hosts a summer institute, and the teachers who complete the programme later lead professional development for local schools. Typically, teachers are invited to apply and must be selected and admitted to the program following interviews. The NWP requires 'one form of participation above all others . . . at NWP staff development: writing teachers must write' (NWP and Nagin, 2006, p. 65).

Hannah's four-week NWP Summer Institute featured digital composition (e.g., blog and Twitter writing, podcast and video composing, simple coding to create online portfolio websites) as a central component of the program. During a typical six-hour day at the Summer Institute, participants wrote independently on topics and in genres of their choice, gave and responded to teacher demonstrations, met in writing feedback or reading discussion groups, and composed 'assigned' digital texts. All teachers were encouraged, but not required, to submit a piece of writing to the NWP website for online publication. As a former participant at this site and to facilitate long-term relationships with participants over time, I engaged in the Summer Institute as a participant observer (Erikson, 1986), participating in all activities as a fellow writer and writing teacher, and offering support with digital composition.

The focal teacher: Hannah

For the larger study, I selected four focal participants to create a mix of elementary and secondary teachers, personal writing (e.g., creative vs. online writing), and instructional experiences (e.g., a focus on writing process pedagogy vs. literary analysis). I focus on Hannah in this piece because out of the focal teachers, she was the most hesitant to identify herself as a writer, but deeply committed to helping her students see themselves as writers. Hannah, a Korean American female, was a fourteenth-year teacher, but it was only her second year in early elementary as a first-grade ESL teacher. Another focal participant from the larger study, Samantha, co-taught with Hannah and makes multiple appearances in the findings. Samantha, a white female, was an eighteenth-year teacher who was pursuing her Master's degree in ESL at the time of the study. She loved to write and saw herself as a writer, but did not have much time for writing on a regular basis. Hannah, Samantha, and I—along with two other teachers—participated in a writing feedback group that met weekly at the NWP Summer Institute. During these meetings, we took turns sharing our morning writing and getting feedback from each other.

Like many people, Hannah did not have positive memories from writing in school, and could not remember much about learning to write (Brandt, 2001). To use Bucholtz and Hall's (2004) framework, Hannah learned to *distinguish* herself from good writers at an early age. Both before and after the NWP Summer Institute, Hannah wrote little outside of school. Aside from social network writing and e-mailing, Hannah cited mentor text writing for students as her primary type of ongoing writing. Mentor texts are pieces of writing that can be used as an example of quality writing. Students study these pieces, reading them like writers, and use them as models to try out related moves in their own writing. At the NWP Summer Institute, Hannah wrote such mentor texts, as well as narrative stories about her international travels, and shared them with our writing group. She did not share any of her digital compositions with the group for feedback.

Although Samantha took up the mantle of writer primarily as an instructional strategy, and did not tend to include 'writer' as part of her own identity, her participation at the NWP did help her see that writing could be fun, and she seemed to be engaged in a slow process of *authentication*, or 'the construction of a credible or genuine identity . . . [which] often involves the rewriting of linguistic and cultural history' (Bucholtz and Hall, 2004, p. 385), a process which will be described in more detail in the findings. Writing and sharing her writing was often very challenging for Hannah. However, she was insistent that her students should have a different experience as writers in schools. Her hope was that all her students would become confident enough to see 'the truth: I'm a writer and a pretty good writer.' In other words, Hannah tended to *distinguish* herself from writers during a slow process of *authenticating* a writerly identity, while simultaneously attempting to *authorize* her students as writers.

Hannah collaborated closely at both the NWP Summer Institute and in her instruction at Garvey Elementary with Samantha. They each pulled small groups of ESL students (seven to eight each) from monolingual classes, and brought these students together to co-teach their first-grade writing class. They attended the NWP Summer Institute together with the intent to collaborate. Hannah and Samantha did not have a writing curriculum, but tended to use aspects of Calkins' (2006) writers' workshop in their classroom, especially encouraging students to write what they know and focus writing on small moments (see Calkins, 2006). They also focused on learning vocabulary through shared language experiences, and writing using newly learned vocabulary. In an interview, Hannah said 'we want to make sure kids have the language skills to define and talk about their world.'

At Garvey Elementary, a school with a focus on multicultural programmes, diversity and multilingualism were celebrated. The student ethnicity breakdown was 57.4 percent black, 25.5 percent Asian, 9.7 percent white, 3.7 percent multiracial, 2.7 percent Hispanic, and 1 percent American Indian, with 86 percent from low-income families. The school was known for and very proud of its multicultural language programmes, including native language, dual language, and ESL instruction. Many international faculty and graduate students from the local university, as well as refugee families, enrolled their children there. In Hannah and Samantha's writing class, students came from Iran, Egypt, Guatemala, India, Turkey, China, Vietnam, Indonesia, and the French Congo. Over twenty-three different native languages were represented in the school.

Data collection

I share data from observations of Hannah's participation at a National Writing Project (NWP) Summer Institute, and from observations of her classroom instruction over the course of seven months to highlight how she positioned her students as writers, and herself as a writer and teacher of writing over time and across spaces. The data collection involved: nineteen days of participant observation with Hannah at the NWP Summer Institute (seven hours each) and thirty-one observations of her writing instruction in her first-grade ESL classroom (thirty minutes each); three formal interviews (thirty minutes each) and one informal interview (twenty minutes); and artefact collection of five blog entries and four writing group pieces at the NWP Summer Institute. Audio-recordings were made of all interviews and classroom observations, and Hannah's writing group meetings and teacher demonstration at the National Writing Project. Interviews focused on current and past experiences with writing, the writing process, Hannah's writing curriculum, and her teaching of writing. Field notes were written as jottings, details, and documentation of conversational turns, which were checked and extended through selected transcriptions. In interviews, I asked Hannah to talk about personal writing, teaching writing and the curriculum.

Data analysis

Consistent with qualitative methods that examine participants' perspectives and meaning-making practices, this analysis focused on identifying how writer and teacher-writer identities were talked about and enacted in interactions across a writing-intensive summer professional development programme and subsequent classroom teaching. Across the observational, interview, and textual data, I identified all instances where Hannah talked or wrote about being a writer (for both herself and her students) or writing teacher. After identifying these instances and examples, I applied Bucholtz and Hall's (2004) analytic framework, 'tactics of intersubjectivity,' to analyze the relational processes through which Hannah carried out her identities in social interactions over time. Because she tended to *distinguish* herself from writers and *denaturalize* her own writing identity when talking with other teachers (including me), but to *authenticate* her identity with students as she attempted to *authorize* them all as writers, I focused the findings on presenting this complex work. I first present her identity enactments as a writer and writing teacher, primarily at the NWP Summer Institute, and then on her intentional work during classroom instruction to foster more positive identity enactments for her first-grade students. Later, in the discussion, I bring this analysis into conversation with the literature and other analytic frameworks that have been used to describe teacher-writers' identity work (e.g., McKinney and Giorgis, 2009, categorization of writer-teacher identities).

Findings

Whereas Hannah never saw herself as a particularly good writer, lacked confidence in writing and sharing writing, and rarely wrote for pleasure before the NWP Summer Institute, she wanted to create a different school experience for her elementary students. Her case highlights not only the relational nature of identity enactment, but also some of the specific moves she made in an intentional attempt to authorize students' writing identities.

Becoming a writer and writing teacher

In our first interview before the NWP Summer Institute, Hannah told me that, 'I don't really personally write. I think part of it is because it is frustrating to think through word choice and things like that.' These ideas about writing were deeply rooted in her experiences writing in school. Although some teachers in the broader study had negative experiences in school, many eventually developed positive writing associations; however, Hannah never did. She was the only teacher in the study who did not have any memories of successful writing from school. When I asked her to talk to me about an experience learning to write, she said:

> To be honest, I don't really have very good memories of writing. I think I really just remember feeling like I'm not very good at it. And I do feel like that's always been a bit of a weakness of my English coursework. I love reading, I love talking about reading, but when it actually comes to writing, I know because I'm not the most ordered person, writing is difficult for me at times, for sure . . . I actually have a very distinct memory from my freshman year of high school . . . There was this guy in my class who wrote the most amazing paragraph responses. They sounded like a teacher. And the teacher would always read them in class as an example, and I was like "oh my gosh I'll never write like that."

In school, Hannah learned to *distinguish* herself from good writers, and came to *denaturalize* her own writing identity. Perhaps unsurprisingly, compared to the other teachers who experienced many successes with writing in their lives, Hannah was the least confident writer, and the teacher who wrote the least for pleasure.

At the NWP Summer Institute, though, Hannah wrote every day, and regularly shared her writing with our writing group. She primarily wrote two types of texts: mentor texts for her students and narrative stories about her international travels. For example, at our first writing group meeting, she shared a mentor text called *My Friend Boo*, a fanfiction series that she had been writing and sharing with her students about herself as a child and the fictional character Batman. She wrote the story from the perspective of herself as Bruce's fictionalized best friend growing up. Hannah told us that she had been writing and sharing these stories with her students and this was 'one of the popular ones.' In her NWP Summer Institute portfolio, she reflected on this writing:

> The main focus of *My Friend Boo* was the idea that Batman was once young and was someone's friend. My students also love superheroes (as do I), so this seemed liked a great way to connect my world and their world. I wrote different vignettes that could be used depending on the goals I have for my students.

When I later asked her about this piece, she told me that she wrote it to help 'students to realize they can write about anything in life.' During the observation school year, I saw Hannah write more mentor texts for her students on other popular characters and incorporating people the students knew. Hannah felt fairly comfortable writing pieces like these to model instructional strategies with her students.

At the NWP Summer Institute, Hannah also shared two narrative stories from her international travels. On her digital portfolio for the NWP Summer Institute, she wrote that, '[t]he second type of writing I did was journaling my personal travel experiences. I really enjoy travelling. Rather than pictures or a scarf, I find that I treasure the memories. To hold onto them, I decided to collect them for myself.' After the NWP Summer Institute, Hannah told me that she had told those stories orally many times, but never written them down, and that they were 'really just for me. I'm not going to publish them.' Writing these stories helped her articulate her experiences and preserve her memories.

Hannah was particularly nervous about sharing her writing with other teachers. For example, at our first weekly small writing group share session, she said, 'Can I go first, just because I am the most nervous about this? I really, I don't do these [things], I'm not [a writer] . . . .' She did not become more comfortable with sharing as the NWP Summer Institute progressed, saying:

> I hate sharing, if you couldn't tell (laughing). It's really uncomfortable because in some ways, your word choice, like everything, says so much about you. And you're just kind of stripped bare. And that was really, I was like, I just met these people, how can I read them what I wrote? . . . That was kind of painful actually.

Because Hannah tended to *distinguish* herself from writers, she was very uncomfortable engaging in writerly practices like sharing with her peers, often feeling that her writing would be judged. However, she did take away a sense from the NWP Summer Institute that writing for yourself was enjoyable, saying, 'I think that is . . . [a] really good thing that I take from here is the sense that I should be writing. . . . Just for fun, you know it doesn't have to [be a big deal], it is really a stress reliever in some ways. It's fun.' Writing intensively at the NWP Summer Institute helped her broaden her ideas about writing beyond just writing for her students to writing for herself and for fun, a 'rewriting of [her own] linguistic history' (Bucholtz and Hall, 2004, p. 385), and perhaps the beginnings of *authenticating* a genuine writerly identity for herself.

Even though Hannah did think of herself as a writer, she loved teaching writing, which is why she initially signed up for the NWP. Particularly as a new ESL teacher, she was interested in learning about new supports for her students. Before the NWP Summer Institute began, she told me:

> I don't particularly have memories about learning to write or writing as a child, but I love doing it with my students now. I think kind of my goal is that they have great memories of writing. I really do feel like it's such a victory when my students are excited to have journal time or free write time. Especially when, for them, language is hard enough . . . I really do enjoy teaching [writing] so I hope that this experience is going to be something I can offer my students.

Like other teacher-writers in the literature (see Cremin and Baker, 2010, 2014; McKinney and Giorgis, 2009) Hannah positioned herself multiply—as the struggling school writer concerned with word choice; the confident writer of mentor texts for students; the world traveller writer documenting her memories and experiences; the very nervous writer who felt 'stripped bare' when encouraged to share with those she did not know well; and a general nonwriter. Hannah primarily positioned herself as a teacher of writing and tended to write out of necessity and her constructions of identities were sometimes contradictory and inconsistent (see McCarthey and Moje, 2002). For example, she tended to identify herself as a nonwriter, but loved teaching writing so much that she sought out graduate writing classes and intensive long-term professional development experiences. She enjoyed writing mentor texts and narrative recounts of her travel, but only liked sharing with students, not her peers. She was just beginning to see writing as fun, low-stakes, and enjoyable, but didn't prioritize it yet as a valued personal activity.

Hannah wanted to create a school experience with writing for her students that was radically different than her own. In her NWP Summer Institute digital portfolio, she wrote, '[a]s I empower my students to speak their voice through writing and technology, their confidence in life will grow and lead them to the truth: I'm a writer and a pretty good writer.' In practice, three ways that Hannah sought to *authorize* her young students' writerly identities included *legitimizing* their diverse personal experiences, fan writing, and drawing.

Legitimizing students' diverse personal experiences as central to writing

Hannah and Samantha, who had both travelled extensively or lived abroad themselves, both used their NWP Summer Institute writing time to write narrative experiences about visiting or living in other cultures. Particularly as ESL teachers, such stories were central to their identities and understandings about teaching and learning. In an interview after the Summer Institute, Samantha told me about her goals for writing a story about living abroad: 'I wanted to have that be a story of many of my kids interacting with kids from the country. I thought that would be instructive and respective as well of both cultures maybe, or of that journey crossing cultures.' Hannah also wrote about her travels crossing cultures, telling our writing group about an awkward interchange between her American friend and a Thai man on a mission trip she took in college when she shared her piece *Ugly American*.

In their writing classroom, Samantha and Hannah similarly encouraged their ESL students who moved to the US from all over the world to celebrate their journeys with culture crossing, positioning them as experts on their cultures. Over the course of the fall semester, Hannah and Samantha developed a country project where students researched, wrote about, and presented on their home countries. During the unit, Hannah told me, 'We're doing country studies of all the kids . . . [we want to] make sure kids have language skills that they can access their background knowledge. And then help them feel like they are an expert, even though English is such a challenge for them.' Samantha also explained to me that the country studies were an important part of building up to testimonio writing in the spring (testimonios are powerful personal narratives used to tell a collective story and history of oppression; see Saavedra, 2011), '[t]he country study I think was major because it connected them with their country and how proud they are, that *they* know things that nobody else knows about their country. And then, their feelings are important because they're going to add that [to the testimonios].' At the end of the project, students did presentations on their countries and the teachers videotaped them.

Hannah and Samantha constantly created opportunities to help their students talk, write, and think about cultural border crossing, much like the writing they enjoyed doing themselves. Observations across the semester made it clear that they created a community of writing where students' languages and cultures were honored. In these ways, Hannah and Samantha lent their authority as teachers to *legitimize/authorize* students' writerly identities by acknowledging their personal experiences as important and positioning them as 'experts' with specific 'language skills' and 'background knowledge' to share.

Legitimizing fan writing

Inspired in part by Dyson's (1997) research documenting young children's appropriation of popular culture in their writing, Hannah wrote numerous mentor texts for students based on characters from popular culture and their favorite authors. Recall, for example, that she loved superheroes and wrote a mentor text about the comic book hero Batman at the NWP Summer Institute to help 'students to realize they can write about anything in life.' During one observation in the fall semester, she shared another example of a mentor text she had written appropriating characters from popular culture. Her story, 'I Need Chocolate!,' was based on Mo Willems' Elephant and Piggie characters (see Figure 8.1). In it, Piggie was sick, and Elephant gave Piggie chocolate to make him feel better.

In Hannah's second blog post at NWP, in response to a teaching demonstration that asked us to consider which three authors we would want to visit our classrooms, she identified Mo Willems as her top choice, calling him her 'children's writer crush' and noting that both she and her students loved all his characters—she was a true fan.

Much like fanfiction writers (Jenkins, 2006), Hannah capitalized on her love of his characters and stories, and expertise in them, as a springboard for her own writing. Her writing, in turn, inspired many Elephant and Piggie stories from her

a
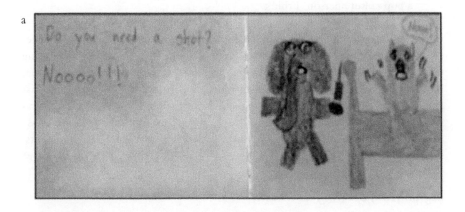

b
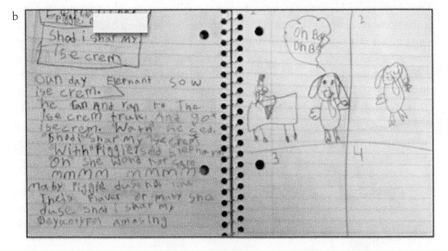

FIGURE 8.1A AND 8.1B   An excerpt from Hannah's mentor text writing based on Mo Willems' characters (above) and her student, Anjali's, related story *Elephant and Piggie: Should I share my ice cream?*

first graders (see Figure 8.1). Hannah and Samantha encouraged these types of stories; both of them saw making students comfortable and helping them talk about their worlds as important elements of writing in early elementary ESL classrooms. In fact, just before Hannah shared her Elephant and Piggie story, Samantha had led the class in writing a shared book on the topic of their choice—Scooby Doo. Regarding her mentor text writing, Hannah reflected:

> The mentor texts, I do pretty often because I mean, I just use it all the time with kids. For me, it's like if it's not fun—if I don't like it, then they're not going to like it. So, I do [them for that reason], and also because I took [a class] with Anne Haas Dyson . . . she did revolutionize my way of thinking about primary literacy, and thinking about how to support and access their [young students'] literacy. And it made a lot of sense because I'm such a pop culture person, I think.

Other teacher participants in the study learned in their own schooling experiences to *distinguish* fanfiction writing from 'original' writing, and writers who came up with 'original' ideas from nonwriters who did not. Hannah and Samantha, however, actively worked against such ideas and *legitimized/authorized* their first graders' writerly identities by showing students that it was okay to be fans who write fun pieces about characters they love, and by making space in their classrooms for writing about popular culture characters that permeated students' worlds (Dyson, 1997).

Legitimizing drawing as writing

After I observed Hannah teaching during the fall semester, she told me that one of the texts she read at the Summer Institute in a book group had been very influential in her instruction—Horn and Giacobbe's (2007) *Talking, Drawing, Writing: Lessons for Our Young Writers*. Right after reading it, Hannah wrote on her blog, 'I was most struck by her [the author's] instruction of specific drawing skills to empower her students.' Samantha also told me how inspired she was by our many discussions at the NWP Summer Institute about broadening conceptions of writing to think about composing. After the Summer Institute, I asked her if she would say anything about writing now that she would not have said before, and she told me:

> I think, one thing that really screamed at me from Sally's demo [was] that drawing is composing. Since I work with young children and children who don't speak English, that's always where we start, we start with their drawings. . . .
>
> Composing is many things . . . many, many things, and I put much more weight into that. Not just for kids, but for everyone. I mean, I compose a lot when I'm out walking.

Hannah and Samantha worked to incorporate and *legitimize* drawing as part of writing in their classroom. For example, Samantha showed me a Drawing Center where they had illustrated guides to help students learn how to draw figures. In an observation at the beginning of the school year, Hannah told a student, 'I like the really nice details on your picture. Drawing helps some people write.' In November, for Garvey Elementary's Family Reading Night, the classes were supposed to focus on folktales from around the world. Samantha and Hannah read *Coyote: A trickster tale from the American Southwest* by Gerald McDermott (1999) to students, and then had them identify and draw important moments from the story, and create speech bubbles to go along with their pictures. They discussed how the pictures and text worked together to create meaning at length, and sequenced the drawings into a class picture book (see Figure 8.2). By the end of the fall semester, both teachers were pleased with the ways their students were intentionally combining pictures and words to communicate.

Hannah understood that *legitimizing/authorizing* drawing as writing is particularly important for emergent writers, who often use combinations of talking, drawing, and writing to convey their meaning (Horn and Giacobbe, 2007), and for ESL writers, who might not yet be able to access vocabulary beyond their native language. Similarly, many types of digital composing include multiple modalities. A shift in

FIGURE 8.2   A student's retelling—in illustrations and dialogue—of an important moment in the book *Coyote*

conceptualization from writing to composing, which Hannah and Samantha were encouraged to grapple with at the NWP Summer Institute, may offer substantial potential openings for identifying oneself and others as writers.

Discussion and implications

Hannah's case offers considerations for teachers intentionally trying to authenticate writerly identities and create classrooms that authorize all students as writers.

Teachers trying to authenticate identities as writers and writing teachers

Hannah, like many of the teachers across the broader study—even those who wrote extensively for pleasure—denaturalized her writing identities from claims of 'realness.' 'Real' writing identities, for many of the teachers, are tied to a view of writers as published professionals or experts engaged in serious, often solitary, paid work (Woodard, 2013). This view stands in contradiction to broadening ideas in the field of writing studies about what writing is and who writers are. As Yancey (2009) writes, 'in the 21st century people write as never before—in print and online' (p. 1).

Today, our field and our society are grappling with—and sometimes broadening—our ideas about writing and writers. In 2011, the National Council of Teachers of English's (NCTE's) National Day on Writing website, for example, suggested that texting, IMing, note jotting, and diary writing might 'count' as writing, and that people are writing today more than ever. For Hannah and Samantha, they worked hard to make sure that personal experiences, fan writing, and drawing 'count' as writing in their classroom. For teachers interested in authenticating identities as writers and writing teachers, it might be productive to closely examine their own beliefs about what counts as writing and who counts as writers, as well as tensions in those beliefs.

As in the existing research literature on teacher-writer identities (see Cremin and Baker, 2010, 2014; McKinney and Giorgis, 2009), Hannah—and the other teachers across the study—expressed multiple, sometimes conflicting writerly identities in interactions with their students and me. To me, Hannah tended to showcase a sort of 'fake it till you make it' identity enactment—often positioning herself as a writer to students, but rarely to me. I saw other teachers taking a similar stance, and have begun to wonder if performing a writerly identity with students, even if you don't believe it yourself, might be an important part of developing a writerly identity for teachers like Hannah, who have negative experiences with writing and don't see themselves as writers but want to support more positive identity work for their students.

Hannah's NWP experience also seemed to be an important part of her developing writerly identity. There, she was challenged to share her writing, even though she was not comfortable, expanded her ideas about what counts as writing (and thus, potentially, who counts as a writer), and began to see writing as relaxing and enjoyable. My own research has shown that teachers who engage deeply and regularly in writing appropriate many textual practices into their instruction, even if they do not see many connections between their writing and teaching of writing (Woodard, 2015). For teachers like Hannah interested in authenticating identities as writers and writing teachers, professional development like the NWP Summer Institute that creates times and spaces for regular writing and sharing broadens conceptualizations of what counts as writers and who counts as writers, and explicitly encouraging teachers to engage with the identity of writer seems particularly important.

Creating classrooms that authorize all students as writers

Hannah's case resonates clearly with the literature on teacher-writers. In McKinney and Giorgis's (2009) research even Erika, one of the teachers they categorized as a 'nonwriter,' expressed a strong desire to 'instill in students the excitement, creativity, and adventures that await them in the written word' (p. 137). Hannah, who might be characterized as bridging from a 'nonwriter' to 'sometimes writer' under their categorization, expressed similar goals to help her students see themselves as writers with important things to say. As a teacher in a school with significant authority over her students, she tried to authorize or legitimize her students' writerly identities in many ways: she positioned them as experts on culture and characters, encouraged them to engage with kinds of fan writing that are often a taboo in school, and helped them to see writing more broadly as a semiotic meaning-making system. While her single case is not broadly generalizable, I do think it warrants some considerations for any teacher hoping to authorize all students as writers, such as:

- What are the messages I am sending students about 'real' and 'good' writers?
- How do I acknowledge and push back on narrower messages that may have already encouraged them to distinguish or denaturalize themselves from writerly identities?
- How do I authenticate myself as a writer in my classroom? How do I present this as a credible, genuine part of my identity?
- What are the specific moves I make—or could make—to legitimate/authorize my students as writers?
- How can I attend to my students' complex, multiple writerly identities that are expressed differently across interactions and contexts?

Conclusion

Hannah's case is interesting because she primarily took up the identity of writer with and for her students; however, this was not just an instructional strategy—she did it to create a space where she could authorize all students as writers. It was an intentional move to provide a different sort of relationship with writing than she herself struggled with. She was in a process of beginning to find writing fun and enjoyable, but it remains to be seen if she ever declares 'writer' as an explicit aspect of her identity. However, multiple classroom practices did emerge from her engagements with writing and writerly identities, particularly related to Hannah's legitimization of many of her first graders' composing practices. In my observations, these practices seemed to positively affect children's sense of themselves as writers, their motivation to write, and their writing performance.

Hannah's case raises a number of questions to ponder more broadly: Is taking on the identity of writer primarily for students an instructional strategy? Or does it also do something for the teacher (if so, what)? How does explicitly naming oneself a writer—or not—matter in the work we do with students? What sorts of classroom practices emerge from teachers' intentional engagement with writing and writerly identities? When teachers attempt to legitimize students' writerly identities, how are students positively—or otherwise—affected? Further studies of teachers attempting to authenticate their own writerly identities, as well as their diverse identity enactments across relationships, time, and space, may shed light on how teachers can best legitimize all students as writers.

References

Alsup, J. (2006) *Teacher Identity Discourses: Negotiating Personal and Professional Spaces*, Mahwah, NJ, Lawrence Erlbaum and the National Council of Teachers of English.

Brandt, D. (2001) *Literacy in American Lives*, New York, Cambridge University Press.

Brooks, G. W. (2007) 'Teachers as readers and writers and as teachers of reading and writing', *The Journal of Educational Research*, vol. 100, no. 3, pp. 177–191.

Bucholtz, M. and Hall, K. (2004) 'Language and identity', in Duranti, A. (ed.) *A Companion to Linguistic Anthropology*, Malden, MA, Blackwell, pp. 369–394.

Calkins, L. M. (2006) *The Units of Study for Teaching Writing, Grades 3–5*, Portsmouth, NH, Heinemann.

Cochran-Smith, M. and Lytle, S. L. (1992) *Inside/Outside: Teacher Research and Knowledge* (Language and Literacy Series), New York, Teachers College Press.

Cremin, T. and Baker, S. (2010) 'Exploring teacher-writer identities in the classroom: Conceptualising the struggle', *English Teaching: Practice and Critique*, vol. 9, no. 3, pp. 8–24.

Cremin, T. and Baker, S. (2014) 'Exploring the discursively constructed identities of a teacher-writer teaching writing', *English Teaching: Practice and Critique*, vol. 13, no. 3, pp. 30–55.

Dawson, C. (2011) *Inventing Teacher-Writers*, PhD, Michigan State University.

Dyson, A. H. (1997) *Writing Superheroes: Contemporary Childhood, Popular Culture, and Classroom Literacy*, New York, Teachers College Press.

Erikson, F. (1986) 'Qualitative methods in research on teaching', in Wittrock, M. (ed.) *Handbook of Research on Teaching* (3rd edn), New York, Macmillan, pp. 119–161.

Gray, J. (2000) *Teachers at the Center: A Memoir of the Early Years of the National Writing Project*, National Writing Project.

Horn, M. and Giacobbe, M. E. (2007) *Talking, Drawing, Writing: Lessons for our Youngest Writers*, Portland, ME, Stenhouse Publishers.

Jenkins, H. (2006) *Convergence Culture: Where Old and New Media Collide*, New York, New York University Press.

McCarthey, S. J. (2001) 'Identity construction in elementary readers and writers', *Reading Research Quarterly*, vol. 36, pp. 122–151.

McCarthey, S. J. and Moje, E. (2002) 'Identity matters', *Reading Research Quarterly*, vol. 37, no. 2, pp. 228–238.

McDermott, G. (1999) *Coyote: A Trickster Tale from the American Southwest*, Singapore, HMH Books for Young Readers.

McKinney, M. and Giorgis, C. (2009) 'Narrating and performing identity: Literacy specialists' writing identities', *Journal of Literacy Research*, vol. 41, no. 1, pp. 104–149.

Murray, D. M. (1968) *A Writer Teaches Writing: A Practical Method of Teaching Composition*, New York, Houghton Mifflin.

National Writing Project and Nagin, C. (2006) *Because Writing Matters: Improving Student Writing in Our Schools*, San Francisco, CA, Jossey-Bass.

Robbins, B. W. (1990) *Teachers as Writers: Relationships Between English Teachers' Own Writing and Instruction*, PhD, Indiana University.

Robbins, B. W. (1996) 'Teachers as writers: Tensions between theory and practice', *Journal of Teaching Writing*, vol. 15, no. 1, pp. 107–128.

Saavedra, C. M. (2011) 'Language and literacy in the borderlands: Acting upon the world through testimonios', *Language Arts*, vol. 88, no. 4, pp. 261–269.

Shea, A., Balkun, M. M., Nolan, S. A., Saccoman, J. T. and Wright, J. (2006) 'One more time: Transforming the curriculum across the disciplines through technology-based faculty development and writing-intensive course redesign', *Across the Disciplines*, vol. 3. Retrieved April 15, 2012, from http://wac.colostate.edu/atd/articles/shea2006.cfm.

Woodard, R. L. (2013) 'Complicating "writing teachers must write": Tensions between teachers' literate and instructional practices', in Dunstonet, P. J., Gambrell, L. B., Headley, K., Fullerton, S. K. and Stecker, P. M. (eds) *62nd Yearbook of the Literacy Research Association*, Oak Creek, WI, Literacy Research Association, pp. 377–390.

Woodard, R. L. (2015) 'The dialogic interplay of writing and teaching writing: Teacher writers' talk and textual practices across contexts', *Research in the Teaching of English*, vol. 50, no. 1, pp. 35–59.

Yancey, K. B. (2009) *Writing in the 21st Century: A Report from the National Council of Teachers of English*, Urbana, IL, National Council of Teachers of English.

9

DEVELOPING A WHOLE-SCHOOL CULTURE OF WRITING

Terry Locke

This chapter begins with a consideration of two broad concepts: teacher professional identity and disciplinary literacy. Building on these two concepts, it envisages what a 'culture of writing' might look like in the secondary school. It then moves to a discussion of a number of case studies, each of which investigates changes in identity, self-efficacy and classroom practice of a range of secondary-school teachers from a range of schools and representing a range of subject areas or disciplines. It reports on transformations in identity and how these can be related to intensive engagement in writing workshop-based professional learning experiences. It also reports on some examples of changed classroom practices that were found to impact on students themselves, in terms of motivation, performance and identity. Finally, it outlines the steps required to produce a whole-school culture of writing.

Introduction

There is a narrative aspect to this chapter, which stems from my sense of it as a work in progress, where I continue to reflect on the conditions necessary for the development of a culture of writing, particularly in the secondary school, and what such a culture would look like in practice. I would have called myself a 'writer' before I called myself a 'teacher', and a teacher before I called myself a 'researcher'. But it is only in the last four years that I have begun systematically reflecting on what it *means* to call oneself a writer in the context of classroom teaching.

One starting point for this chapter was a two-year research project I led in 2010–11 entitled 'Teachers as writers: Transforming professional identity and classroom practice'. This action research project involving 13 teachers from three secondary and four primary schools investigated how intensive participation in writing workshops impacted on the competence and confidence of teachers as writers, and sought to demonstrate positive effects in the writing performance and motivation of students in the classrooms of participating teacher-researchers. There is an ample literature on the way Writing Project practices and principles can transform the teaching and learning of writing in a range of contexts (see Wood and Lieberman 2000; Andrews 2008). Indeed, in the 'Teachers as writers' project, findings suggested that teachers found the intensive, writing workshop-based, professional learning beneficial (Locke, Whitehead, Dix and Cawkwell 2011). In addition, researchers involved in the project found a range of positive, 'flow-on' effects on student motivation and learning through a range of case studies conducted along action research lines (e.g., Whitehead and Murphy 2012; Locke and Kato 2012; Dix and Cawkwell 2011). Teachers engaged in the project experienced enhanced self-efficacy (Bandura 1997) in relation to both writing and the teaching of writing (Locke, Whitehead and Dix 2013).

Among the seven National Writing Project tenets Andrews (2008, p. 5) identified were the following:

1. To teach writing, you need to be able to write;
2. Students should respond to each other's writing;
3. The teacher should act as writer alongside the students, and be prepared to undertake the same assignments as the students.

The participants in the 'Teachers as writers' project engaged in writing workshops for a total of 13 days (including two six-day workshops in successive Januaries). In keeping with the above tenets, they engaged in writing a range of genres and participated in peer-response either in groups (Pritchard and Honeycutt 2007) or via 'Author's Chair' (McCallister 2008). Even though the phrase 'professional identity' occurred in the project title, our research focus was on self-efficacy as both writer and teacher of writing (Locke et al. 2013). As Fairclough (1992) points out, the same word can have multiple meanings, something he refers to as its *meaning potential*. Even though in our interviews we explored participants' changing feelings about themselves as writers, we did not explore the meanings they ascribed to such phrases as 'identity as a writer'.

The focus in 'Teachers as writers' was teachers rather than schools. However, it became apparent that seeding effects were occurring as participants shared beliefs, attitudes and practices with colleagues in their own schools (Locke and Kato 2014). Other trends occurred also. The meaning potential of the word *writing* expanded to include multimodal textual production. (Teachers spent two days on digital story-telling.) Sometimes the word *composition* was used in preference to 'writing'. What I'll call 'grammar anxiety' was widespread, but was especially evident among primary teachers and for the project teacher who taught secondary chemistry. (The other secondary participants taught either English or History.) Clear differences emerged among teachers in terms of the types of text and text functions they were required to teach in their professional lives. The mantra 'Every teacher is a teacher of writing' changed to 'Every teacher is a teacher of certain types of writing'.

A subsequent project (co-led with Shaun Hawthorne), which produced find-ings more germane to the problematics associated with developing a whole-school culture of writing, was situated in an inner-city, co-educational Auckland second-ary school, we'll call Huia College. This two-year project (2013–14) was entitled: 'A culture of writing: Impacting on teacher and student performance across the curriculum' (Locke and Hawthorne 2015). Because the school had a Rumaki,[1] it offered the opportunity to address specifically the needs of Māori students. The project investigated the writing workshop-based practices that enhanced teacher self-efficacy in respect of writing and the teaching of writing and, in particular, practices which appeared to have a positive impact on student (including indig-enous Māori students) motivation and performance in writing. It also investigated ways in which a cross-disciplinary 'culture of writing' might be seeded and devel-oped in a secondary school. Teachers participating over 2013 and 2014 represented a range of subjects: English, Geography, Science, ESOL, Media Studies, Visual Art and Mathematics. All had volunteered following a briefing meeting where the project was explained to them and the required commitment spelled out. In the context of regular professional learning community (PLC) meetings, participat-ing teachers collaborated in drawing on their writing workshop experiences to design, introduce and evaluate a writing-focused intervention in just one of their classrooms. In effect, the classrooms these teachers selected became single cases in a collective case study (Yin 1989; Heigham and Croker 2009).

Later, I will share findings from this project that tell us something about how these eight teachers viewed the concept of *writer identification*, and whether their involvement in writing workshop professional learning impacted on this. I will also draw on ongoing research at a central North Island school I will call Manāki College, which began with a five-day writing workshop for 18 staff in December 2014, in the first few days of their summer vacation. These staff also volunteered as a result of a briefing session, which spelled out the parameters of the project, which also explores ways of developing a community of writing in a secondary school. I will also have something to say about teacher efficacy around the teaching of writ-ing, and the relationship of this to specific subject/disciplinary areas. Inevitably, the question of metalinguistic competence will arise. But first, let me turn to the question of identity and its various meaning potentials (ascribed meanings).

Identity

I want to make a number of claims that establish the premises upon which this section of the chapter rests. For all of us, identities (and subjectivities) are multiple and dynamic. I concur with Ferreira's (2014) distinction between 'subjectivity as an open-ended process of becoming and *identities* as "points of suture" (citing Hall 1996) along this process when particular subject positions are taken up' (p. 176). As Gee (2000) implies, in defining identity as 'acting and interacting as a "certain kind of person"' (p. 100), the subject positions we take up vary from context to context. As this book has asserted throughout, there is, then, no single 'who'. However, there is, as Damasio (2000) theorises, a single *autobiographical self* that endures, 'based on autobiographical memory which is constituted by implicit memories of multiple instances of individual experience of the past and of the anticipated future' (p. 174). We are social beings as well as biological organisms. All of us, consciously or unconsciously, subscribe to a range of discourses or stories, which make sense of some aspect of our experience. We are in this sense socially and historically *constructed* creatures. I am using the term *discourse* here in its Foucaultian sense, defined neatly by Fairclough (1992) as 'a practice not just of representing the world, but of signifying the world, constituting and constructing the world in meaning' (p. 64). However, we are also creatures with agency. 'I use the term *self as negotiator* to suggest that as individuals we have agency over the subscription process and can contest the way the world is storied in discourse' (Locke 2015a, p. 44).

Identifying as a writer

A common reference point for this topic is Ivanič's *Writing and Identity* (1998), where she argued that four dimensions of identity are involved in the act of writing:

1. An autobiographical self (similar to Damasio's concept);
2. A discoursal self which relates to how we position ourselves in relation to an anticipated audience by the discourses we subscribe to and project outwards;
3. An authorial self (akin to Elbow's 'voice with authority' (2000, p. 193)); and
4. Possibilities for selfhood.

As I understand the last of these, it suggests that there are certain social conditions that favour our willingness to take risks in trying out or asserting or discovering identities (or 'selves') in the act of writing itself (finding our 'voice').

I argue that this is valuable work, but is only tangentially about identifying as a writer. Rather it tells a story about the kinds of selves potentially involved in the act of writing. It seems to me that all of these dimensions of identity could be found in the act of constructing a landscaped flower garden. For example, the *discoursal self* would be indicated by the kind of landscaping discourse subscribed to (e.g. English cottage garden). Ivanič's framework doesn't actually tell a story about what it means to write or *be* a writer.

At this point, then, I offer a definition of writer identity as *the subscribed-to discourse or story about what it means to be a writer that is implicit in one's own beliefs and practices*. These stories are likely to be complex and to change over time. They are likely to be variable and have their origins in a range of experiences and cultural contexts. They are also likely to have an affective aspect, in that these stories about what it means to write and be a writer will be connected with certain emotions, some negative, some positive. Everyone who has learnt to read and write has a writer identity of some kind. But self-doubt, a lack of self-efficacy and a history of painful experiences, which may have implanted a fear of being judged, will discourage many people from acknowledging the writer identity they *do* have.

I distinguish writer identity thus defined from the way one positions oneself (or not) as a writer in various contexts; the latter can be viewed as the public face of writer identity and bears some relationship with Ivanič's discoursal self. The distinction was captured by a Huia College teacher who described herself as having 'an identity as a writer but not really – a writer who doesn't write much'.

Teacher (professional) identity

Teacher professional identity is a construct subsumed under the larger construct of teacher identity. To remain consistent with my own practice, I should define teacher identity as *the subscribed-to discourse or story about what it means to be a teacher that is implicit in a teacher's own beliefs and practices*. As Beijaard, Meijer and Verloop (2004) point out in their review of research on teachers' professional identity, the concept is used in various ways in the educational domain. However, there is broad agreement that it is multifaceted and dynamic. In synthesising findings across 22 studies, they identified four features deemed to be essential for teacher professional identity:

1. It involves 'an *ongoing process* of interpretation and re-interpretation of experiences';
2. It is context-bound, suggesting both constraints and affordances;
3. It is made up of '*sub-identities* that more or less harmonize';
4. Teachers have *agency* in their identity formation.

(p. 122; italics theirs)

By way of comment, I would note that the dynamic quality indicated in the first feature derives from continual engagement with new experiences and the way teachers' beliefs (discourses) are subject to change. The second point is a reminder that there are discursive forces at work that constrain the professional identification process; for example, working in settings characterised by standardised assessment regimes. In relation to the third feature, there are plenty of instances where sub-identities co-exist in ways that are difficult to reconcile (see Locke 2013). The fourth feature is consistent with Bernstein's assertion that 'identity positions the teacher as a dynamic and agentive individual who actively mediates the diversity of input—from students, curricula, standards, administration—through the lens of their lived experience and sense of self' (2014, p. 111). I will have more to say about agency below.

Consistent with my own definition above, Mockler (2011) uses the term *teacher professional identity* to refer to the way that 'teachers, both individually and collectively, view and understand themselves as teachers' (p. 519). She views teacher professional identity as 'constituted across and out of the three key domains of . . . personal experience, professional context, and the external political environment' (p. 520). Like any map, her way of expressing this in diagrammatic form has its strengths and limitations in helping us explore the territory of teacher identity. However, her concept of 'domain' is a useful way of identifying contextual feeders into a teacher's discursive make-up.

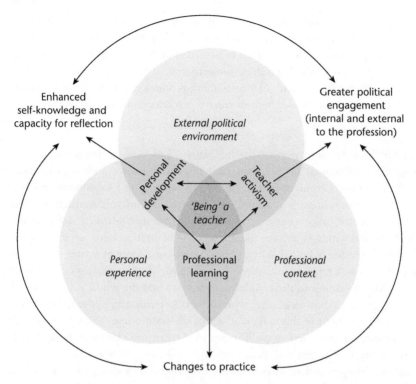

FIGURE 9.1   The formation and mediation of teacher professional identity (Mockler 2011, p. 521)

We would locate Shulman's (1986) well-known professional knowledge trio of *content knowledge*, *pedagogical content knowledge* and *curricular knowledge* in the domain of 'professional context' and the segment of 'professional learning'. In Locke (2004), I suggested that there is a fourth kind of knowledge teachers need, namely *critically strategic knowledge*. Such knowledge enables teachers to make critical connections between the 'professional learning' segment in Mockler's diagram and the external political environment. In particular it draws attention to discourses operating in the educational policy environment that play a role in shaping the work teachers. The self-reflexive *self as negotiator* has the capacity to identify the discourses or stories we tell ourselves about some aspect of teaching; for example, writing and the teaching of writing. It also provides a sense of where these discourses or stories originate—who or what out there has *designs* on how we think and practise our art. Because writing is a widespread, meaning-making activity, we can expect a teacher to draw on personal experiences (as per Figure 9.1) in the formation of their sub-identities as writers.

I can come at this another way by citing Hall (1996), mentioned at the start of this section. Referencing Althusser (1971), Hall deploys the word *identity* to refer to:

the meeting point, the point of *suture*, between, on the one hand, the discourses and practices which attempt to 'interpellate', speak to us or hail us into place as the social subjects of particular discourses, and on the other hand, the processes which produce subjectivities, which construct us as subjects which can be 'spoken'. Identities are thus points of temporary attachment to the subject positions which discursive practices construct for us.

(p. 19)

I prefer the term 'subscription' to 'attachment' and have a stronger sense of the possibilities of human agency than Hall implies. However, his deployment of this term invites a connection with *positioning theory*. Van Langenhove and Harré (1999) describe *positioning* as a fluid process—'the discursive construction of personal stories that make a person's actions intelligible and relatively determinate as social acts and within which the members of a conversation have specific locations' (p. 16). A teacher who sub-identifies as a particular kind of writer—the public face of identity I referred to earlier—can be thought of as *speaking* or positioning themselves in relation to their students, institution and the world at large, and also as *speaking back* to those discourses which, in Hall's terms, attempt to speak to or for us. Agency, thought of this way, is an act of self-positioning (and self-fashioning). The fluidity of these acts of positioning in the writing classroom is highlighted in the work of Cremin and Baker (2014), who show how teachers experience tensions as they negotiate ways of positioning themselves along a teacher-writer/writer-teacher continuum.

Disciplinary literacy

Shulman's categories were a response to the question: 'Where did the subject matter go?' (p. 5), a question as pertinent today as it was in 1986, if not more so. I want to continue with Shulman's trio and relate it to writing.

Content knowledge

The comment below was written in the response journal of a pre-service primary teacher, who was participating in a writing workshop as part of a course entitled 'The teacher as writer'. She wrote:

> What I did notice today was that, not for lack of trying, no one in my peer-response group including myself felt particularly confident in giving specific feedback, positive or constructive, for our poems. There was a lot of uncertainty around what merited a strength/weakness and what indicators can be identified for a good poem. Everyone just kind of mumbled, 'Good work, yep that was good', or 'Oh yeah, I really liked that poem'.

(Karen)[2]

Karen is experiencing a gap here in 'content knowledge'—what I'd prefer to call *disciplinary* knowledge, in this case the discipline of literary criticism (one of the discourses that contributes to the construction of subject English). As an aside, it is a discipline whose contribution to the teaching of literature has been marginalised as 'literacy' takes over centre-stage from literary studies (Locke 2009). Literary criticism, in its various forms, provides a specialised language for talking about literary texts (*content knowledge base*) and how they are composed (*rhetorical content base*), a distinction drawn from Bereiter and Scardamalia (1987). Specifically, it offers a language for talking about the content of literary texts (e.g. *theme*) and a language for talking about the textual practices associated with literary criticism (a metalanguage to talk about disciplinary literacy practices). In a similar way, the discipline of biology provides a specialised language for talking about such things as the human digestive system (content) *and* how biologists talk and write about the subject (the discipline-specific rhetorical content base) (see Figure 9.2).

Pedagogical content knowledge

Both a teacher's content knowledge base and rhetorical knowledge base can be associated with pedagogical content knowledge—more or less effective ways of helping students master the content, skills and dispositions related to each. New Zealand research suggests that teachers in secondary schools are more secure in the pedagogical content knowledge (PCK) associated with their content knowledge base than the PCK associated with their rhetorical knowledge base, and generally lack confidence in teaching disciplinary literacy practices, particularly writing. In addition, the degree of (in)security is generally subject-related, with mathematics teachers least secure (Locke and Johnston 2016).[3]

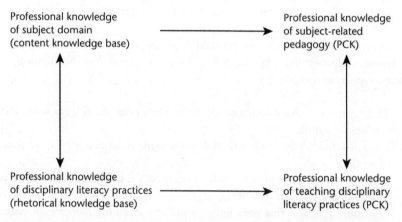

FIGURE 9.2 Professional and metalinguistic knowledge (Locke 2015b, p. 150)

Curricular knowledge

In most Anglophone countries, the State has assumed virtually total control of the official curriculum and its attendant assessment regimes. In terms of Mockler's diagram, the official curriculum is a locus for overlap between the external political environment and the professional context. Many of us have become so used to stepped ladders of skills or competencies that we have perhaps forgotten how flawed these constructions of knowledge/skills progression *are* that underpin these structures. While Shulman suggested that teachers need to have a good knowledge of the curriculum, he doesn't spell out *which* curriculum teachers should teach. The question becomes: 'In what ways might the official curriculum be operationalised in schools so that the learning needs of students are adequately met?' For many of us, this means: 'How can we ring-fence sound practices around the teaching of writing in the context of standardised testing regimes?'

Developing a culture of writing

The 'Culture of Writing' research at Huia College (2013–14) involving eight teachers was conducted in line with a participatory action research ethos and is described in detail in Locke and Hawthorne (2015). It set out to identify:

1. The writing workshop features and practices viewed positively by teacher-participants as contributing to increased self-efficacy as writers and teachers of writing;
2. Pedagogical strategies that enhanced the motivation and writing performance of students (including Māori students) in case-study classrooms which were attributable to changes in classroom practice prompted by engagement in the writing workshop experience; and
3. How writing workshop-based principles and practices might be embedded within a school culture as a community of writing practice.

Adopting a similar ethos, the Manāki College project (2015–16), involving 12 teachers representing English, Māori, Science, Visual Art, Accounting and Technology, is investigating:

1. The experiences that contribute to teachers assuming identities as writers and teachers of writing;
2. The self-efficacy effects when teachers assume identities as writers and teachers of writing;
3. Changes in classroom practices which occur when teachers assume identities as writers and teachers of writing;
4. Classroom practices that contribute to students assuming identities as writers both generally and in relation to the production of discipline-specific text-types;

5. Classroom practices that appear to enhance students' self-efficacy, motivation and performance as writers; and
6. Steps needed to enable a school to become a community of writing practice.

The project ethos positioned teachers to view themselves as researchers who were involved in decisions related to which of their classes became case studies employing mixed methods, the interventions they would trial with their students and the evidence that would be collected and analysed as a way of ascertaining whether and how the intervention had worked. In this sense, both projects were multiple case studies. In addition, participants in both projects completed self-efficacy questionnaires related to themselves as teachers of writing and questionnaires related to their writing workshop experiences, and were also interviewed by me one year into the project. Both principals were also interviewed one year into the project. All qualitative data were subject to thematic analysis (Braun and Clarke 2006).

In what follows, I reflect briefly on five topics: the challenges secondary schools face in becoming cultures of writing; the transformative potential of ongoing writing workshop professional learning in the context of a professional learning community (PLC); the importance of classroom-based inquiry; a focus on cross-disciplinarity; and the need for a whole-school and community 'buy-in'.

Challenges to the development of a culture of writing

There is ample evidence globally suggesting a reluctance on the part of many subject teachers to see themselves as teachers of writing. When interviewed, the principal of Huia College certainly did not see such a self-perception as 'widespread' in his staff. In part he attributed the resistance to this identity position as stemming from a gap in professional development: 'I'm not to be judged as a teacher of writing because I haven't been trained as such; I've had little or no PD as such since I began teaching.' The school's Deputy Principal, in contrast, suggested that 'all of the humanities-based subject teachers would absolutely identity themselves as teachers of writing', contrasting them to Maths teachers who would be less likely to do so. Interestingly, in reflecting further on the word 'identity', he commented that though teachers might describe themselves as 'teaching writing to a certain extent', they would not '*label* themselves as teachers of writing' [my emphasis]. He had this to say about identifying as a writer *per se*:

> I think there'd be far fewer teachers who would claim the identity or feel comfortable with the identity of calling themselves a writer. . . . It's almost in contradiction to the fact that everyone is a teacher of writing but they . . . don't identify as a writer themselves.

The words 'label' and 'claim' draw attention to the act of deliberate self-positioning around the taking up of an identity. As discussed earlier, while all teachers have identities as writers and teachers of writing in some way, this is a different matter from *claiming* or *proclaiming* these identities in one's professional context.

In reality, patterns of teacher sub-identification in any secondary school are likely to be complex and shifting. Manāki College is located in a rural service town and has a small roll of around 340. Over half its students identify as Māori. The 12 teachers engaged in the 'Culture of Writing' project constituted a significant percentage of staff and, as a PLC within the school, a potentially strong voice for advocating changes in practice (see below). In the New Zealand context, secondary teachers prepared to forgo five days of their summer vacation to participate in a writing workshop are unlikely to be typical. Baseline data for these teachers revealed a somewhat unexpected pattern of teacher sub-identification. All were asked to indicate how strongly they identified as teachers of writing and writers on a 0–10 scale. In relation to the former, three (25 per cent) identified weakly as teachers of writing, 17 per cent moderately, and 58 per cent strongly. The three teachers who identified weakly were from Accounting and Technology. (No surprise there.) In relation to the latter (i.e. as writers), two (17 per cent) identified weakly, three (33 per cent) moderately and six (50 per cent) strongly. Three teachers rated themselves equally as teachers of writing and writers, four rated themselves as writers more strongly and five rated themselves as teachers of writing more strongly. The likelihood is that this is an atypical pattern of sub-identification reflecting a predisposition already evident in the teachers' willingness to engage in the writing workshop experience. This is certainly true in terms of the strength with which certain of these teachers identified as writers.

There are other challenges to the development of a culture of writing, which I will mention briefly here. One is the absence of opportunities for cross-curriculum dialogue around issues of professional learning and practice. Compared to Manāki College, Huia College had a well-developed system of PLCs representing a large range of professional development priorities. Cross-curriculum (or interdisciplinary) dialogue was rare at Manāki College prior to the project discussed here. Typically at Manāki College, the teaching of writing would have been seen as the province of the English Department by many staff, who would not have viewed *themselves* as teachers of writing. Where Manāki differed from Huia, however, was its decision to prioritise writing instruction as a professional development priority, something prompted by its most recent Educational Review Office report indicating writing performance as an area of concern.

Transforming professional practice and identity

The development of a culture of writing in a school begins with teachers themselves, ideally supported by a whole-school plan (see Ings 2009 for an English example). As mentioned in my introduction, the success of the National Writing Project in the US in transforming professional practice and identity around writing and the teaching of writing is widely attested (Wood and Lieberman 2000; Whitney 2008) with similar findings reported in New Zealand writing workshop research (Locke et al. 2011), including with teachers at Huia College (Locke 2015b). Drawing on qualitative data and an analysis of a customised writing/ teacher of writing self-efficacy scale, a study of five high-school teacher-researchers engaged in the 'Teachers as Writers' project found positive and frequently significant effects in terms of self-efficacy as writers and teachers of writing (Locke et al. 2013). However, the interview data showed how changes in self-efficacy were moderated by the way individual teachers cognitively processed 'source' data (e.g. mastery experiences, verbal persuasion), and highlighted the complex nature of domain-specific self-efficacy beliefs. For example, a negative shift in self-efficacy around writing and teaching writing may arise because of an increased awareness of the challenges both these activities pose (the writing workshop as reality check!).

Since 2010, despite small modifications arising from participant feedback, the basic shape of the NZ writing workshop model used in the research reported here has remained unchanged. Over five or six days, participants engage in writing genres beginning with the personal/literary and progressing to the rhetorical/ expositional/argumentational, while addressing the major language functions of description, narration, explanation and argumentation. Debates around the privileging of 'personal' over 'professional' writing in the American NWP context as reported by Whitney (2009) have not occurred in New Zealand. As I see it, there are two reasons for this. The first is that regardless of the discipline(s) they represent, workshop participants have enjoyed a sense of enlargement of their identities as writers as a result of the personal/creative writing they undertook. Such writing was also viewed as a safe entry-point into more impersonal genres. Second, because of the cross-disciplinary composition of the group and the interdisciplinary nature of the talk *around* writing and the teaching of writing, participants began to see possibilities for *transgressive genre practices* in their own teaching; for example, using creative narratives in science and poetry in woodwork technology.

One prompt for the 'Culture of Writing' research was an awareness of the way writing workshop professional development for teachers produced a ripple effect in schools where teacher-participants were based. Reporting on the first New Zealand Writing Project, Scanlan and Carruthers (1990) described this process as 'seeding'. In Locke and Kato (2014), we describe the seeding impact of Helen Kato's involvement in the 'Teachers as Writers' project on members of the English Department at her own school.

For the two 'Culture of Writing' projects, the organisational hub was a PLC (DuFour 2004; Locke and Hawthorne 2015) established in the aftermath of the initial writing workshop. The PLC performed a number of functions:

- It afforded writing workshop participants structural visibility within the school's organisational structure;
- It afforded sustainability for the writing workshop ethos, while allowing for a transition into a group focused on action research aimed at changes in classroom practice, fostered by a spirit of analytical reflection and inquiry;
- It fostered cross-disciplinary dialogue;

- It enabled the induction of new PLC members;
- It provided a collective voice within the school advocating evidence-based policies and practices related to the teaching of writing across the disciplines; and
- Above all, it offered emotional support to teachers who were taking risks in evaluating their old practices and trialling new ones.

In all these ways, the PLCs have been change agents within these two schools.

Interviews with teacher-researchers from each school one year into their respective projects indicated a number of trends in relation to changes in identity as both writers and teachers of writing.

- Teachers' feelings about themselves as writers changed. For example, some teachers became more aware of who they were as writers (including aspects of their writing histories). Others viewed themselves as having an enhanced genre range. (A mathematics teacher commented that he 'managed to rewire my brain to redoing' creative literary writing in the context of the writing workshop.)
- Teachers generally developed a deeper understanding of writing and the writing process, including greater empathy for students' struggles as writers and an enhanced understanding of particular genres.
- Teachers' feelings about themselves as teachers of writing changed, with changes ranging from enhanced self-confidence to decreased confidence in the face of difficulties they faced, for example from the constraints of the assessment regime they worked with.
- Teachers' classroom practices changed, and included a greater willingness to write alongside students, and focus more time on process and the use of metalanguage. Some changes were discipline-specific. A Media Studies teacher changed the way she taught argumentation, while a mathematics teacher used writing to develop conceptual understanding in algebra.
- Teachers refined their understanding of what it means to be a writer. One teacher, in equating identification as a writer with a belief that 'you can express yourself clearly in writing', maintained that self-belief was different from self-confidence. 'It's not necessarily confidence because sometimes it's still hard. But it's thinking I can do this, I can write this. If you write you are a writer.'

Classroom-based inquiry

Effective classroom practices around writing pedagogy are the acid test in the development of a culture of writing in a secondary school. There is ample research on self-reported changes in classroom practice, including my own (e.g. Locke et al. 2013). However, classroom-based research, with teachers collectively assuming the role as teacher-researchers, is a *sine qua non* of a culture of writing. Multiple, small-scale case-study management is a key function of the PLC, where interventions are planned, learning activities are designed in accordance with specific learning objectives, and evidence is collected and analysed to ascertain changes in motivation, performance and to have students share their responses to aspects of the intervention.

In relation to the projects referred to here, we have been learning more about the importance of function words in assisting chemistry students to write lab reports (Whitehead and Murphy 2012), and how an English teacher writing poetry alongside her students can spark an interest in writing (Locke and Kato 2012). We have discovered that Māori students respond well to writing creative narratives to build their confidence in using science discourse in Biology, and that using written language to explain algebraic concepts can enhance students' mathematical understanding. We have refined our understanding of what works and what doesn't when response groups are used in the context of creative writing in English (Hawthorne, Locke and Tai 2015). And so on, as we seek to develop a multifaceted, cross-disciplinary picture of what seems to work in secondary classrooms.

An emphasis on cross-disciplinarity

Quite simply, a culture of writing in a secondary school is necessarily cross-disciplinary. This has always been implicit in the writing workshop ethos. Making it *explicit* requires the facilitation of a particular kind of cross-disciplinary dialogue that compares and contrasts such disciplinary characteristics as typical genres, typical functions, the range of modalities (verbal, symbolic, pictorial, gestural, auditory and so on) and threshold concepts (that is, those key concepts whose mastery is key to grasping the particular way a discipline makes sense of the world). As mentioned above, the PLC is the key locus for this kind of dialogue to occur.

Whole-school and community buy-in

While the initial embodiment of a culture of writing may be in the context of a PLC, there need to be organisational mechanisms which allow for the ethos underpinning the PLC and the practices/discourses adopted by it to permeate the school. All schools are different, but without a commitment from the principal and the senior management team, it will be impossible to achieve a school-wide community of writing, where all staff identify as teachers of writing in *some* way, even in a way that acknowledges reluctance, apprehension and that *all* staff are on a writing journey. Once a whole-school commitment is in place, and reflected in the school's systems, management of release time, professional learning and so on, then there will be opportunities for the school to invite its local community *in* as a way of extending the school's community of writing outwards into homes, organisations and businesses.

Conclusion

The situation where many teachers resist thinking of themselves as teachers of writing and writers of particular kinds of texts, and in some cases are crippled with writing and grammar anxiety, is likely to persist for some time yet. I argue, then, that to ignite the process of developing a culture of writing requires initially some kind of intense, transformational, professional learning on the part of a core group of staff, along writing workshop or comparable lines.

The next step is to accept that a cultural change in any school requires time. Having this core group constitute a PLC within the school's overall professional development strategy is vital to ensuring that members are supported, sustained and enabled to develop what Ball (2009) terms their *generative knowledge* as change agents. The PLC is also a way of ensuring that a vision can be developed regarding the key requirements for developing a culture of writing in *this* particular school, since no two schools are the same. These requirements would include: designing classroom-based case studies along action research principles; seeking academic advice beyond the school; building professional reading resources; planning ongoing professional learning for the PLC itself; widening the scope of the PLC to involve and integrate other staff; community outreach; and disseminating findings and resources within and beyond the school community.

Critical inquiry in the context of a developing action research agenda is crucial in both ascertaining the needs of particular groups of students and resisting some of the discourses at play in the educational and wider context that are currently having negative consequences for teachers and students. The development in teachers of secure identities as writers (people who know what writing entails, both generally and in terms of their disciplinary orientation) is central to such inquiry.

The development of a culture of writing also depends on the facilitation of cross-disciplinary dialogue within the PLC and the wider school environment. There is a growing literature on the discipline-specific literacy demands (including writing demands) of various school subjects which needs to be engaged with and drawn on as the school, assisted by the PLC, reassesses the way teachers and students engage with the writing requirements of different learning areas.

Finally, a secondary school aiming to develop a culture of writing cannot afford to be a house divided. Yes, there will be teachers who will secretly feel antagonised by the efforts of the kind of PLC I have described here, fearing that certain failings will be exposed, or that their autonomy will be threatened. Such teachers must be treated kindly and in a manner that is non-coercive, by senior management (including the principal) and by PLC colleagues. Having said that, school and subject leaders should not let teacher resistance deter them from developing policies and strategies along the lines advocated here, which will, in time, transform the classroom experiences of students of all ages as they learn to write, write to learn and discover the joys and satisfactions of what it truly *means* to be a writer.

Notes

1 A Māori immersion unit catering for the special needs of Māori students through Māori-medium instruction.
2 All teacher names in this chapter are pseudonyms.
3 See Siebert and Draper 2008 for a view of the situation with Mathematics teachers in the US.

References

Althusser, L. 1971. 'Ideology and ideological state apparatuses (Notes towards an investigation)', in L. Althusser (ed), *Lenin and philosophy and other essays* (Trans B. Brewster), NLB, London, pp. 121–173.

Andrews, R. 2008. *The case for a National Writing Project for teachers.* CfBT Education Trust, Reading.

Ball, A. 2009. 'Toward a theory of generative change in culturally and linguistically complex classrooms', *American Educational Research Journal*, vol. 46, no. 1, pp. 45–72.

Bandura, A. 1997. *Self-efficacy: The exercise of control*, W. H. Freeman, New York.

Beijaard, D., Meijer, P.C. and Verloop, N. 2004. 'Reconsidering research on teachers' professional identity', *Teaching and Teacher Education*, vol. 20, pp. 107–128.

Bereiter, C. and Scardamalia, M. 1987. *The psychology of written composition*, Lawrence Erlbaum, Hillsdale, NJ.

Bernstein, M. 2014. 'Three planes of practice: Examining intersections of reading identity and pedagogy', *English Teaching: Practice and Critique*, vol. 13, no. 2, pp. 110–129.

Braun, V. and Clarke, V. 2006. 'Using thematic analysis in psychology', *Qualitative Research in Psychology*, vol. 3, no. 2, pp. 77–101.

Cremin, T. and Baker, S. 2014. 'Exploring the discursively constructed identities of a teacher-writer teaching writing', *English Teaching: Practice and Critique*, vol. 13, no. 3, pp. 30–55.

Damasio, A. 2000. *The feeling of what happens: Body, emotion and the making of consciousness*, Vintage, London.

Dix, S. and Cawkwell, G. 2011. 'The influence of peer group response: Building a teacher and students' expertise in the writing classroom', *English Teaching: Practice and Critique*, vol. 10, no. 4, pp. 41–57.

DuFour, R. 2004. 'What is a "professional learning community"?' *Educational Leadership*, vol. 61, no. 8, pp. 6–11.

Elbow, P. 2000. *Everyone can write: Essays toward a hopeful theory of writing and teaching writing*, Oxford University Press, New York.

Fairclough, N. 1992. *Discourse and social change*, Polity Press, Cambridge.

Ferreira, A. 2014. 'Negotiating Afrikaner subjectivity from the post-apartheid margins: One student's subject positions in the discursively constructed classroom space at an elite English high school', *English Teaching: Practice and Critique*, vol. 13, no. 3, pp. 173–190.

Gee, J.P. 2000. 'Identity as an analytic lens for research in education', *Review of Research in Education*, vol. 25, pp. 99–125.

Hall, S. 1996. 'Who needs identity?' in S. Hall and P. du Gay (eds), *Questions of cultural identity*, Sage, London, pp. 1–17.

Hawthorne, S., Locke, T. and Tai, T. 2015. 'Using response groups in the junior English classroom', *English in Aotearoa*, vol. 85, pp. 35–49.

Heigham, J. and Croker, R. (eds), 2009. *Qualitative research in applied linguistics*, Palgrave Macmillan, Basingstoke, Hampshire.

Ings, R. 2009. *Writing is primary*, Esmée Fairbairn Foundation, London.

Ivanič, R. 1998. *Writing and identity: The discoursal construction of identity in academic writing*, Benjamins, Amsterdam.

Locke, T. 2004. 'Reshaping classical professionalism in the aftermath of neo-liberal reform', *Literacy Learning: The Middle Years*, vol. 1, no. 1/*English in Australia*, vol. 139, pp. 113–121.

Locke, T. 2009. 'The disappearance of enjoyment: How literature went wandering in the literacy woods and got lost', in J. Manuel, P. Brock, D. Carter and W. Sawyer (eds), *Imagination, innovation, creativity: Re-visioning English in education*, Phoenix Education, Putney, pp. 123–138.

Locke, T. 2013. 'Assessing student poetry: Balancing the demands of two masters', *English Teaching: Practice and Critique*, vol. 12, no. 1, pp. 23–45.

Locke, T. 2015a. *Developing writing teachers: Practical ways for teacher-writers to transform their classroom practice*, Routledge, New York.

Locke, T. 2015b. 'The impact of intensive Writing Workshop professional development on a cross-curricular group of secondary teachers', *New Zealand Journal of Educational Studies*, vol. 50, no. 1, pp. 137–151.

Locke, T. and Kato, H. 2012. 'Poetry for the broken-hearted: How a marginal Year 12 English class was turned on to writing', *English in Australia*, vol. 47, no. 1, pp. 61–79.

Locke, T. and Kato, H. 2014. 'Seeding Writing Project principles and practices in a school community: A case study', *Teacher Development: An International Journal of Teachers' Professional Development*, vol. 18, no. 4, pp. 449–465.

Locke, T. and Hawthorne, S. 2015. 'Effecting a high-school culture of writing: Issues and dilemmas in participatory action research', in L Rowell, C Bruce, J Shosh and M Riel (eds), *Palgrave international handbook of action research*, Palgrave, New York.

Locke, T. and Johnston, M. 2016. 'Developing an individual and collective self-efficacy scale for the teaching of writing in high schools', *Assessing Writing*, vol. 28, pp. 1–14.

Locke, T., Whitehead, D. and Dix, S. 2013. 'The impact of "Writing Project" professional development on teachers' self-efficacy as writers and teachers of writing', *English in Australia*, vol. 48, no. 2, pp. 55–69.

Locke, T., Whitehead, D., Dix, S. and Cawkwell, G. 2011. 'New Zealand teachers respond to the "National Writing Project" experience', *Teacher Development*, vol. 15, no. 3, pp. 273–291.

McCallister, C. 2008. '"The author's chair" revisited', *Curriculum Inquiry*, vol. 38, no. 4, pp. 455–471.

Mockler, N. 2011. 'Beyond "what works": Understanding teacher identity as a practical and political tool', *Teachers and Teaching: Theory and Practice*, vol. 17, no. 5, pp. 517–528.

Pritchard, R. and Honeycutt, R. 2007. 'Best practices in implementing a process approach to teaching writing', in S. Graham, C. MacArthur and J. Fitzgerald (eds), *Best practices in writing instruction*, Guilford Press, New York, pp. 28–49.

Scanlan, P. and Carruthers, A. 1990. 'Report on the New Zealand Writing Project: An informal evaluation', *English in Aotearoa*, vol. 11, pp. 14–18.

Shulman, L.S. 1986. 'Those who understand: Knowledge growth in teaching', *Educational Researcher*, vol. 15, no. 2, pp. 4–14.

Siebert, D. and Draper, R. 2008. 'Why content-area literacy messages do not speak to mathematics teachers: A critical content analysis', *Literacy Research and Instruction*, vol. 47, no. 4, pp. 229–245.

van Langenhove, L. and Harré, R. 1999. 'Introducing positioning theory', in R. Harré and L van Langenhove (eds), *Positioning theory: Moral contexts of intentional action*, Blackwell, Maldon, pp. 14–31.

Whitehead, D. and Murphy, F. 2012. 'Teaching causal text connectives in chemistry', *NZ Science Teacher*, vol. 129, pp. 36–38.

Whitney, A. 2008. 'Teacher transformation in the National Writing Project', *Research in the Teaching of English*, vol. 43, no. 2, pp. 144–187.

Whitney, A. 2009. 'Writer, teacher, person: Tensions between personal and professional writing in a National Writing Project summer institute', *English Education*, vol. 41, no. 3, pp. 235–258.

Wood, D. and Lieberman, A. 2000. 'Teachers as authors: The National Writing Project's approach to professional development', *International Journal of Leadership in Education*, vol. 3, no. 3, pp. 255–273.

Yin, R. 1989. *Case study research: Design and methods*, Sage, Thousand Oaks, CA.

SECTION D
Students' writing identities

10

BEING IN THE WORLD

Students' writing identities beyond school

Josephine Brady

Introduction

This chapter examines the ways in which the context of children's writing shapes their relationship with their work. Its starting point is the seminal work of Clark (1976), who asked, 'What can we learn from young fluent home readers?' and the suggestion is that we should similarly ask, 'What we can learn from young people who "home" write?' Despite the burgeoning number of creative writing websites, the increasing demand for young writers' groups and the unprecedented success of national writing competitions such as, in the UK, BBC Radio 2's '500 Words', home writing is still the poor relation of home reading and there is little qualitative research examining how students experience and engage with writing outside of school.

The longitudinal ethnographic study reported in this chapter investigated the role of writing in the lives of fifteen self-identified home writers aged between 7 and 13 years old in England. In a deliberate steer away from school, the sample was located through a local library system and children's writing events. Purposive sampling resulted in a group of female participants who attended different schools across the West Midlands region. The three main research questions were:

1. What can we learn from the experiences and understandings of young home writers?
2. How, if at all, do young writers' attitudes towards home writing differ from their attitudes towards school writing?
3. What theories can be used to conceptualise their experiences/understandings and what gaps exist in these theories?

A grounded theory approach was adopted and the constant comparative method was used to analyse the three datasets: semi-structured interviews, field notes and samples of the participants' writing. Quality checks were implemented to increase the validity of the analysis. The chapter initially explores the conceptual underpinning of the work.

The literature reviewed

Writing as social and personal

Drawing upon the conceptual frameworks of Brice Heath (1983), Street (1984, 1993) and Barton and Hamilton (1998), writing can be understood as a context-bound activity, linked to the domains of home, school or community. Studies of children and young people's writing predominantly take place in school; however, within the last twenty years, there has been a growing body of research focused on adolescent writing practices outside of school (Alvermann et al., 1998; Hull and Schultz, 2002; Moje et al., 2004) and children's writing in home and community settings (Kenner, 2004; Pahl, 2012, 2014). There has been a renewed interest in researching children's literacy lives (Cremin et al., 2014) to 'find out about the children's lived experiences of literacy, consider their own conceptualisations of literacy, and question the continued dominance of school literacy activities framed around an autonomous model' (ibid: 13). Increasingly, children's writing is re-positioned as an expressive art, which is connected to the outside world yet undeniably 'close to self' (Britton et al., 1975: 96). But how does that unifying concept of 'self' situate itself in terms of the 'other'? In *Developing Writing Teachers*, Locke (2014) weaves existing theories of writing into a new interactional framework of understandings (see in particular chapter 5, p. 94), encouraging us to re-invigorate the term 'expressive' or 'creative' writing by moving beyond the dualisms of mind/environment, home/school or expert/novice. One way of embracing this interactional model is to draw on third space theory, for as Bhabha explains, "by exploring third space we may elude the politics of polarity and emerge as the others of ourselves" (1994: 56).

Third space theory and home writing

Third space theory has its origins in philosophical studies of power and identity in a postcolonial world. According to Bhabha (1994), 'third space' emerges from the hybridity of 'first' and 'second' space, and is expressive and creative for it is the fusion of old and new ideas from a personal perspective. As Black (2008: 25) reflects:

> The notion of a 'third space' entails a meeting place or a convergence of sorts where diverse mindsets, perspectives and materialities can come together and be articulated in new interconnected and hybrid frames of mind.

Challenging the binarisms that often dominate our understandings, literacy researchers have used third space theory to explore multiliteracies (New London

Group, 1996), 'border crossings' between academic and everyday literacies (Gutiérrez et al., 1999; Moje et al., 2004), and individual expressions of hybrid cultural identities (Pahl, 2007, 2014). In this chapter, third space theory is used specifically to enrich our conceptual understanding of 'home'.

Home, as it is referred to in this study, is conceptualised as a psychological rather than physical space. In accord with Bhabha's understanding of third space as 'the terrain for elaborating strategies of selfhood that initiate new signs of identity' (1994: 1), it consists of two critical aspects: a person's relationship with the external world (surroundings/others), and their relationship with self. These relationships are inextricably linked as home is 'not the place we "come from"; it is a place we are' (Wise, 2000: 297). We make ourselves 'at home' as home is fluid and dynamic, it is never an absolute ('home is not authentic or inauthentic, it does not exist a priori, naturally or inevitably'; ibid: 300).

Home is our individual way of 'being in the world' and thus can be 'taken along wherever one decamps' (Rapport, 1997: 73). In this way, Rapport (1997) conveys the closeness to everyday experiences; it is anchored to one's sense of self in the world rather than a geographical location:

> This wonderful word 'home' . . . connotes a physical space but also has the more abstract sense of a 'state of being.'
>
> *(Rybczynski, 1987: 61)*

It defies reification as it is 'an abstract signifier of a wide set of associations and meanings' (Moore, 2000: 208). It is the individual who decides what constitutes home or what gives rise to feelings of being 'at home'. Seamon (1979: 70) defines 'at-homeness' as:

> The usually unnoticed, taken-for-granted situation of being comfortable in, and familiar with the everyday world in which one lives, and outside of which one is visiting.

This sense of familiarity and ordinariness is embodied in Berger's concept of home as he argues it does not exist in time and space but rather 'in words, jokes, opinions, gestures, actions, even the way one wears a hat' (1984: 64). Home is rooted in our routine ways of being-in-the-world:

> It is the known as opposed to the unknown; it is certainty as opposed to uncertainty, security rather than insecurity. . . . It is familiar and predictable.
>
> *(Shaw, 1990: 227)*

To be 'at home' or 'to make oneself at home' means to be 'at ease' (Kron, 1983) or to 'come closer to oneself' (Dovey, 1978: 28). Frank develops this by suggesting that 'home equals self' because 'when we are not at home we are not experiencing our true personhood' (2005: 190). He argues that a person affirms their sense of self through the attributes of home. Over the years, the attributes of home have been identified in numerous studies (to name but a few: Appleyard, 1979; Sixsmith, 1986; Putnam and Newton, 1990). However, as Putnam and Newton point out, terms such as 'privacy, security, family, intimacy, comfort, and control' (1990: 8) recur in most of the findings. Home is thus a combination of cognitive, social, emotional and existential aspects yet at the same time the concept is beyond this for, as Moore cautions, 'to focus strongly on one part, it is possible to lose sight of the whole concept itself' (2000: 208).

The starting point then is that home writing is far more complex than it first appears. The central argument is that home writing takes place where and when a person feels 'at home'. This could be in the physical space called home, in school, in the library, on the bus or in the car. The significance rests in the conceptual aspects of home (security, warmth, feeling comfortable) as 'it was not the space itself . . . but the *way of inhabiting* it that made it a home' (Boym, 1994: 166).

In this way, this conceptual understanding of 'home' is distinct from third space theory as home is a marker; it is the subjective set of thoughts and feelings transferred onto a space, person or object which marks and shapes it (though not in absolute terms). In other words, it is representable; it is brought into existence in time and space. In comparison, in Bhabha's terms, third space is an 'indeterminate' or 'unrepresentable' space (1994: 37). Nevertheless the concept of third space is critically important as in agreement with the view that 'third space' is the space 'where agency is gained' and 'transformations' take place (Bhabha, 1994: 175), I would suggest that 'home' writing emerges from a third space, with the first and second spaces being the two critical aspects of home: a person's relationship with the external world (surroundings/others) and a person's relationship with self. In recent years, social scientists (Giddens, 1991; Archer, 2000, 2003, 2007) have sought to understand the process whereby individuals gain agency in relation to structural constraints. Archer (2000, 2003, 2007) in particular has dedicated her research career to the study of human agency which she conceptualises in terms of the process of reflexivity.

Third space theory, reflexivity and home writing

Archer's empirical research on reflexivity takes us further by drawing our attention to the process by which creative agentic acts, in this case writing, emerge or evolve from a third space. Archer (2007: 4) defines this process as:

> The regular exercise of the mental ability, shared by all normal people, to consider themselves in relation to their (social) contexts and vice versa.

Reflexivity is integral to third space theory as it is the dynamic, mediatory process by which 'we interrogate the world we inhabit' (2007: 63). Archer identifies three elements of reflexivity: agency, structure and the relationship between the two.

In emphasising this, Archer achieves two things: first, she reinforces the view that 'structure' and 'agency' constitute two distinct forces and second, she emphasises the existence and importance of the third – the interrelationship. Agency is gained through reflexive acts as we do not simply reflect upon a pre-ordered world; we actively participate in the process of creating and shaping it for ourselves via conscious deliberations. Our personal power comes from our ability to engage in these continuous reflexive deliberations from an early age so that we are neither simply reactive to situations nor reflexive in a general self-aware manner. In this way, Archer's work connects with Vygotskian theory as Vygotsky argued that speech plays a central role in self-regulated, self-directed action. Drawing a clear distinction between inner speech, 'speech for oneself', and external speech, 'speech for others' (1962: 149), he believed that 'inner speech' plays a crucial role in human's capacity to plan, regulate and revise their everyday activities. Archer advances this position as she places greater emphasis on the dynamic nature of this engagement by referring specifically to internal conversations/dialogue.

Drawing on Archer's theory, Ryan (2014: 135) posits that the process of reflexivity is at the heart of writing as:

> Effective writers in any context are active decision makers who mediate their own concerns and considerations . . . and their particular circumstances to write in certain ways.

This resonates with the idea of writers as active designers of text (Maun and Myhill, 2005; Sharples, 1999) and problem-solvers (Sharples, 1999; Hayes and Flower, 1980); writers identify goals for their texts and then identify how they can be achieved, and our inner dialogue (or reflexivity) is driven by a personal trajectory of 'concerns-projects-practices':

> No one can have an ultimate concern and fail to do something about it. Instead, each person seeks to develop a concrete course of action to realise that concern by elaborating a 'project', in the (fallible) belief that to accomplish this project is to realise one's concern.
>
> *(Archer, 2007: 7)*

The emphasis is on the agency of the individual which in turn leads us to reflect upon the qualitative difference between writing 'to comply' and writing of 'one's own volition'. Or, to put it another way, the distinction between 'writing because I want to, not because I have to' (Garrett and Moltzen, 2011).

The study

The aim of the study was to gain a comprehensive understanding of the experiences and views of young home writers. It was ethnographic in that the intention was to describe in as much detail as possible through fieldwork the perspectives and practices of a group of young home writers aged between 7 and 13 years old. In seeking the rich accounts necessary for genuine understandings to emerge, the young people were encouraged to express themselves freely and the findings presented here are largely provided in their own words. The goal was not to generalise, but rather to make tentative steps to theorise the ways in which home writing is experienced by young people.

Participants

As the study was predicated on the desire to encounter young home writers in an authentic way, participants were recruited outside of school via posters in libraries and bookstores, leafleting at young readers' festivals, and contact with local professional writers. The criteria for participation were: young people aged between 7 and 13 years old who enjoyed writing creatively in their own time and freely chose to home-write on a regular basis. Potential participants were screened during the preliminary phone conversation and initial interview. However, on the one occasion when it became clear during the second interview that the participant did not fulfil the criteria, the data was not included in the study. After a period of approximately nine months, fifteen females, who satisfied the criteria and were interested in taking part, were recruited to the study. The participants were drawn from five different areas within the West Midlands region. Four of the participants were aged 13; three aged 12; two aged 11; one aged 10; one aged 9; three aged 8; and one aged 7. Eleven of the participants attended comprehensive schools, two public schools, one grammar and one Steiner.

Ethical considerations

The project was conducted within a carefully considered ethical framework, in accordance with British Education Research Association (BERA) guidelines. The participants and their parents/guardians were fully briefed prior to their involvement, and were given an opportunity to ask questions. They were also made aware that consent was ongoing and could be withdrawn at any point. Anonymity and confidentiality were sought through the use of pseudonyms, and all data collected was stored in a secure place and used only for the purposes explained to the participants. Throughout, I sought to acknowledge and be responsive to the uniqueness and complexity of each situation as it emerged (Simons and Usher, 2000).

Data collection and analysis

Three different qualitative data sets were collected: field notes – transcripts of 54 in-depth interviews and an average of three home writing pieces per participant. Over the course of a year, participants were interviewed three/four times either in their own home or a local library; the average length of each open-ended interview was 65 minutes, with a range from 45 to 110 minutes. Field notes were recorded immediately after each interview and alongside the home writing pieces, they were used to guide subsequent interviews. Home writing pieces (poetry, prose, non-fiction) were collected at various points throughout the study.

In light of the exploratory nature of my research, I adopted a particular interview approach known as 'convergent interviewing' (Dick, 1990, 1999). The advantage of this form over other interview approaches was its progressive nature:

> At its beginning, each interview is almost completely unstructured and then proceeds into more specific questions to which the interviewer adds as s/he conducts more interviews and differences of opinions and beliefs begin to emerge. That is, later interviews start in the unstructured way of earlier ones but become more focused as the interviewer learns more and more about the topic.
>
> *(Riege and Nair, 2004: 75)*

Questions are added to the 'conversation' where appropriate and refined after each interview to converge on the issues emerging. In this way, convergent interviewing combines elements of both structured and unstructured interviews. Its appeal was that it encouraged a co-constructed approach within interviews (Sankaran, 2001).

From the outset, I introduced myself as an educational researcher/fellow writer interested in their writing outside of school. I met the young writers over an extended period as I felt it was important to establish a rapport/relationship with each girl and reach a position where they felt comfortable to talk freely about their home writing practices.

As the study was exploratory in its design and the intention was to understand home writing from the point of view of the home writer, a grounded theory approach (Glaser and Strauss, 1967) was adopted. Analysis of the data followed an iterative process in accordance with this approach. The three datasets were analysed using the constant comparative method which meant that coded categories from one interview or piece of home writing were compared with categories developed from other interviews or home writing pieces to identify emergent themes.

Findings and discussion

This section is divided into two parts. The first part reveals the participants' views on home and school writing; the second explores the different forms and functions of home writing, and the concept of a home writing continuum. The continuum emerged from the iterative analysis of all the datasets, and its value will be illustrated here by focusing on one young writer, Ruth, aged 13.

Before discussing the findings, it is important to remember that my relationship with participants developed over an extended period of time, and data collection and analysis was a shared process evolving within the wider context of this ongoing relationship. The process was co-constructed as it was circular in nature;

experiences, feelings and thoughts were explored and discussed collaboratively, and possible themes were identified, clarified, confirmed or refuted collaboratively over time until this process became established as a cycle of shared knowledge and understanding.

Moreover, as relationships evolved, the quality of interactions changed as participants invited me further into their worlds of home writing, some further than others. In some instances, contact outside of the interviews increased (emails, texts and phone calls initiated by them) and while meanings were still openly explored, reflected upon, negotiated and re-negotiated, tacit knowledge became more important as participants shared or made visible writing which was more personal to them. In contrast to the earlier interviews where the participants were generally more talkative and descriptive, the participants became more tentative and absorbed in self-reflection. In response, some areas were explored further while other potential lines of enquiry were not pursued.

Home writing and school writing

One of the key issues concerning home writing was our conceptual understanding of 'home'. From the point of view of the young home writers, what does it actually mean to them? How, if at all, does their home writing differ from school writing? Five participants described the difference as follows:

> I can really tell what I've done at school and what I haven't; my home stuff is like the better stuff I'm writing. The school stuff is fairly good but *I don't like putting everything I could put in the school ones.*
>
> *(Nicole, 13)*

> It [school writing] *is not as imaginative as when I write for myself,* my imagination goes a lot further when I'm writing for myself . . . my home writing is better. I am very self-critical, I don't like rubbish writing.
>
> *(Kate, 13)*

> *It is like whatever I feel is the matter, whatever issues are important to me I can write about that.* I can incorporate other people's problems and sometimes I like give advice in my writing that can help other people. . . . If I'm in an angry mood than I write something with anger. I write diaries, I write stories, I write romance, anything really.
>
> *(Amelia, 12)*

> I quite like to *just write by myself, see what comes up,* and then maybe swap things around and you don't have what you are writing about, you get to think about what it is.
>
> *(Lucie, 11)*

At home, there is no limit to what I do whereas at school I think 'oh, is that alright? *Will the teacher like this? Does that fit the criteria?*' So my creative writing is quite limited in school.

(Emma, 11)

The data showed that all of the participants had a different relationship with their home writing than their school writing. They described two distinct types of writing: writing for self ('whatever I feel is the matter') and writing for others. The contrast between their sense of personal agency in home writing and the perceived lack of choice and control regarding school writing is striking. One form emerged from a space where they felt empowered and the other, powerless. Indeed, according to the young writers, a key affordance of home writing is freedom: freedom to choose the genre, style and content; and freedom to allow their thoughts and emotions to infuse their writing. School writing was generally experienced as rushed; Alice (7) was conscious of 'quickness' and Simone (9) remarked without a hint of irony: 'You really don't have time to write at school'. Michelle (12) disliked it when the 'teachers say "everyone stop now"' – she wanted them to just leave her alone – and Amelia (12) remarked: 'There is a deadline'.

All expressed the view that the process of writing in school is closely regulated and restricted and that this lack of personal power and control over the process affected their motivation and enjoyment. These findings corroborate the research carried out by Garrett and Moltzen who point out that the participants in their study perceived school-based writing as being 'less experimental and more focused on responding to a specific assessment brief to suit "teacher wants"' (2011: 174).

In addition, a surprising finding was that most of the participants saw home writing as an iterative process, placing considerable emphasis on editing, revising or developing multiple versions of some pieces.

I have had the book going for like half a year now. It has come so far and it has become so complicated, it is difficult to let go of it.

(Alex, 11)

I like editing them over time. If I can't think anymore I put the piece of paper to the side in my book and just leave it there. And sometimes I come back to it and I'll be able to expand on whatever I've written or sometimes I get a new idea and I just write it down so I haven't discarded the paper, I just can't think anymore at that point.

(Samantha, 12)

Like this story, I have a notebook that I was writing it in but I'd only done some of it . . . and basically most of that is just changed from my book. If I brought my book you would be amazed at how much that's changed.

(Alice, 7)

What we start to see here is high levels of reflexivity in their responses; they reflect at length upon their home and school writing, and the marked differences between the two processes.

> In school, I don't write things that I know are going to be fantastic, I just write any old ones that I know the teachers are going to think are good.
>
> *(Matilda, 8)*

> I like to save the best ones [ideas] for me even though it is not going to get any grades or anything.
>
> *(Emma, 11)*

For the purposes of clarity and brevity, I have summarised in the Figure 10.1 the perceived differences between home and school writing as revealed in this study.

Home writing continuum

The home writing continuum, which emerged from the collaborative research journey, seeks to capture and display information about the home writing, the home writer and, most importantly, the relationship between the home writers and their home writing. The positioning of the 'texts' is always an approximation informed by a number of factors: the participants' comments regarding their home writing and themselves; when they chose to discuss or share pieces with me (first meeting? fourth meeting?) and how they related to them (shared freely or more cautiously?). The continuum is a practical tool as it captures and synthesises the data collected over an extended period of time without overly simplifying it and it also allows the data to be compared with greater clarity.

The home writing continuum shows that young people's home writing is multifunctional and there is a distinct strand which is specifically for the purpose of communication with self rather than others. It illuminates the sheer diversity and complexity of texts created by home writers in terms of range, audience and function.

Ruth's home writing continuum

During our first meeting, Ruth gave me three poems her mother had selected from her PoemHunter.com account. Towards the end of the meeting, she shared her account name and directed me to look at one or two specific poems. Initially, Ruth told me:

> I joined it [PoemHunter.com] in July last year and *I post all my poems on there under my pseudonym.*

At our second meeting, however, she confided that:

> *Some I keep back* because there are one or two I don't want all my family reading.

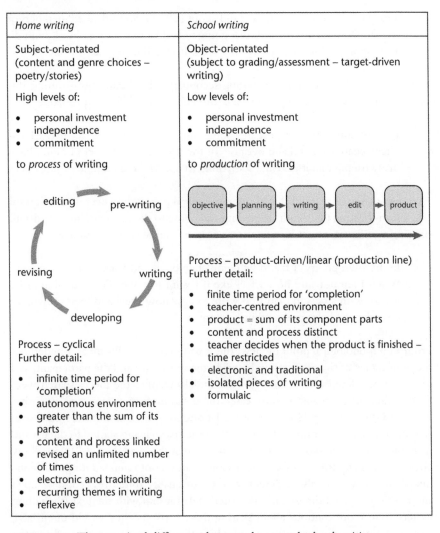

Home writing	School writing
Subject-orientated (content and genre choices – poetry/stories)	Object-orientated (subject to grading/assessment – target-driven writing)
High levels of:	Low levels of:
• personal investment • independence • commitment	• personal investment • independence • commitment
to *process* of writing	to *production* of writing

FIGURE 10.1 The perceived differences between home and school writing

She also added:

> It's quite important to me that people *respect my privacy and don't ask me to share all my writing*. I mean I share most of it with someone but . . . (her voice trails off)

Ruth is making deliberate choices about her writing; from the outset she makes it clear that some of her writing is private and her right to privacy should be respected.

Ruth explains that she began by 'writing creative prose for ages' which she used to 'share and sometimes bring into school'; she then started writing magazines, 'The Family Gazettes', which she shared and discussed at our second meeting:

> I used to give it to my family. I did about half of it and I'd asked members of
> my family to do bits for it. It was going to be like twice a year but I don't do
> it anymore, I don't really have the time. It would take quite a while.

She felt she had less time since starting secondary school and it was during this
period that her writing changed and she 'turned to poetry'. She explained:

> I'm not sure why but probably something to do with the fact that I liked
> Shakespeare a lot and also because for the first couple of weeks I didn't have
> many friends and it gave me something to do. And then it kind of just stuck.

At our third meeting, Ruth shared three additional poems; however, it wasn't until
our fourth meeting that Ruth opened up and chose to discuss them in some detail,
offering significant insight into her more personal home writing practices:

> In my own poetry, I try to be completely open and true, honest to myself.
> When I am not sure how I feel like if I want to say or do something or be
> friends with a person than I do write exactly how I feel and then sometimes
> it works and helps me see things or not.

From a methodological point of view, this is particularly significant as it underlines
the importance of the relationship between the researcher and the participant, and
the value of a longitudinal study. At the initial meeting, the pieces shared were
for general readership and, in most cases, there was no firm reference to any other
forms of home writing. However, as a relationship of trust and mutual interest in
writing developed over time, Ruth and the other participants started to discuss and
share pieces of home writing which perhaps at first they had denied ('I post all my
poems'). These texts were of a more personal nature, not intended for public consumption. They were also different in terms of quality (often revised, developed
and rewritten several times) and the writer's relationship with the text (the young
writers were more cautious about sharing these texts yet they would often have
more to say about the circumstances in which these pieces were produced and the
meanings they attached to them). For example, as illustrated above, Ruth revealed
that her poetry is closely connected to her sense of self: her thoughts, feelings,
pent-up emotions. She relates to her poems in an 'open' and 'honest' way and
when faced with difficult situations and complex emotions, they help her greatly.

Thus it becomes quite clear that home writing practices fall across a very broad
continuum. At one end, home writing is a social literacy practice with texts produced for different audiences and at the other, home writing is a highly personal and
reflexive practice. However, these 'practices' do not exist as two binary categories –
the social and the private – as varying degrees exist in between, as Ruth revealed:

> Most of my poems you can tell what emotion I'm feeling, I think. And when
> I do write when I am upset or angry, I do feel better afterwards, more relaxed

and calm. Sometimes, I do say things in my writing that I would never ever, ever say in person but I do say through poems. It is like a secret that you need to say but you don't really want the whole world knowing. It is just kind of veiling your secret really. Hiding it really but you still have the comfort of saying it and sometimes sharing it.

I write more personal things now but occasionally it is in the middle, not really personal but it is not impersonal either. Like I wrote one a while ago called a 'Recipe for a Smile' which just like listed things that if you added them together would make someone smile which was personal but not like about my feelings.

Thus the production of text can be seen in a fluid rather than static way, which in turn underlines the value of the home writing spectrum as it maps out the developments over time, and draws our attention to the subtle yet distinct shifts in the purpose, form and quality of the texts shared. To aid understanding, Figure 10.2 below offers a visual representation of the home writing continuum with suggested markers, and Figure 10.3 presents a visual summary of Ruth's home writing spectrum.

Crucially, the home writing continuum is underpinned by the process of reflexivity as home writing is distinctive from other forms, particularly school writing, as it is self-generated, self-motivated and self-directed. However, the degree of reflexivity varies across the continuum with higher levels present in the more private and personal pieces, as illustrated in the following examples.

Ruth's veiled writing

At our third meeting, Ruth shared three additional poems which she explained she had written a while ago, and had not shared with anyone. A common theme of these three poems is the sense of potentiality and transition. Something is going to happen, but it hasn't happened yet:

> When the withered fruits of time have bloomed their fill
> When the River of the People's run its course
> When the World will never rise from being ill . . .
> Then we shall know that the Fields of Life have gone
>
> *(extract from 'When the withered fruits of time')*

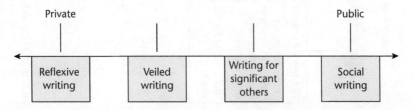

FIGURE 10.2 A representation of the home writing continuum

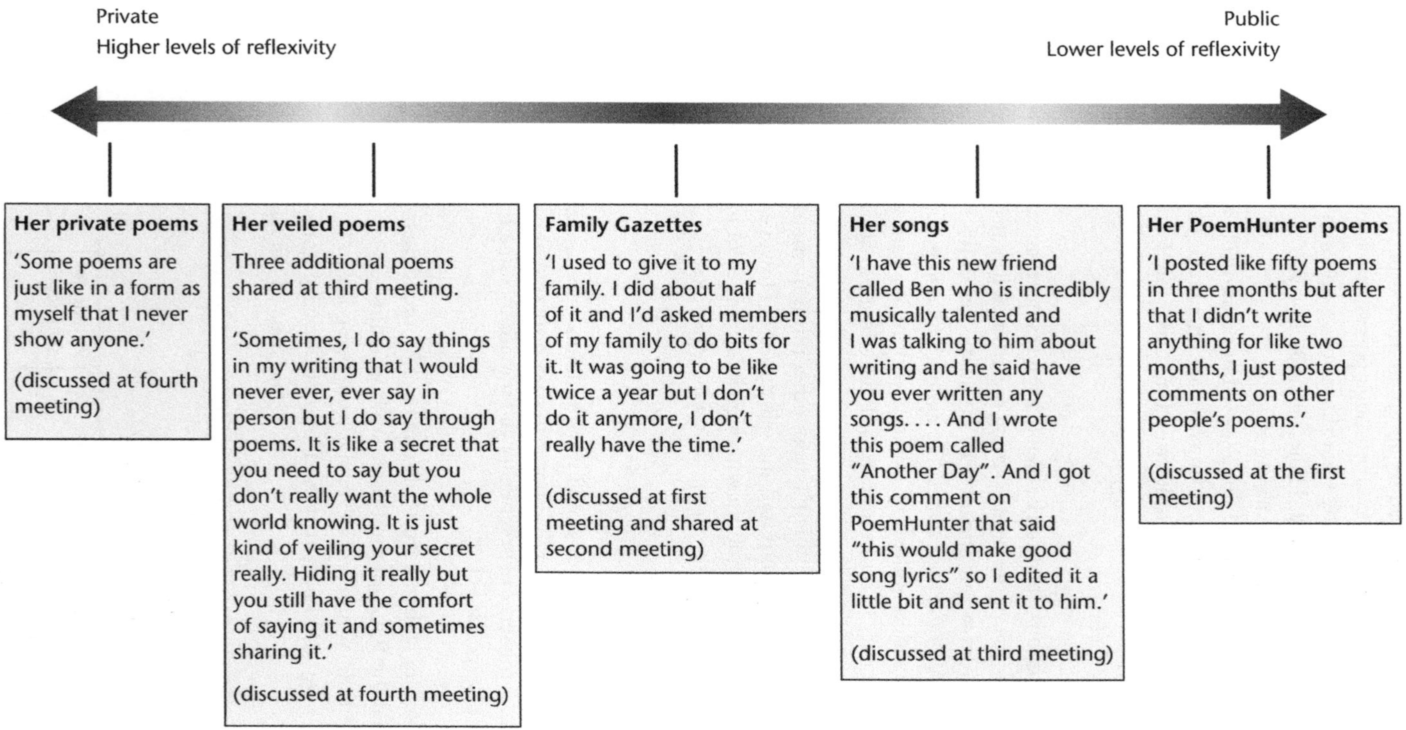

Private
Higher levels of reflexivity

Public
Lower levels of reflexivity

Her private poems

'Some poems are just like in a form as myself that I never show anyone.'

(discussed at fourth meeting)

Her veiled poems

Three additional poems shared at third meeting.

'Sometimes, I do say things in my writing that I would never ever, ever say in person but I do say through poems. It is like a secret that you need to say but you don't really want the whole world knowing. It is just kind of veiling your secret really. Hiding it really but you still have the comfort of saying it and sometimes sharing it.'

(discussed at fourth meeting)

Family Gazettes

'I used to give it to my family. I did about half of it and I'd asked members of my family to do bits for it. It was going to be like twice a year but I don't do it anymore, I don't really have the time.'

(discussed at first meeting and shared at second meeting)

Her songs

'I have this new friend called Ben who is incredibly musically talented and I was talking to him about writing and he said have you ever written any songs. . . . And I wrote this poem called "Another Day". And I got this comment on PoemHunter that said "this would make good song lyrics" so I edited it a little bit and sent it to him.'

(discussed at third meeting)

Her PoemHunter poems

'I posted like fifty poems in three months but after that I didn't write anything for like two months, I just posted comments on other people's poems.'

(discussed at the first meeting)

FIGURE 10.3 Ruth's home writing continuum

Sometimes it feels as if the frozen snow
Has melted and there's nowhere left to go,
Sometimes it feels as if the long ago dead
Have risen and they're somewhere close ahead,
Sometimes it seems as if Winter long
Will never succumb to Spring's pleading song,
Sometimes it's as though the last thread left
Snaps and leaves my soul bereft

(extract from 'Sometimes')

I see you, and sometimes you call
But I can only watch you silently –
Tiptoeing through the long grass.

How I long to meet you, how I long to come,
But all I can do is watch you silently –
Tiptoeing through the long grass.

(extract from 'The Mystery Being')

These are poems of 'the cusp'; there is a path to be taken, but at the moment, this path is unknown and there is a potent sense of waiting. The content is highly speculative and there is a sense that the writer is looking to the future for the answers. There is the promise of movement and change but this is yet to be realised. The poems are philosophical in tone and there is a sense of uncertainty. This is supported by Ruth's own reflections around her veiled writing.

> I can like realise/recognise thoughts that I have that I wouldn't want to recognise or point out that I have in real life. It is just a way of expressing myself that I can't really say. Things that I don't always want to recognise but I need to recognise so I can move on. I don't know.

Conclusion

The study overall highlighted a significant gulf between home and school writing. The level of commitment and the quality of the writing is different. The young writers took pride in their home writing and crafted it in a way that was distinctive from their routine and formulaic approach towards school writing. The question that naturally arises, then, is what can we learn from this? How can we begin to encourage the same level of engagement in school writing?

The study has indicated that the quality of the relationship home writers have with their texts can be both strong and highly reflexive. The girls involved in this study were not budding professional writers – they were, first and foremost, interested and engaged in the process of reflexivity – and engaged in multiple inner conversations with themselves on the page. Home writing offered the girls a space for self-reflection and an opportunity to consider their position in the world.

Archer's (2000, 2003) theory of reflexivity enables us to examine and recognise this micro-level identity work as important, and perhaps it can offer insight into how identities become 'sedimented' in text (Rowsell and Pahl, 2007). For writing can be a powerful expression of reflexivity, as others also recognise:

> Writing is a mirror of the self, the soul and the world. Through writing we can give voice to our most intimate thoughts and give free rein to our imagination; through writing we can shape and articulate new knowledge, new ideas, and new philosophies; through writing, we can reflect on the past and imagine the future.
>
> *(Myhill and Watson, 2011: 58)*

I argue that reflexivity, to varying degrees, is the primary process at the very heart of young people's home writing practices and that more attention needs to be given to their reflexivity as part of supporting their writing identities 'at home' and at school.

References

Appleyard, D. (1979) 'The Environment as a Social Symbol: Within a Theory of Environmental Action and Perception', *Journal of the American Planning Association*, vol. 45, no. 2, pp. 143–153.

Alvermann, D.E., Moon, J.S., and Hagood, M.C. (1998) *Popular Culture in the Classroom: Teaching and Researching Critical Media Literacy*. Newark, DE: International Reading Association.

Archer, M.S. (2000) *Being Human: The Problem of Agency*, Cambridge, Cambridge University Press.

Archer, M.S. (2003) *Structure, Agency and the Internal Conversation*, Cambridge, Cambridge University Press.

Archer, M.S. (2007) *Making Our Way Through the World: Human Reflexivity and Social Mobility*, Cambridge, Cambridge University Press.

Barton, D. and Hamilton, M. (1998) *Local Literacies: Reading and Writing in One Community*, 1st edn, London, Routledge.

Berger, J. (1984) *And Our Faces, My Heart, Brief as Photos*, London, Writers and Readers.

Bhabha, H.K. (1994) *The Location of Culture*, London, Routledge.

Black, R.W. (2008) *Adolescents and Online Fan Fiction*, New York, Peter Lang.

Boym, S. (1994) *Common Places: Mythologies of Everyday Life in Russia*, Cambridge, MA, Harvard University Press.

Brice Heath, S. (1983) *Ways with Words: Language, Life and Work in Communities and Classrooms*, Cambridge, Cambridge University Press.

Britton, J., Burgess, T., Martin, N., McLeod, A. and Rosen, N. (1975) *The Development of Writing Abilities*, pp. 11–18, London, Macmillan Education Ltd.

Clark, M. (1976) *Young Fluent Readers: What Can They Teach Us?*, London, Heinemann Educational.

Cremin, T. and Myhill, D. (2013) *Writing Voices: Creating Communities of Writers*, London, Routledge.

Cremin, T., Mottram, M., Collins, F.M., Powell, S. and Drury, R. (2014) *Researching Literacy Lives: Building Communities Between Home and School*, London, Routledge.

Dick, B. (1990) *Convergent Interviewing*, Brisbane, Interchange.

Dick, B. (1999) *Rigour Without Numbers: The Potential of Dialectical Processes as Qualitative Research Tools*, Brisbane, Interchange.

Dovey K. (1978) 'Home: An Ordering Principle in Space', *Landscape*, vol. 22, pp. 27–30.

Frank, J. (2005) 'Semiotic Use of the Word "Home" Among People with Alzheimer's Disease: A Plea for Selfhood', in Rowles, G.D. and Chaudhury, H. (eds) *Home and Identity in Late Life: International Perspectives*, New York, Springer Publishing, pp. 171–197.

Garrett, L. and Moltzen, R. (2011) 'Writing Because I Want To, Not Because I Have To: Young Gifted Writers' Perspectives on the Factors that "Matter" in Developing Expertise', *English Teaching*, vol. 10, no. 1, p. 165.

Giddens, A. (1991) *Modernity and Self-Identity*, Cambridge, Polity.

Glaser, B.G. and Strauss, A.L. (1967) *The Discovery of Grounded Theory: Strategies for Qualitative Research*, Chicago, IL, Aldine Publishers.

Gutiérrez, K.D., Baquedano-López, P. and Tejeda, C. (1999) 'Rethinking Diversity: Hybridity and Hybrid Language Practices in the Third Space', *Mind, Culture, and Activity*, vol. 6, no. 4, pp. 286–303.

Hayes, J. and Flower, L. (1980) 'Identifying the Organization of Writing Processes', in Gregg, L. and Steinberg, E. (eds) *Cognitive Processes in Writing: An Interdisciplinary Approach*, Hillsdale, NJ, Lawrence Erlbaum Associates, pp. 3–30.

Hull, G.A. and Schultz, K. (2002) *School's Out: Bridging Out-Of-School Literacies With Classroom Practice*, New York, Teachers College Press.

Kenner, C. (2004) *Becoming Biliterate: Young Children Learning Different Writing Systems*, Stoke on Trent, Trentham Books.

Kron, J. (1983) *Home-psych: The Social Psychology of Home and Decoration*, Danvers, MA, Clarkson Potter.

Locke, T. (2014) *Developing Writing Teachers: Practical Ways for Teacher-writers to Transform their Classroom Practice*, London, Routledge.

Maun, I. and Myhill, D. (2005) 'Text as Design, Writers as Designers', *English in Education*, vol. 39, no. 2, pp. 5–21.

Moje, E.B., Ciechanowski, K.M., Kramer, K., Ellis, L., Carrillo, R. and Collazo, T. (2004) 'Working Toward Third Space in Content Area Literacy: An Examination of Everyday Funds of Knowledge and Discourse', *Reading Research Quarterly*, vol. 39, pp. 38–70.

Moore, J. (2000) 'Placing Home In Context', *Journal of Environmental Psychology*, vol. 20, no. 3, pp. 207–217.

Myhill, D. and Watson, A. (2011) 'Teaching Writing', in Green, A. (ed) *Becoming a Reflective English Teacher*, Maidenhead, England, and New York, Open University Press, pp. 58–72.

New London Group. (1996) 'A Pedagogy of Multiliteracies: Designing Social Futures', *Harvard Educational Review*, vol. 66, no. 1, pp. 60–93.

Pahl, K. (2007) 'Creativity in Events and Practices: A Lens for Understanding Children's Multimodal Texts', *Literacy*, vol. 41, no. 2, pp. 86–92.

Pahl, K. (2012) '"A Reason to Write": Exploring Writing Epistemologies in Two Contexts', *Pedagogies: An International Journal*, vol. 7, no. 3, pp. 209–228.

Pahl, K. (2014) 'The Aesthetics of Everyday Literacies: Home Writing Practices in a British Asian Household', *Anthropology and Education Quarterly*, vol. 45, no. 3, pp. 293–311.

Putnam, T. and Newton, C. (1990) *Household Choices*, London, Futures Publications.

Rapport, N. (1997) *Transcendent Individual: Towards a Literary and Liberal Anthropology*, London, Routledge.

Riege, A.M. and Nair, G. (2004) 'The Diversity of Convergent Interviewing: Applications for Early Researchers and Postgraduate Students', *The Marketing Review*, vol. 4, no. 1, pp. 73–85.

‎

Rowsell, J. and Pahl, K. (2007) 'Sedimented identities in texts: Instances of practice', *Reading Research Quarterly*, vol. 42, no. 3, pp. 388–404.

Ryan, M. (2014) 'Reflexivity and Aesthetic Inquiry: Building Dialogues Between the Arts and Literacy', *English Teaching*, vol. 13, no. 2, p. 5.

Rybczynski, W. (1987) *Home: A Short History of an Idea*, New York, Penguin.

Sankaran, S. (2001) *Effective Change Management Using Action Learning and Action Research: Concepts, Frameworks, Processes, Applications*, Lismore, Australia, Southern Cross.

Seamon, D. (1979) *A Geography of the Lifeworld: Movement, Rest, and Encounter*, New York, St. Martin's Press.

Sharples, M. (1999) *How We Write: Writing as Creative Design*, London, Routledge.

Shaw, S. (1990) 'Returning Home', *Phenomenology and Pedagogy*, vol. 8, pp. 224–236.

Simons, H. and Usher, R. (2000) *Situated Ethics in Educational Research*, London, Routledge.

Sixsmith, J. (1986) 'The Meaning of Home: An Exploratory Study of Environmental Experience', *Journal of Environmental Psychology*, vol. 6, no. 4, pp. 281–298.

Street, B.V. (1984) *Literacy in Theory and Practice*, Cambridge, Cambridge University Press.

Street, B.V. (1993) *Cross-cultural Approaches to Literacy*, Cambridge, Cambridge University Press.

Vygotsky, L.S. (1962) *Thought and Language*, Cambridge, MA, MIT Press.

Wise, J.M. (2000) 'Home: Territory and Identity', *Cultural Studies*, vol. 14, no. 2, pp. 295–310.

11

GLANCING SIDEWAYS AT YOUNG WRITERS BECOMING

Diane R. Collier

Introduction

Writers are always in a state of becoming; in classrooms, teacher-writers and student-writers are always *becoming* writers and their social and academic identities are intertwined with their writer identities. In this chapter, I use a methodology of 'glancing sideways' to look at the writing trajectories of Stephanie and Kyle.[1] They were 9 years old, in the same class and engaged in a range of writing activities during the school year, including short pieces about 'someone I admire', a favorite winter activity, various journal entries, retelling, and group story writing.

I attempted to interview Kyle and Stephanie directly about their sense of themselves as writers, as well as what they thought key others (i.e., parent, teacher, friend) might think of them as writers, but I gained little insight from this approach. As others have found when observing children in play (Kendrick, 2005), a 'sideways glance' (Schwartzman, 1976) at writing-in-motion was more effective, as I positioned myself alongside children while they wrote in the classroom and in the computer lab at school, to discern what was happening as they engaged in writing practices. This analysis examines what was happening and how writers are constructed through particular practices and relationships. Locating myself as a becoming writer also, I briefly share some of my writing journey.

Considering Kyle and Stephanie as *becoming* writers at a point in their academic lives—in the middle years of elementary school—when they are no longer beginners, this chapter focuses on Kyle's and Stephanie's literacy challenges and successes in writing. The chapter begins with a review of relevant literature on young writers and writing practices, and related fields of play and identity. It then proceeds with an exploration of a developing methodology of 'glancing sideways' and ways that ethnographic researchers as well as classroom teachers might learn from children writing. Next, the larger context of a two-year ethnographic study of children's textmaking is presented along with the data highlighted here, and the ways in which data were generated and analyzed. Finally, findings are connected to beginning writer identities, Kyle's and Stephanie's writing choices, writing voice, and writing trajectories over the course of a school year. Implications for how researchers and writing teachers might support children who are becoming writers are discussed.

Writer identities and writing practices

The twentieth and twenty-first centuries have seen fluctuations in dominant pedagogies, and thereby writing practices, in elementary classrooms. The most notable of these practices are 1) writers' workshop approaches that often include a focus on the writing process and children as authors (i.e., Lensmire, 1997; Whitney et al., 2008); and 2) the pressures of an increasingly test-focused curriculum where teachers are often under demands to conform to narrow interpretations of literacy, as defined by state-mandated testing, especially in the United States (e.g., Dutro, Selland and Bien, 2013; Lund, 2008) but also in Australia (e.g. Frawley, 2014), Canada (e.g., Peterson, McClay and Main, 2011), and the United Kingdom (e.g., Burke, 2011).

In addition to the narrowing of curriculum, which is sometimes accepted and sometimes resisted by teachers, certain kinds of writing genres and daily writing practices tend to be preferred in classrooms (Collier, 2010). Journal writing and narrative forms continue to be favored and writing process approaches are understood and implemented in very different ways (Strachan, 2014). Although an interest in inquiry and a focus on reading nonfiction have increased in Canada and the United States (e.g., Coleman, Bradley and Donovan, 2012; Ministry of Education, Ontario, 2011; Witmer, Duke, Billman and Betts, 2014), it is unclear whether the classroom writing practices that might accompany these pedagogies and forms have changed alongside these trends.

In the late twentieth and early twenty-first century, there has been a proliferation of research about the writing and writer identities of youth, as they express their social identities through their writing and literacies (e.g., Lewis, Enciso and Moje, 2007; McLean and Rowsell, 2015; Snow and Moje, 2010). Often writing from a sociocultural perspective, these studies have focused on negotiating the writing curriculum, peer relations and the circulation of power in classrooms, and youth ownership of writing. Other research has focused on multimodal writing and embodiment (Wager and Perry, 2015), writing and emotions (Lewis and Tierney, 2013), and the importance of choice and a variety of possible and available writer positions as integral to sustained and meaningful engagement with writing (Dutro, Kazemi and Balf, 2006; Grainger, Goouch and Lambirth, 2002).

The analysis that follows relies heavily on two ideas about writers: 1) an understanding of writers as 'becoming' and therefore writer identities as fluid, and 2) a framing of writing as a form of narrative play. Conceiving of children as engaged in a 'writers-in-becoming process' (p. 306), Hong (2015) describes how English language learners developed their writer identities in a classroom where the teacher explicitly taught children about their role/authority as writers/authors. Hong uses

Bakhtin's (1986) dialogism to document how the teacher explicitly engaged students in conversations about their ongoing writing process and process of becoming writers. Nonetheless, within the flows of power in educational institutions, and particularly within the discourse of assessment, narrow labels are often ascribed. Dutro, Selland, and Bien (2013) disrupt binaries of proficient and non-proficient that are often implied and constructed through large-scale assessments by examining the subtleties of students' writing and emphasize the many things that students can do. Looking at *voice*—rather than grammatical correctness—to understand competence, Carbone and Orellana (2010) highlight emergent academic identities that are more visible when close examinations are made.

Important explorations of literacy as play and play as literacy in early childhood describe play as a form of narrative and as an expression of literate identity (Kendrick, 2005; Wohlwend, 2009, 2011). These explorations and others suggest an expansion of literacy to include embodied modes. Thiel (2015), describing superhero play, states that 'play is one of the ways children actively engage in and perform complex, embodied literacy work' (p. 46). In the analysis that follows, I look for the playfulness that happens in more conventional literacy practices, when children are writing in more formalized ways in classrooms. In the next section, I also continue to explore how the observation of writing practices can occur in the same ways that play can be seen when 'glancing sideways'.

Methodology of 'glancing sideways'

When interviewing young children, it is not always possible, or desirable, to take a head-on view to topics of interest. In fact, when interviewing children about their literacy practices, and their identities as readers and writers, a 'sideways glance' (Kendrick, 2005; Schwartzman, 1976) may be more desirable. Just as interviews with adults can be viewed as constructions (Lemke, Kelly and Roth, 2006), interviews with children can be constructions, especially in spaces where adult–child conversations are not the norm.

Schwartzman (1976) introduced the term 'sideways glance' (p. 211) to disrupt conventional understandings of children's play that were held at the time. Instead of play as future-oriented (preparing for adulthood), play as an expression of inner life/expression, or play as inversion of cultural systems, Schwartzman introduced the notion of the (at least) two versions of child (child as self and child as actor) that could be viewed simultaneously when taking a sideways glance at play. In play, she argued, children were simultaneously themselves and someone else, introducing a dialectic of self. This important inversion of our usual thinking about play, from imitative to productive, has implications for how children can be considered as writers and the complex ways in which their writer identities might be manifested and interpreted. Drawing on Schwartzman's description of a sideways glance, Kendrick (2005) described how a young girl's play could be interpreted 'as a literary and social text' (p. 5) about her position in her family and her imagined future roles. How does glancing sideways help in this case? Through children's writing, and the use of a longitudinal, ethnographic approach to generating data, one might view the young writers' multiple identities through the intersection of their writing, their social identities, and their talk about both of these.

A sideways glance focuses on ongoing processes. Ellsworth (2005) and Davies (2014) frame learning with a future orientation and the learner as always *becoming*. When talking about particular pedagogical moments, Ellsworth suggests that the learner 'invite[s] the sensation of a mind/brain/body simultaneously in both suspension *and* animation in the interval of change from the person one has been to the person that one has yet to become' (p. 17). This future orientation and expectation of change and flux allows for disruption of any identities as stable or fixed. Likewise, when referring to play, Ellsworth describes 'play [as] the experience of the learning self in its incompleteness' (p. 142). What happens as we engage in 'emergent listening' (Davies, 2014, p. 1)—an openness to others—in our encounters with children?

In this research, I started with conventional interviews with Kyle and Stephanie, where I devised semi-structured interview questions to ask about their writer identities. Deliberately positioning myself as learner and follower in these interviews, these events took on a more random, sometimes recursive trajectory, where other interests, agendas, identities, and interactions sometimes pushed questions aside.

Generating data about writers: methods

The two-year ethnographic study from which these data are drawn builds specifically upon the research of Dyson (2003) and Hicks (2002), and is particularly interested in the literacy narratives and trajectories of children from low-income and/or minority backgrounds. Hicks describes her retellings of children's stories of early literacy as a focus on 'the smallness of situated lives' (p. 33). She argues for the richness of this approach for theorizing about power relations because of the ways in which one can trace histories and the shaping of practices and subjectivities through the everyday observation of these relations.

Kyle and Stephanie, the focal participants, were both in Grade 4[2] at the time of this research and both lived in a low-income housing project, located on the eastern coast of Canada in an urban setting. I had previously been a Grade 3 teacher in their school for six years and engaged in this research during my doctoral studies, several years later. I moved in and out of observer and participant roles, as I made notes or audio-recorded as children worked. During this year, I spent two to five days a week in this classroom, engaged in monthly informal conversations with Kyle and Stephanie (at school but outside of their classroom), and visited them at home monthly when possible.

During the Grade 4 year, children engaged in a range of writing activities. Derived from prompts from mandated writing assessments that occurred in Grade 3, children were asked to respond to similar prompts provided by the teacher. These *demand*[3] writing pieces, similar to journal writing prompts, were often free writing exercises and sometimes students created a brainstorming web. Students also wrote responses to questions about stories they had read and wrote in preparation for talk (once about a show and tell object and once about a bag of personal items from home that were shared with others).

Writing and talking about writing: findings and potentials

The findings that follow are divided into three sections. The first section discusses what was gleaned from interviews and informal conversations with Kyle and Stephanie over one year, both inside and outside of their classroom. The second and third are generated from classroom writing processes and Kyle's and Stephanie's responses to two prompts: the first to write about 'a person I admire' and the second to write about 'my favorite winter activity'. All of these argue for a sideways glance as a method for understanding writer identities as becoming.

From ongoing, sideways conversations

In the initial stages of working with Kyle and Stephanie, I attempted to conduct semi-structured interviews. To understand how writers were constructed within particular writing practices, and to understand how they perceived certain ways of writing as more or less valuable, I asked them about the kinds of writing in which they engaged at school, in their class, and outside of school. To understand what they valued in writing and how they knew when writing was successful, I asked about good writers they knew, and about how others (their parents, friends, or teacher) would describe them as a writer.

My attempts to solicit information using these kinds of questions were possibly in direct opposition to my desire to follow the children's lead in the study more generally. From the beginning, Kyle and Stephanie wholeheartedly embraced my statements that I wanted to learn from them. I do not know if it was for this reason, or for some other, but asking direct questions (as described above) received minimal responses or attempts to change the subject. Instead of relying on interviews, I pieced together their understanding of their writer identities across a number of sessions over a year. When I met with Kyle and Stephanie, each on their own, in the computer lab, or an empty classroom, we sometimes engaged in online games or other activities of their choice. We also talked about and reflected upon the pieces of writing (as well as other multimodal compositions) that they produced.

From Kyle I received an interesting range of responses. He often referred to the mechanics of writing such as the need for neat, small work. He demonstrated his ability to form cursive letters when I asked him about his writing. On occasion, in class, he had difficulty generating topics for writing. When asked about what others might think about him as a writer he replied, 'I guess I don't pay attention to that stuff . . . the world doesn't go around me'. He was unsure of what others might think of his writing, but was more sure about himself as a reader when he drew a picture of a chapter book from a popular book series and the letter 'O' to represent the reading level assigned for his in-class and home reading.

On other occasions he seemed to enjoy writing about topics that were discussed and explored in detail in class (such as about African animals, Martin Luther King, or politicians), and he sometimes wondered about the purposes for writing. On one occasion, students were asked to write to politicians about something they wanted changed. Kyle wrote about needed repairs for his housing complex. Later when we looked at this piece, he wondered why they wrote the letters if they never sent them. Often conversations would turn to Kyle's desire to stay out of trouble. When writing or when generating ideas (whether at home or at school), Kyle would often ask for help from his mother, his teacher, or me.

As a becoming writer Kyle was someone who worked well with the support of others, and enjoyed producing work that was neat and sometimes humorous. He showed an interest in learning about new topics, and demonstrated concern and caring for his family in his writing. Often he seemed interested in the superficial aspects of writing and sometimes the authentic purposes were paramount. In the sections that follow this one, his writing plans and drafts show his ability to act as a writer.

Interview-style conversations with Stephanie were even more difficult in terms of my initial and ongoing intentions to elicit information about how she thought of herself as a writer. Many times she would nod, say yes or no or quickly change the topic. Stephanie was happy to talk, but seemed to find it difficult to reflect upon her own progress. Her mother did report that she mentioned at home that she was not smart, but Stephanie did not talk about these concerns with me. Her insecurity about her academic writer identity may have been the reason for her hesitancies. Stephanie was happy to report on a dispute that happened earlier that day or to talk about her new puppy, amongst other ranges of topics. Stephanie often used our time together to ensure that I would agree to sit next to her on the next occasion like recess or lunch and would ask me to reiterate who was included in my study (her). Stephanie was knowledgeable about her relations, her family finances, and shopping needs. She told me stories about the tooth fairy and explained that her mom said I had chosen her because of her excellent drawing abilities. Stephanie had recently been chosen to have her drawing reproduced for a fund-raising calendar and this appeared to enhance her sense of herself as a drawer. Good drawers, she said, do not draw stick people and include necks. Stephanie was an effusive storyteller, but she talked more at length when the topics were of her choosing. She often told stories about her family, her friends, or a new pet. I was struck by her ability to paint a picture with words (e.g., when describing her new dog: 'He got a twirl on his tail that's white') and tell an elaborated and compelling story.

Stephanie seemed engaged in writing about personal topics. She often chose to read to me during our sessions, whether at home or at school, and read often to her young nephew. Stephanie was happy to read to me from her school journals and started keeping a journal at home. In some ways, I often felt that Stephanie was a competent and eager beginning writer, and she also happily adopted school practices, such as dating each page in her coloring book at home (in the way that teachers often ask students to do in school). When I asked Stephanie about a good reader she knew, she pointed me to a community volunteer pictured on a poster in the school hall, who came to read to the children one day. When I asked her about her own writing, she changed the topic. I mentioned that she seemed engrossed when writing and she affirmed. She explained that her mom would say she is a 'good worker' and 'checks her work' but was unable or unwilling to say what her teacher might think.

What are Stephanie and Kyle becoming as writers and where might their talents be valued? Both seemed interested in following conventions and expectations, as they perceived them. For Kyle, authentic and purposeful writing seemed integral to his interests and, for Stephanie, personal topics, about her interpersonal relations and home life, appeared to be primary.

Looking close-up at writing processes: drafts and final products

Writing process 1: writing about 'someone I admire'

In this section, I make connections gleaned from the interviews above to the specific texts that Kyle and Stephanie produced. Early in the school year, Kyle and Stephanie's teacher asked them to write about 'someone I admire'. The teacher had taken the prompt from a sample performance assessment (provincially mandated) from the previous school year. The teacher's focus was on detail:

> We're not going to be so particular over our—our—our spelling and punctuation the whole idea is to get lots of ideas down. A nice beginning, middle and an end. To have a focused piece of writing. . . . With many details, many interesting details that would be interesting to us to read.

Children were invited to make a list of ideas and the teacher and students brainstormed ideas together (see Figure 11.1). Although there was always the option of writing about a famous figure, most of the children wrote about someone in their personal lives. Kyle and Stephanie both wrote lists as part of their brainstorming, shown in Figure 11.1. Beneath these brainstorming lists are their finished drafts. Through the analysis that follows, I attempt to listen to Kyle's and Stephanie's voices, to see what can be found about their identities as writers. At first glance, these seem to be mundane lists about important people in the children's lives.

Kyle listed a wide range of things that his mother did for him, from the grand— 'gives me food and shelter—to the everyday—'plays basketball with me'. His list could easily be titled 'what my mother does for me' rather than 'a person I admire'. If one looks back to the brainstorming chart, 'when I was sick' is one of the items and one that Kyle replicated in his writing. Kyle lived with his mother and one brother, but most of the time Kyle and his mother were alone. Kyle's mother sat with him to help with homework or to supervise his online time and they also sang along to rap songs together. Kyle helped his mom with the cleaning and tidying. They worked together, and often.

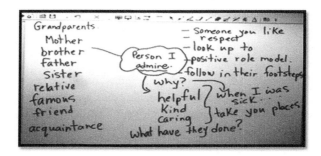

Whole Class Brainstorming – 'Person I Admire'

Instructions:
Write about a person you admire. Who is this person? What is it that you admire about this person and why?

Kyle's brainstorming chart	Stephanie's brainstorming chart
The person I admire is my Mother - ~~helps me if I am hurt~~ ~~helps me with homework~~ - ~~helps me when I am hurt~~ - ~~takes care of me when I am sick~~ - ~~buys me toys~~ - ~~gives me food and shelter~~ - ~~plays basketball with me~~ - ~~does housekeeping~~	Person I Admire My sister -helpful -kind -caring -respectful -loving -sweat -thankful -looks up to me -thinks about me -pick me up when it is raining -take me places
Kyle's writing - 'Person I Admire'	Stephanie's writing - 'Person I Admire'
The person I a admire is my Mother because she helps me with my homework and if I don't know a word she helps me to. When I am bleeding or hurt she comes to see if I am all right. The next thing I admire about my mom is she takes care of me when I am sick. Every time I am sick she brings me to the doctor. The next thing is she buys me GREAT! toys like wrestilers and other toys to. My mom also gives me the basic things like a shelter to live in and food to eat so I won't starv to death. Every night if I get my Socil Studies right we will play basket ball with my little net, me, her and my father plays. But the most important things of all and I am sires [serious] the most important job is house cleaning for us, like if we spill something they need to help us clear it up. If the house is dirty they need to clean the house. and that's who I admire.	The person I admire is my sister because she is helpful, caring and best of all loving, My sister named is Jane she is twenty one years old she is tall pretty sometimes gets me in a lot of trouble. When it was Chistmas day I went down staries and said wake up sleeping head and she said be up in a minute I did not know how to ride a bike so my sister helped me and I was just five years old it was really hard. My sister brings me to the cabin in the winter and it is a bit and that's were I go slideing to and it is really fun and when I go back my sister cooks me some hot choclate. In the summer we go to the park and play and when it is time to go swimming then we go in the pool. When I wants someon to come over my sister say yes and sometims she says no. She went to East Coast school and know I do too and that is very cool. My sister takes me out to lunch a lot and she lets me pick were we go and I pick McDonalds. My sister loves me because when she don't get up I bring her breakfast and lunch and sometimes ever supper. And I get very tied when I get up stairs and mom said Stephanie are you ok and I say do I look ok she says no you don't. This is why I admire my sister Jane.

FIGURE 11.1 Class brainstorming, independent brainstorming, and drafts of 'person I admire'

Stephanie chose her sister as the person she admired. In contrast to Kyle, she listed a series of attributes that made her sister admirable, that she looked up to (even though she said her sister looked up to her, Stephanie recanted that point later), and then, like Kyle, stated what her sister did for her. Indeed Stephanie often spoke about her sister, who did not live at home, and who was ten years older than her. Looking back to the whole-class brainstorming chart, it seems that Stephanie took her cues from the items listed there: 'respect', 'look up to', and 'take me places'.

So where might writer identities come into play in these pieces? When Kyle writes about his mother, he writes first about how she helped him with his home-work. His writing connects back to Kyle's desire for help and support from others when working. Kyle accompanied by his mother writing and working at home is not the same as Kyle writing alone at school.

In Kyle's draft he returns to the brainstorming list and writes about the first item, when he was hurt. He expands his response to each item on the list into a full sen-tence. Then he reminds the reader of the topic, 'a person I admire', and how she cared for him when he was ill. New elements are added when he reminds the reader that his mom bought him GREAT toys! Kyle had a collection of wrestler figures in his room, and his mom planned her savings carefully so that she could occasionally buy a new one for him. Kyle's slightly humorous and energetic tone continues into the next sentence when he tells how she prevented him from 'starve[ing] to death'. His written thoughts follow the original brainstorming list but are elaborated. He explains how they played basketball with the mini plastic net in his bedroom. Then, he ends with her role as house cleaner. It may seem that he is telling of a role that many mothers or parents do but in Kyle's house, housecleaning and tidiness were paramount and toys, furniture, and other objects were always organized and immacu-late. Kyle ends the writing and reminds the audience of the subject of his admiration. In conversations with Kyle later, he said he only wrote about his mom because he could not think of anyone else. He could have been downplaying his mother's role, as he did on other occasions, or his decision to write about her could have been a matter of convenience. Nonetheless, his mother was very pleased when she got to read the story, when I brought it home to share, along with other texts from school.

Stephanie's very brief brainstorming list was translated into a lengthy final piece. She also began with a statement about the topic assigned. She used the descrip-tors from her list to introduce her sister. Then she moved on to details about her sister's age and appearance. These ideas do not appear on the brainstorming chart but are perhaps included so that the reader can imagine the sister. She alludes to her sister having gotten her in trouble but does not tell how. Stephanie then writes a list of things that she and her sister did together – they went to the cabin, went sliding, and made hot chocolate. She describes winter then summer activities. She explains how her sister took on a mothering role, deciding whether she could have friends over. Her sister took her out to eat and indulged her choices. Then she explains what she did for her sister, as a demonstration of her caring for her sister. She ends with a humorous anecdote about her mother who had asked if she was okay. Stephanie represents herself as competent, loved, and loving in this story. Like Kyle, she knows how to bring her story back to the assigned topic.

Both Kyle and Stephanie, as writers, are able to meet many of the expectations of them in their academic writing, especially when looking up close. Kyle was able to encapsulate many of his social roles in this piece of writing that is detailed, humorous, and describes his relationship with his mother while also following the instructions for the assignment given to the students. He often focused on objects and activities. Stephanie represented her intense and close relationships in her writing and her description flows from a relational, perhaps even emotional, stance.

Writing process 2: writing about 'a favorite winter activity'

When Stephanie and Kyle's teacher gave instructions for a favorite winter activity during the same school year, she encouraged them to plan with a web 'if you want' and to think about adding details that are interesting to the reader. She suggested that they 'compile great ideas in your own head about what you're going to write about'. Together, with the teacher, they brainstormed potential winter sports, as shown in Figure 11.2. Additionally, they brainstormed what could be included: many details as well as when, where, why, and with whom, as well as how they felt about it. Again, the teacher created a brainstorming web with the children.

In Kyle's web, he replicated the brainstormed ideas/questions, and then answered each one with brief one or two-word responses. As he moved forward with his draft, Kyle then proceeded methodically to elaborate on each of these bullet points. His writing has an explanatory tone, in almost an encyclopedic way, and he seems to have built on or responded to the teacher's suggestion that he explain the details. In his writing, he positions himself as knowledgeable about the topic, and powerful as a hockey player. In the end, he mentioned his favorite team—also his father's favorite team—and how he would lead them to victory. Although on the surface this text seems predictable, there are elements of connection across home and school that the topic actually encourages, and elements of Kyle's humor and closeness with his family that pervade his talk and texts at school.

When Stephanie completed her brainstorming chart, which she embellished with curvy 'y's and boxes around the shape of each word, she wrote about figure skating during public skate events at a local arena. As with Kyle, her brainstorming chart led her about halfway through the draft and the rest was more improvised. Stephanie explains the events that allowed her winter skating to happen and the role of each person in the scenario. She describes the tricks she can do in figure skating terms. Anticipating and imagining the reader's questions ('Stephanie, how do you know these figure skating tricks?'), Stephanie explains that they are gleaned from the skating movies that she and her sister watched. Stephanie emphasizes the large number of times she could skate around and how doing all those tricks, spinning around, made her so dizzy. She sums it up neatly at the end with a restatement of the questions posed. Like Kyle, a portrait of Stephanie as competent and in a loving supportive family is painted through her writing.

At school, Kyle's easy and humorous interactions with adults positioned him as competent, with academic potential, and he did not always get the writing

Whole Class Brainstorming – 'Favourite Winter Activity'

Instructions:
Tell about your favourite winter activity. Remember to include lots of description in your writing to make it interesting to your reader.

Kyle's brainstorming chart	Stephanie's brainstorming chart

Kyle's writing - 'Favourite Winter Activity'	Stephanie's writing - 'Favourite Winter Activity'
My favourite winter sport is Hockey I play it in my parking lot for about a hour. I play it with my brother, his friend robert or robbie and a lot more people. In Hockey you need a puck or a hard ball, hockey sticks, two net's and to goaldy's in the net so the the other team won't shoot the puck in that's a goald. In Hockey you play 5 on 5 me and my friends sometimes play 6 on 6. You can play Hockey anytime winter, spring summer or fall. When you Play it in winter it's called ice Hockey any other time it's called street Hockey. Hockey to me is one of the best sports every and it is really fun to play. I hope I am in the NHl one and if I am I'm going to bring my team to victory. My team would be the NyISLANDERS because My dad likes them so I like them and Hockey to. The End.	My favourite winter activity is figure skating. I go with my sister and mom but mom watches us. We only go in the winter and weekends because sister and mom aren't working. We go to the Stadium because it is all most by us. We go figure skating because it is my sister's and me favorite winter sport. When I'm on the ice and can do tricks like twirles and other things figure skaters do. And my sister helps me do all those tricks it was hard but I did it. Me and my sister are really good at figure skateing because we watches a lot of skateing movies and that's how we get all the tricks from a lot of them because they are very good at it. We go around the hole ice rike but sometimes I get very dizzing to. If I go around a lot of times. This is why figure skating is my favorite winter sport of all times!!

FIGURE 11.2 Class brainstorming, independent brainstorming, and drafts of 'favorite winter sport'

feedback that might have challenged his writing or support he may have wanted. At school, Stephanie experienced challenges relating to her peers, and sometimes to adults, and was positioned as less mature and more imitative in her writing, as well as in other academic areas. Her academic identity contrasted sharply with her more lively, engaged, and literate identities at home, with her family. These three aspects of Kyle's and Stephanie's writing processes, and their talk about their writing, pieced together from glancing sideways, show how Kyle and Stephanie were becoming writers and how their potentials and multi-faceted writer identities can be perceived in positive ways.

Valuing writers: developing writer identities

This discussion began with an interest in what a sideways glance at writing, like a sideways glance at play, might reveal about children's writing. Through the analysis and the lens of a sideways glance I attempted to find a way to listen to children's voices, as they were and are becoming writers. Within this close-up, sideways examination, children insert themselves, and their social and academic identities, into their texts and talk in personalized ways that represent their identities outside of their classrooms and schools. In the same way, they display their competence in doing what writers do; they plan ideas, they expand ideas, they tell stories, and they learn how to focus on a topic. They learn to listen to their own voices as they write and, in these examples, regardless of the generic or prescriptive nature of the task, they develop personal styles and personal narratives.

Revisiting our conversations and the texts produced allows for an examination that is both close (looking at drafts of writing) and wide (looking at events across space and time). Although not the primary focus of this analysis, the varied elements that move in and out of and contribute to children's textmaking argue for the consideration of the contribution of multiple modes or a multimodal perspective (Collier and Kendrick, in press; Kress, 1997; Miller and McVee, 2012). Written texts are much more than a two-dimensional printed product.

Stephanie and Kyle have fluid and moving writer identities and are on a journey of becoming writers where there are still many things to learn and try and be. Schwartzman's notion of a sideways glance at children engaged in play allows for a view on children's developing social and academic identities. Thinking of learning from children in this way is not altogether different from the observational, 'kidwatching' (Owocki and Goodman, 2002) stance of many early childhood educators and some more formalized educational stances. In contrast to formalized, standardized, or mandated assessment, which tends to categorize writers in more fixed ways, from a sideways glance writers can be seen in ways that complement and enhance how students' writers can be seen as becoming.

A theme of this volume is how teachers' investments in writing and personal engagement with writing might enhance both their experiences and their students' experiences as writers. Teachers who write alongside their students, whether or not they write outside of their roles as teachers, are, at the very least, engaged in the kinds of decision-making and problem-solving in which they ask their students to engage. As Cremin (2006) found, teachers who engage in their own writing may find themselves engaging in written composition 'alongside the children' (p. 428) and entering the kinds of journeys that we often ask children to take. Furthermore, they are better positioned to understand what it might feel like to identify as a becoming writer and to see what writers might do as they are becoming. The cost of ignoring what writers do is too high to dismiss in an educational field where written products are the currency that counts.

Notes

1 All names are pseudonyms.
2 Children in Grade 4 in Canada are usually 9 years old and this is their 5th year of formal schooling.
3 *Demand* writing is writing in response to a provided prompt, usually completed in one session without brainstorming, revising, or editing sessions.

References

Bakhtin, M.M. (1986) *Speech genres and other essays*. University of Texas Press, Austin, TX.

Burke, W. (2011) 'Log jammed by standard assessment tests: How feedback can help writers', *Literacy*, vol. 45, pp. 19–24.

Carbone, P.M. and Orellana, M. (2010) 'Developing academic identities: Persuasive writing as a tool to strengthen emergent academic identities', *Research in the Teaching of English*, vol. 44, pp. 292–316.

Coleman, J.M., Bradley, L.G. and Donovan, C.A. (2012) 'Visual representations in second graders' information book compositions', *Reading Teacher*, vol. 66, pp. 31–45.

Collier, D.R. (2010) 'Journey to becoming a writer: Review of research about children's identities as writers', *Language and Literacy: A Canadian Educational E-Journal*, vol. 12, no. 1, pp. 147–164.

Collier, D.R. and Kendrick M. (in press) 'I wish I was ~~a lion~~, a puppy: A multimodal view of writing-process assessment', *Pedagogies*.

Cremin, T. (2006) 'Creativity, uncertainty and discomfort: Teachers as writers', *Cambridge Journal of Education*, vol. 36, pp. 415–433.

Davies, B. (2014) *Listening to children: Being and becoming*. Routledge, London.

Dutro, E., Kazemi, E. and Balf, R. (2006) 'Making sense of "The boy who died": Tales of a struggling successful writer', *Reading and Writing Quarterly*, vol. 22, no. 4, pp. 325–356.

Dutro, E., Selland, M., & Bien, A. (2013) 'Revealing Writing, Concealing Writers: High-Stakes Assessment in an Urban Elementary Classroom', *Journal Of Literacy Research*, vol. 45, no. 2, pp. 99–141.

Dyson, A.H. (2003) *The brothers and sisters learn to write*. Teachers College Press, New York.

Ellsworth, E.A. (2005) *Places of learning: Media, architecture, pedagogy*. Routledge, London.

Frawley, E. and McLean Davies, L. (2015) 'Assessing the field', *English Teaching: Practice & Critique (Emerald Group Publishing Limited)*, vol. 14, no. 2, pp. 83–99.

Grainger, T., Goouch, K. and Lambirth, A. (2002) 'The voice of the child: "We're writers" project', *Reading: Literacy and Language*, vol. 36, no. 3, pp. 135–139.

Hicks, D. (2002) *Reading lives: Working-class children and literacy learning*. Teachers College Press, New York.

Hong, H. (2015) 'Exploring young children's writer identity: Construction through the lens of dialogism', *International Journal of Early Childhood*, vol. 47, no. 2, pp. 301–316.

Kendrick, M. (2005) 'Playing house: A "sideways" glance at literacy and identity in early childhood', *Journal of Early Childhood Literacy*, vol. 5, no. 1, pp. 5–28.

Kress, G. (1997) Before Writing – Rethinking the Paths to Literacy. Routledge, London.

Lemke, J., Kelly, G. and Roth, W.M. (2006) 'Forum: Toward a phenomenology of interviews; Lessons from the phenomenology of interviews', *Cultural Studies of Science Education*, vol. 1, pp. 83–106.

Lensmire, T.J. (1997) *Powerful writing, responsible teaching.* Teachers College Press, New York.

Lewis, C., Enciso, P.E., and Moje, E.B. (2007) (eds) *Reframing sociocultural research on literacy: Identity, agency, and power* (1st edn). Lawrence Erlbaum Associates, Mahwah, NJ.

Lewis, C. and Tierney J.D. (2013) 'Mobilizing emotion in an urban classroom: Producing identities and transforming signs in a race-related discussion', *Linguistics and Education*, vol. 24, pp. 289–304.

Lund, A. (2008) 'Assessment made visible: Individual and collective practices', *Mind, Culture, and Activity*, vol. 15, pp. 32–51.

McLean, C. and Rowsell, J. (2015) 'Imagining writing futures: Photography, writing, and technology', *Reading and Writing Quarterly*, vol. 31, no. 2, pp. 102–118.

Miller, S. and McVee, M. (2012) *Multimodal Composing In Classrooms: Learning and Teaching for the Digital World.* Routledge, New York.

Ministry of Education, Government of Ontario. (October 2011) 'Getting started with student inquiry', Capacity Building Series.

Owocki, G. and Goodman, Y. (2002) *Kidwatching: Documenting children's literacy development.* Heinemann, Portsmouth, NH.

Peterson, S.S., McClay, J. and Main, K. (2011) 'An analysis of large-scale writing assessments in Canada (Grades 5–8)', *Alberta Journal of Educational Research*, vol. 57, pp. 424–445.

Schwartzman, H. (1976) 'Children's play: A sideways glance at make-believe' in Lancy, D.F., and Tindall, B.A. (eds) *The study of play: Problems and prospects*, Leisure Press, New York, pp. 208–215.

Snow, C. and Moje, E. (2010) 'Why is everyone talking about adolescent literacy?', *Phi Delta Kappan*, vol. 91, no. 6, pp. 66–69.

Strachan, S.L. (2014/2015) 'Expanding the Range of Text Types Used in the Primary Grades', *Reading Teacher*, vol. 68, no. 4, pp. 303–311.

Thiel, J.J. (2015) '"Bumblebee's in trouble!" Embodied literacies during imaginative super-hero play', *Language Arts*, vol. 93, no. 1, pp. 38–49.

Wager, A. and Perry, M. (2015) 'Resisting the script: An experiment in assuming embodiment in literacy education' in Enriquez, G., Johnson, E., Kontovourki, S., and Mallozzi, C.A. (eds) *Literacies, learning, and the body: Putting theory and research into pedagogical practice*, Routledge, New York, pp. 252–268.

Whitney, A., Blau, S., Bright, A., Cabe, R., Dewar, T., Levin, J., Macias, R. and Rogers, P. (2008) 'Beyond strategies: Teacher practice, writing process, and the influence of inquiry', *English Education*, vol. 40, no. 3, pp. 201–230.

Witmer, S.E. (2014) 'Using assessment to improve early elementary students' knowledge and skills for comprehending informational text', *Journal of Applied School Psychology*, vol. 30, no. 3, pp. 223–253.

Wohlwend, K.E. (2009) 'Damsels in discourse: Girls consuming and producing identity texts through Disney princess play', *Reading Research Quarterly*, vol. 44, no. 1, pp. 57–83.

Wohlwend, K.E. (2011) *Playing their way into literacies: Reading, writing, and belonging in the early childhood classroom.* Teachers College Press, New York.

12

TAUGHT BY BITTER EXPERIENCE

A timescales analysis of Amalie's development of writer identity

Nikolaj Elf

Introduction

The development of students' writer identities is always unique and at the same time socially and culturally typified. This study explores an adolescent Danish student's development of writer identity. More specifically, it is a case study of Amalie's development of writer identity during four years in the context of Danish secondary and upper-secondary education.

I got to know Amalie at the age of 15 through the large-scale longitudinal research project Writing to Learn, Learning to Write (hereafter WLLW). Within WLLW we take as a point of departure that the technological development in communication has altered the nature and practice of writing and brought with it a dramatic increase in the spread and significance of writing (Christensen et al., 2014; Krogh et al., 2015). This calls for more knowledge on what this means for the individual in the context of a learner biography and how the challenge is met at subject and educational levels (Krogh, forthcoming). The purpose of WLLW is to explore, in qualitative ways, how students learn subjects through writing and learn writing through subjects.

The present study reflects this research interest as it draws on ethnographic data collected from 2009–13. More specifically, I followed Amalie from her last year in the so-called Folkeskolen, a compulsory school system in Denmark that takes 10 years, and further on in the transition to the upper-secondary education system, the education programme called htx, which is a three-year higher technical education programme that prepares students for further education at university, technical engineering or college levels. In the course of the four years – with extensive field-work, including continuous participant observation of Amalie writing at school, a collection of (in principle) all writing prompts for assignments in htx, all her written assignments, all feedback she received on the assignments, and ongoing interviews – it was quite easy to observe that Amalie made some rather dramatic turns in terms of writer identification. How and why these turns occur is what I will explore in detail in this chapter.

Now, what is meant, in writing research, by 'development of writer identity' is contested. The broader purpose of the chapter is to elaborate on this question, theoretically and empirically analytically. In the theoretical section that follows, four claims of writer development are outlined based on a sociocultural and social semiotic approach. These lead to a heuristic model and a tool for analysing writer development as a sociocultural and textual practice in school.

The empirical analysis finds that Amalie was 'taught by bitter experience' to write, as she puts it in an interview at the end of htx. She makes some rather dramatic turns in terms of writer identification, from 'loving' writing in science in Folkeskolen to 'hating it' in htx. However, we also find signs, at the end of her upper-secondary career, of Amalie restoring her old love through the writing of and reflection upon an interdisciplinary writing project – a so-called *Study Line Project* (SLP) – that includes social science and science. This finding suggests that we, as researchers, should be careful not to make too definitive conclusions on students' developments of writer identity. Findings also suggest that teachers and students – including Amalie – should be careful not to do this. Identities are, indeed, dynamic and susceptible to change.

Theoretical framework

The study positions itself within a sociocultural and social semiotic approach to literacy and learning (Prior, 2006). We know from a sociocultural approach to literacy research that it is crucial to acknowledge contextual features of literacy which co-shape writing in 'ideological' ways (Street, 1984, p. 7). Consequently, a sociocultural perspective emphasises that learning occurs through participation and use of mediating tools in a situated community (Gee and Green, 1998).

Sociocultural and social semiotic theory devotes considerable attention to an analysis of literacy practices, i.e. writing as a social practice (Barton, 1994). In a school's social practices, mediating tools such as learning resources and writing are central to a student's learning (Kress, 1997). A sociocultural perspective gives explanatory power to help analyse how these tools are employed in literacy practices. This leads to a first claim that informs the study: *learning literacy over time may be understood as a change in the observed action in the use of mediating tools among those participating in the community.*

In recent decades we have observed a shift in literacy research from a focus on text production to a focus on the individual writer and how and why (s)he writes (Lillis, 2013). Roz Ivanič's research has played an important role in this shift. As she argues, writer identity can be identified through the analysis of four interwoven aspects: 1) how a student constructs writer identity as an 'autobiographical self', 2) how she constructs through concrete writing a 'discoursal self' and a 3) 'self-as-author', and how her writing is framed by 4) 'prototypical possibilities of selfhood' embedded in the writing context (Ivanič, 1998, p. 23ff). Ivanič later argued that instead of using the noun 'identity', it is perhaps more appropriate to use 'identification', as a verb, stressing the ongoing contextualised *process* of identity building (Ivanič, 2006, p. 7). This leads to a second claim that informs the study: *writing must be understood in relation to processes of identification.*

Analysing writing within a social semiotic perspective requires an understanding of how signs and signage as material elements are assembled in students' texts and resources for learning. Semiotic and material resources are termed modalities within social semiotics (Kress, 2010). Resources such as verbal writing, use of pictures and diagrams represent possible resources for communication and learning. In school all such modalities are shaped through and within disciplinary literacy practices (Mojé, 2008). This leads to a third claim: *disciplinary, subject-related writing must be understood from a multimodal perspective.*

The final claim relates to the fact that the present longitudinal study explores writer development over an extended period of time. As Rogers' (2010) review of US research on longitudinal studies of student writer development revealed, such studies struggle with the basic question: how do we analytically frame a longitudinal analysis of writer development? I will argue that developments of writer identification could be analysed in meaningful ways within a timescales analytical framework (Burgess and Ivanič, 2010; Lemke, 2000). Such a framework – which will be further elaborated on in the next section – distinguishes, and at the same time explores relations between, a student's writing and identification processes on different timescales. As Burgess and Ivanič explain, 'all written texts are heterochronous artifacts because they are written in relatively short-term events but have the capacity to persist on longer timescales' (2010, p. 233). Furthermore, they link the heterochronous nature of written texts with the *coordination* of identification processes:

> We agree with Lemke that writing contributes to identity formation in that it enables us to coordinate our identities across different interactions and activities (Lemke, 2000). In other words, due to their capacity to endure over time, written texts are able to coordinate events (including acts of writing and reading) that occur at different points in time. However, we argue that in producing texts, writers also coordinate processes (of identification) that unfold over multiple timescales.
>
> *(Burgess and Ivanič, 2010, p. 234)*

This leads to the fourth claim: *student writers coordinate writing and identification processes that unfold on many timescales in contexts inside and outside school.*

These claims imply that processes of coordination develop, and should be studied, in non-linear, heterochronous ways. For concrete timescales analysis of a student's identity development, both Burgess and Ivanič (2010) and Lemke (2000) suggest that it should be narrowed down in pragmatic ways and could include three dimensions: a microgenetic timescale (minutes, hours, days), a mesolevel timescale (weeks, months, years) and a sociocultural timescale (decades, centuries).

The next two sections further elaborate on how a concrete timescales analysis of student writer identification could be developed, suggesting a heuristic model for analysing student writing as social practice and a tool for the analysis of Amalie's specific writing across four years.

Framing the analysis of Amalie's writer development

Figure 12.1 (below) depicts a model developed in WLLW (Krogh et al., 2015) that represents the basic entities and relations that co-shape a student's writer development within a school context.

The minimal unit of analysis of the model is the 'writing event' placed in the centre. The writing event is defined as *any event within which the student writes something in a school-related context* (both at school and at home or elsewhere). The writing event, we assume, is informed by the student's writer identification, which is inferable through analysis of student writing within social practice. Moreover, the model specifies, in greater detail, the social practices that co-shape writing events over time. If one looks at the triad's three corners, we suggest that the writing event at the same time actualises and is moderated by three domains, 'SCHOOL', 'SUBJECT' and 'YOUTH'. These domains, which we argue operate on a socio-cultural timescale, are related to contexts outside school, and at the same time they contextualise, and are linked in dynamic ways, with three types of writing cultures that contextualise writing events.

The triad's three sides indicate that the three domains are balanced in a specific school setting by three types of writing culture, 'Local school . . . ', 'Instructionally

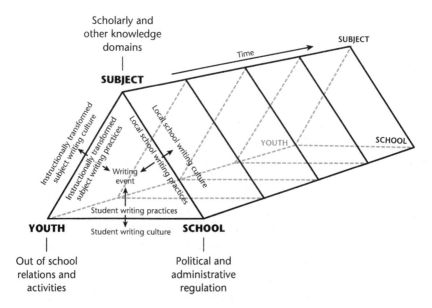

FIGURE 12.1 Model for analysing writer development as a social practice in school

transformed . . . ' and 'Student writing culture'. The model further suggests – moving towards its centre – that these three types of cultures are related to three types of writing practices, i.e. repeated patterns of how student writing is regulated, respectively, within a 'local school writing practice' (e.g. norms of writing inferred from school tutorials on how to write assignments), an 'instructionally transformed writing practice' (e.g. norms inferred from writing recipes found within a subject, such as a recipe for reports in science) and a 'student writing practice' (such as students' shared understandings of how one goes about writing a report in science).

As can be seen in the model, arrows point from 'cultures' and 'practices' towards writing events, suggesting that cultures and practices shape and to some extent exercise hegemonic dominance over events. However, arrows also point the other way around, reminding us of the basic Bakhtinian point that utterances are always embedded in socially and culturally typified practices (or 'genres'), but also that practices and cultures are in dialogue with and changeable through utterances (Bakhtin, 1986).

As a final point, there is a 'time' perspective installed in the model (the long diagonal arrow), indicating, in a somewhat mechanical way, that a student's writing events develop, in multiple and complex ways, over time. Consequently, student writer identification also develops in similar ways over time. This implies that writer development occurs through writing events that operate on a microgenetic timescale (cf. above), taking place here and now, and that these events are in dialogue with writing practices and cultures operating on a mesolevel timescale, which are, again, linked with the domains of SCHOOL, YOUTH and SUBJECT operating on a sociocultural timescale. From a student perspective, I further argue that such dialogue is coordinated by the student and her production of texts on an ontogenetic timescale (Wertsch, 1993; Vygotsky, 1986) shaped by the mind of the student and her meaning-making processes taking place in places and spaces inside and outside school in an ongoing construction of writer identification. In other words, coordination takes place in the interior domain of ontogenesis, which is in complex dialogue with the three other exterior timescales described above. The question is: how can we analyse this empirically?

How to analyse Amalie's writer development within constellations of literacy events

Basic advice from sociocultural timescales analysis, as suggested above, is that one cannot speak of a student in general autonomous ways; specificity is needed. Consequently, in the Amalie case, we should ask: who is Amalie as a writer within a specific (Danish) educational context, what characterises her autobiographical self, how does she write and how does she reflect as a writer in the course of student life, and, more specifically, in the transition from Folkeskolen to htx? Such questions are addressed in the mesolevel analyses that follow.

However, in a microgenetic analysis of how writing events, including assignments, position – and are being positioned by – Amalie, and in a broader timescales analysis of how writing on microgenetic levels is related to, or coordinated by,

writing on mesolevel and sociocultural timescales, we need a more text-based analytical framework than the model for analysing writing events as social practice
offers (Figure 12.1). Thus, in WLLW (Krogh et al., 2015), we have developed
a tool for analysing what we refer to as *constellations of literacy events*, or simply 'a
constellation' (Table 12.1). The tool represents the basic units and analytical perspectives for analysing a student's meaning making within a writing event. How
to use the tool is illustrated with the case of Amalie writing the SLP in Year 3 htx.

TABLE 12.1 Tool for analysing constellations of literacy events; exemplified with Amalie
writing the Study Line Project (SLP)

Analytical unit	*Analytical perspective*		
	Viewed as text	*Viewed as discourse*	*Viewed as social act*
Assignment	One page entitled Study Line Project with a detailed writing prompt	Prompts exploratory writing on 'Nuclear energy in Denmark' that integrates Physics and Social Science (inter)disciplinary discourse	Handed out in Year 3; reflects mandatory school goals of developing student writing competence and personal development; teacher-student guidance focusing on Amalie's interests
Student text(s)	Three versions of the text (vers. 1: 4 pages, 8340 signs with space; vers. 2, 18 pages, 33947 s.w.s.; vers. 3: 18 pages, 39873 s.w.s. + ill.)	Integrates disciplinary discourse in increasingly interdisciplinary and explorative ways from Versions 1–3	Student develops individually, through reading and writing and emotional ups and downs, a mediated understanding of the theme and question prompted by the assignment
Teacher feedback	Grade: 10 (equivalent: B)	Quantified evaluative discourse	Evaluation exercising power-related recognition related to final exam results
Interview(s) with student	Several interviews, before, during and after writing student text	Reflects writing process and outcome; positions herself in different ways	Interprets how writing event is related to and has impact on writer identification on different timescales

As indicated in the far left column, a constellation comprises four empirical units, well known to all in school: an *assignment* written by teachers, the *student text(s)*, i.e. the writing of the assignment (which may include several texts), the *teacher feedback* and *student reflections* on writing the assignment, which is catalysed, in the case of this study, by 'talk around text' (Lillis, 2009, p. 169) with me as participant observer. Along the horizontal axis of this table are listed the analytical viewpoints that we can bring to bear on constellations of literacy events. Each analytical unit can be viewed as different types of instantiations of the analytical unit: as text; as discourse; and as social act.

When taking the *text* view, we study aspects of textual structure and style as these are initiated by the assignment, realised in the student text, subsequently commented upon by the teacher and eventually discussed by the student participant in interviews (examples of this and the two other 'views' will be offered later in analyses). The privileged interest is in the student's selection of linguistic and other multimodal resources viewed as a response to the framing requirements of the assignment, and as an expression of intentions and patterns of identification with these. Through this textual analysis we also attempt to pin down what Ivanič terms the writer's discoursal self. According to Ivanič, this aspect of self 'is concerned with the writer's "voice" in the sense of the way they want to sound, rather than in the sense of the stance they are taking' (Ivanič, 1998, p. 25). One should add, from a multimodal perspective, that a discoursal self is constructed not only in the way students want to sound, but also in the way they want to *look*, aesthetically.

When the analytical unit is viewed as *discourse* (cf. Table 12.1, third column), we focus on a student's positioning of themself in relation to disciplinary discourse. We are interested in the student's ways of handling knowledge and in their construction of writer authority in this respect. This dimension may pin down, to some degree, what Ivanič terms self as author. Notably, the self as author is the most complex of Ivanič's concepts of writer identity. She explains that it 'concerns the writer's "voice" in the sense of the writer's position, opinions and beliefs: a different sense of "voice" from the one associated with the discoursal self' (op.cit., p. 26).

Taking the social act view, we focus on a student's *use* of and *reflection* on writing in the social and cultural context as this can be traced in their texts, observations and interviews. Important questions are: how do students negotiate the local school culture, the instructionally transformed culture, and student writing culture available in the school setting, and how do they position themselves in relation to their addressee(s)? Answering such questions pins down, at least to some extent, Ivanič's concept of autobiographical self (op.cit., p. 24f).

In the three analytical sections that follow, the analytical framework will be applied. I will analyse Amalie's writer development in the following contexts: i) Amalie's writer development in Folkeskolen; ii) Amalie as a science writer in the first half of htx; and iii) Amalie's coordinated development of writer identification through the SLP in the second half of htx. Due to limits of space, only a few authentic text examples are offered below; however, all examples referred to can be downloaded from the project website www.sdu.dk/wllw.

Timescales analysis I: Amalie's writer development in Folkeskolen

As I met 15-year-old Amalie in Folkeskolen's last year (termed Grade 9 in Denmark), she identified strongly with the science subject called Physics/Chemistry. In general, Amalie was proficient in all subjects in Folkeskolen. But as she states in an interview, she 'loved' writing science reports (interview 13/02/2010), and she was good at it. When asked in the interview, 'what has been the best writing experience?', she highlights the writing of a report on acid in Grade 8. Let us analyse how this writer identification is constructed on a microgenetic timescale through an analysis of the acid report.

Viewing the acid report as *text*, the report is dominated by expository writing acts, of objective, non-personal style, verbal communication and a bit of visual communication using lab icons. For example, the first line of her answer to the first question, 'what is acid?', is: 'Acid is a substance that belongs to the category "acid substances"'. In her answer to the second question, '[w]here is acid found in everyday life?', she states, among other things, that 'sulphuric acid is mainly used for industrial purposes', adding a black-and-white 'Danger Acid' icon next to the text. In brief, she attempts to sound and look like a recognisable scientific self in writing.

The text viewed as *discourse* reveals that Amalie accommodates to, i.e. aligns with, the disciplinary discourse of the writing prompt and, more generally, the subject as represented in learning resources handed out in class. It should be noted, though, that she has difficulties related to the construction of explanations in science discourse. Her continued answer to the first question offers an example, as she states in somewhat illogical Danish language, which is difficult to translate into English:[1] 'By finding out whether the substance is acid, base or neutral, you can put a drop on a pH litmus paper'. One would think that the causal relation works the other way around. Still, what dominates in the text as a whole is the construction of an exploring, quasi researching self as author, focused on the subject *matter*, not herself as an individual with personal interests.

This is backed by the analysis of the report viewed as *social act* and Amalie's construction of an autobiographical self. Unlike others in class, she answers all questions in the assignment in systematic and elaborated ways, drawing on, and quoting, the text book offered by the teacher. She stores this and other assignments in binders, which is an act that relates to Amalie being self-aware of the strategic function of writing reports that could be useful for her later development in education, not the least her planned future in the higher technical examination education system (htx). Interviews and observations from Grade 9 throughout the year back this interpretation. Amalie positions herself, and is being positioned at school, particularly by her physics/chemistry teacher, as a serious and ambitious nerd-like student, who wants and should be allowed to work individually, thus realising her writer-researcher-like aspirations. So, at the end of Folkeskolen Amalie identifies with the instructionally transformed science writing practice. This developed science writer identity defines her writer identity, as if it were a stable entity.

Timescales analysis II: Amalie as a science writer in the first half of htx

Such a writer identity makes it understandable that she chooses htx as her next education programme at the upper-secondary education level. However, as Amalie moves into htx, including two specialised subjects, Physics and Science, taught by teachers educated at university level, her strong identification with science alters. In the course of two years' experience of being taught and learning chemistry and physics, including writing a number of assignments and getting feedback on them, she slowly, but steadily, alters her identification with science subjects, eventually stating explicitly at the end of Year 2: 'I hate Chemistry' (interview, 27/03/2012).

One important reason for making such a dramatic turn suggested in the data is that Amalie continues to experience an epistemological challenge in writing scientific explanations, and more generally, to theorise within the science subjects. One example is the writing of a chemistry report, 'Changing a Homogeneous Equipoise', in first half of Year 2 of htx. In the writing prompt, the teacher stresses the importance of being able to master explanations in chemistry. The teacher also positions the students in class as writers who are expected to, as the last line says, 'write the way a report should be written'. This line refers intertextually, I learned from fieldwork, to a strict genre norm found in the instructionally transformed science writing practices, which students were taught – and offered recipes for – at the beginning of the first year of htx. In other words, a rigorist formulaic writing practice is expected, as is often seen in science writing, and like many other science students around the world, Amalie has trouble dealing with this (e.g. Wellington and Osborne, 2001).

Amalie hands in a text that looks almost the same as the writing prompt. Some questions are answered, many are not. Viewed as a social act, she does not comply fully with expectations. Using a digital Learning Management System (LMS), the teacher offers individual feedback to Amalie. The student text is assessed with a '7' (C). In the comments, the teacher acknowledges, to some extent, Amalie's ability to explain. But he also points out that there are some parts she does not explain at all. As an additional type of feedback, the teacher offers a several-pages-long 'standard response', as he puts it, for all students in class, in which he demonstrates, in all aspects of content and form, how questions are answered, and more generally how a report should be written. In my interpretation, the teacher spells out for students how one should represent disciplinary knowledge as a kind of 'repositories of content knowledge', instead of constructing it as a more open-ended mediating tool for learning disciplinary literacy among students (Mojé, 2008, p. 100). Fieldwork found that this is a repeated instructionally transformed writing practice within science subjects at Amalie's school and at other schools that were part of the WLLW project.

In interviews, Amalie explained that she had a hard time understanding and identifying with this kind of instructionally transformed writing, feedback and, generally speaking, positioning practices that the htx chemistry subject establishes.

On a broader mesolevel timescale, I found that Amalie's problem of constructing science explanations observed in Folkeskolen carries on and is exacerbated in upper-secondary education chemistry writing events. In brief, Amalie is positioned by the chemistry teacher as a student with a voice that does not quite align with the acknowledged subject discourse. Consequently, Amalie has severe trouble learning to write in the science subjects. As she concludes in an interview as early as the end of Year 1, anticipating future writer development: 'Chemistry is like . . . you mix two liquids that look like water, and then it becomes a fire, but it does not?! Things like that, I cannot really relate to that' (16/06/2011). Similar reflections could be inferred from analysing Amalie's writing in physics, and how she comments on that in interviews.

Amalie not being able to 'relate' to science eventually leads to a more permanent non-identification with writing in the specialised science subjects. This is reflected as an erosion of writer identity. From the middle of second-year htx, she no longer considers herself 'a science girl'. There is no writer *identity*, as a noun. Rather, Amalie starts orientating herself, in probing ways, towards new possibilities of writer *identification*, as a verb. Mesolevel analyses based on observations and interviews suggest that Amalie does in fact start identifying (with) new contexts of disciplinary writing. In particular, Amalie made a turn, in the same period, towards becoming a social science writer, or 'even a humanitarian', as she put it self-ironically in interviews (see later). In part, this development was related to student writing practices she was involved in both at school and outside school. One important aspect that should be highlighted is that Amalie became interested in politics, partly due to the social science subject she took at a high level. She became a member of a political party and of the school's student council, and, in the third year, even the leader of the council. Another important aspect, which she was quite open about in class, was that her father and mother are divorced and that her father became mentally ill and had to go to the hospital. This rather personal event made her reflect a lot on psychological issues. This was nurtured, to some extent, by the optional school subject psychology, which she had chosen to follow, and which gave her assignments on psychological issues about which she liked writing. So, through such subtle dynamic developments in practices and activities outside and inside school and school subjects related to writing as a social act, Amalie's writer identification did indeed take on new trajectories of writing and learning.

Timescales analysis III: Amalie's development of writer identification through the SLP in the second half of htx

Negating a science writing identity, however, is not the whole story of Amalie's coordination of writer identification during htx. This becomes clear if we move one year forward to the third and last year of htx and direct our attention towards the SLP writing event, and more specifically the microgenetic timescale of the seven days during which Amalie wrote the SLP assignment. Let's analyse the event as a constellation of literacy events:

The assignment. Viewed as social act, the SLP assignment that Amalie received on 11/01/2013 is a mandatory examination project in the third and final year of htx and as such an aspect of the local school writing culture. The broader purpose of the writing practice, as stated in national curriculum documents, is to develop student writing competence and personal development (termed Bildung in a Nordic context, cf. Gundem, 2000). Considering the instructionally transformed writing practice, it is a multi-subject, interdisciplinary and explorative project. The student is asked to suggest a topic and problem that requires the integration of two subjects. The two subjects must be so-called high-level 'A' subjects (taken for three years in htx). Amalie started thinking about her topic one year in advance, that is, in the middle of Year 2. More specifically, she wondered whether she should write a SLP about 'nuclear power in Denmark'. The backdrop is that an anti-nuclear power political movement in the 1970s led to the rejection of nuclear power in Denmark, which was an issue that had been taught and referred to in her social science class. Amalie had four A subjects, including Danish (L1), maths, social science and physics, and she eventually decided to stick with the suggested topic and integrate social science and physics. Reflecting a distinction required in the setup of the assignment, Amalie chose social science as the 'primary subject' and physics as the 'secondary subject'. In the primary subject, she was expected to draw on resources and knowledge *beyond* what she had been taught in social science; in the secondary subject she was only expected to draw on resources already taught *within* physics.

As part of the writing practice, formal guidance on the SLP started in Year 3 almost half a year before the actual week of writing. It included individual talks with teachers, process-oriented work, drafts and formative feedback, with which Amalie was very content. The guidance finally led to the writing prompt formulated solely by the teachers and handed to the student on a Friday morning in January. Students then had one week to write the assignment. The final text is expected to have a length of approximately 20 pages. After a few weeks, the student receives a grade as feedback (and nothing else). The grade affects final examination results.

From a textual view, the assignment handed out to Amalie is a one-page official-looking document, which included school logo, writing prompt and evaluation criteria. The prompt first introduces the topic of nuclear power in Denmark and asks why the debate has become so one-sided. It then specifies five tasks, written in imperative form: 1) 'account for what is meant by discourse analysis'; 2) 'account for the way nuclear power functions focusing on nuclear radiation'; 3) 'offer an analysis of the factors that have led to the current Danish discourse on nuclear power'; 4) 'discuss the effect of the discourse on dividing lines in Danish politics'; and 5) 'evaluate how Danish discourse on nuclear power distinguishes itself from international discourse'. Viewed as discourse, it is quite clear that the assignment prompts explorative writing and both disciplinary and interdisciplinary writing for answering the question.

Summing up on the assignment viewed as social act, text and discourse, this is clearly a challenging and important writing assignment within the local school and instructionally transformed writing practices, and it is also a writing practice that is taken seriously in the student writing practices, including by Amalie as an individual writer. The exciting question is: what happened when she started writing the assignment?

Student texts. During the seven-day period of writing, Amalie sent me the assignment and two draft versions, *Version 1* Monday 14 January, and *Version 2* Thursday 17 January At the end of the week, on Friday morning, I conducted an interview with Amalie a few hours before she handed in the final version of the assignment, *Version 3*. Comparing the three versions as *texts* makes it clear that Amalie develops her writing in interesting ways, both quantitatively and qualitatively, and at the same time develops writer identification. Among many other aspects, I note that Version 1 is a four-page document, which comprises note-like incomplete sentences. In Version 2, it expands to 18 pages, with complete paragraphs and sentences. Version 3 is further expanded and refined. All three versions basically reproduce the prompt's 1–5 scaffolding of questions as subtitles; however, Version 3 transforms the prompt's imperative form into a nominalisation form, as seen in Figure 12.2.

The subtitle reads, in my translation: '2. Account: How does nuclear power function with a particular focus on radiation?' The picture is cited from http://www.freeinfosociety.com/images/science/nuclearenergy1.jpg, a note on page 6 explains. All three versions include a large number of academic notes, as indicated in Figure 12.2; notes refer to learning resources on a high academic level both in social science and physics, way beyond what were made available to her in prior teaching. Nowhere in the three versions is 'I' used as a personal pronominal. The style is depersonalised and objective, in an even more radical way than found in the acid report. From a multimodal perspective it is interesting to observe that Version 3 includes illustrations, as demonstrated in Figure 12.2, and verbal commenting on illustrations. This is *not* found in Versions 1 and 2. Amalie explains

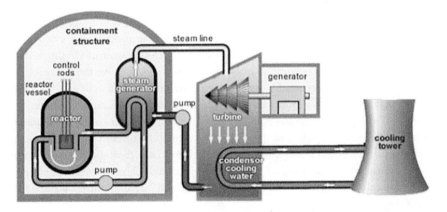

FIGURE 12.2 Excerpt from Amalie's SLP, final version (Version 3), bottom of page 5 of 18

in the Friday morning interview that she started reflecting on Thursday that she should probably add some 'hardcore physics' (int. 18/01/2013) in her disciplinary account of nuclear power. She then adds the picture and explains it in verbal writing. So, clearly, from a textual view, Amalie develops and attempts to construct a discoursal self that looks and sounds like an academic.

The developments in the student texts' multimodal resources and construction of discoursal self are, of course, related to the development of self as author. If we view the three versions as a development of self as author, Amalie increasingly develops a disciplinary and also interdisciplinary explorative discourse that is in dialogue with and transforms the prompt's discourse. One good example of Amalie constructing disciplinary discourse is found in the already cited Section 2 in Version 3 with its visual illustration of nuclear power (Figure 12.2), and also, later in that section, the use of *formulas* and *symbols* from physics (which are not found in Version 2). In the Friday morning interview she reflects that she has now managed to develop an interdisciplinary discussion – which is indeed found in Version 3.

Such reflections and writing processes reflect that the student texts must also be analysed as a social act. The student texts and the Friday morning interview document that during these seven days, Amalie intensely reads and writes, primarily on her own, with the aim of submitting a piece of work that addresses the SLP writing practice, and more specifically a school- and subject-related addressee in the shape of teachers who are going to evaluate her. While she does that, she also addresses her own writing process and reflects about herself as writer, i.e. how writing allows her to learn about life/the world, as explored through subjects, and about herself. For example, she starts discussing, both in Version 3 and in the Friday interview, whether it is a good idea that there is no nuclear power in Denmark. She starts doubting this *matter*. She also reflects on her writer identification in a broader mesolevel perspective, i.e. her autobiographical self, as suggested in this excerpt from the Friday morning interview:

> Interviewer/Nikolaj: Why is it that you have made a turn from physics disciplinarity to social science disciplinarity as primary?
>
> Amalie: Hmm, well, I am not sure, I guess I have become more humanistic during my htx days, my old htx days – however, there was a reason why I started at a science gymnasium in the first place, and there also has been one – can you imagine, I even chose a science line, with physics and math as specialised subjects?! how stupid that was, now that I think about it, ha! but there had always been a reason for that – but then again not – I guess I found out I was a glowing humanist, when it comes to, well, when it comes to it all – it is psychology and Danish as subjects, partly technology history and social science that interests me a lot now – in Folkeskolen it was physics and math – but you know, yes – taught by bitter experience.

(18/01/2013)

In the quote, Amalie confirms that she has stopped identifying strongly with science subjects. *Not* to identify with writing within these subjects is something she has been 'taught by bitter experience', as she expresses it. On the other hand, she also utters a sort of reminiscence of identification with science. We note that even though Amalie rejects identifying with science subjects in general, she does negotiate with herself – back and forth, using different tenses and, hence, constructing different timescales, e.g. in the formulation: 'there was a reason why I started at a science gymnasium in the first place, and there also has been one' – whether she *was* or still *is* somehow a science girl, and not simply a 'glowing humanitarian'. That she expresses such doubts, I will argue, is related to the context of the interview, namely the writing of the SLP, which turns out to be a good learning experience.

This interpretation is backed by an analytical focus on the *feedback* she gets, and how she talks about the SLP in later *interviews*. Amalie receives a high grade (10 = B) for the SLP. In the final interview at the end of Year 3, she comments on the grade, and on the SLP and her overall development as a writer. I ask her the same question I asked at the end of secondary education:

Nikolaj: What was your best writing experience?

Amalie: I liked the SLP, but that one also drove me, like I always do, it drove me completely down, and I say, no, this won't work, and you'll flunk and blablablabla, and then things still work out well after – it was not until I got the grade that I thought the SLP was a good writing experience, I mean, I thought it was interesting, *that* I wish to say, I think it was very interesting, but I was also, like, hell, this can go either way, and then I would have felt that it was a total waste of work having worked my butt for so long – but hey, I guess it is a good writing experience, and *everything* that leads to a good result is, in my view, a good experience, that's, you know – *that's* how I am, results – it's a lot about results, and it's what's on the examination diploma, and that's okay – but perhaps I ought to reflect more on that.

(19/06/2013)

This is a radical comment, in several ways. First of all, Amalie confirms that the SLP was a good writing experience. This is an impression that lasts, on a mesolevel timescale, from January to June. On the other hand, she argues that whether something is a positive writing experience with which she identifies depends on the social recognition of her writing, which is related to different timescales and contexts. Her emotionally oriented inner sense of the writing process during and immediately after the SLP is somehow not to be trusted. It does not really count, in Amalie's view. What counts is what those external evaluators of writing in power acknowledge; the quote certainly backs the claim that writer development is shaped by social practices! Finally, Amalie leaves us with an open question on her writer identity/identification: Is she, or is she not, a science, social science and/or humanitarian writer?

Conclusions and implications: writer identification found, lost and re-found

This chapter has explored how an adolescent student develops writer identity in school. The meso- and microlevel timescales analyses of Amalie's writer development find that her writer identification alters quite dramatically in the transition from secondary to upper-secondary education. Amalie's strong identification with science writing in secondary education is, to some extent, dismantled in upper-secondary education, shaped as it is by local writing events and writing practices that she participates in. Amalie is taught by bitter experience to leave behind a strong identification with science writing. Instead, she searches, and finds, alternative disciplinary contexts in upper-secondary education that offer possibilities for selfhood; that is, positive writer identification.

As highlighted in the analysis of constellations of literacy events, the explorative, interdisciplinary SLP writing event makes it possible for her to re-integrate her prior identification with science writing. This writing event becomes a 'key incident' (Erickson, 1977) for the ethnographically based analysis of writer development in school. Both the SLP and the acid report are such key incidents of writing that function as a mediating tool (Wertsch, 1993) for Amalie in her ongoing process, on an ontogenetic timescale, of identifying or not identifying herself as a science and/or social science/humanistic writer – or more generally, in the process of developing identity in adolescence. The acid report and SLP are also *linked* key incidents in the trajectory of Amalie's trajectory of writing to learn, and learning to write. As Burgess and Ivanič put it (2010), written texts are able to coordinate events that occur at different points in time due to their capacity to endure over time, and in that process they enable a student's identity formation. This is precisely how these two writing events function for Amalie in her identity formation during four years.

As Burgess and Burgess noted, however, writers too have agency that allows them to coordinate processes of identification that unfold over multiple timescales. Considering this point, one could argue that the Amalie-initiated prioritisations found in the SLP assignment reflect, in reciprocal ways, the turn in writer identification that Amalie develops negatively in the two science subjects. The choice Amalie makes on the early mesolevel timescale of the SLP allows her to position herself in subtle ways that balance and coordinate her *increasing* identification with (writing in) social science with her *decreasing*, 'lost' identification with science. As Kress (2010) has pointed out, *choice* – related to existential insecurity or agency through communicative participation and connection – is a fundamental means among adolescent students in contemporary education for expressing subjectivity. They can choose – and they do. As in the case of Amalie.

Considering implications on the level of writing research, the Amalie case backs a general timescales approach towards writer development and offers new methodological, analytical and empirical insights into how to understand such developments in practice. Findings suggest that teachers and students – including Amalie – should be careful not to make too definitive conclusions on student developments of writer identity. Findings also suggest that we, as researchers, should be careful in doing that. It is tempting to ask what might have occurred to have prevented Amalie having the 'bitter experience' in respect of her writing in science and her not quite mastering the 'explanatory function'. A research-based answer, reflecting Amalie's own interpretation, would be to offer more formative feedback on student texts (Applebee and Langer, 2013). Of course, this is easier said than done. On a local school level, it would require a change in the instructionally transformed writing culture of the science subjects – and, I would argue, more broadly in Danish upper-secondary education. Researchers found within the emerging paradigm of disciplinary literacy (see, for example, Mojé, 2008) would argue that it also requires a deeper rethinking of teaching subjects at school. We would have to move from viewing subjects as repositories of knowledge content which should be reproduced by students towards a view on subjects as social practices that are constructed, communicated and learned in situated contexts. As Mojé puts it, '[t]he work of reconceptualising will require that teachers, teacher educators, and researchers alike recognise the role of three central aspects of disciplinary learning: discourses and practices, identities and identifications, and knowledge' (p. 100). Such an approach resonates well with the claims and models developed within the WLLW project and used here for the analysis of Amalie's writer development.

Note

1 Note on translation: Translating and, in the case of speech, transcribing Danish into English is challenging and a matter of interpretation. In translations, I have attempted to represent and communicate the unique mix of content, form and style, which characterises any utterance. In transcriptions, I represent the flow of utterances using normal orthography for words, two symbols for indicating pauses ([,] = short break; [–] = longer break), italics for emphasis, and question and exclamation marks.

References

Applebee, A. N. and Langer, J. A. (2013) *Writing Instruction That Works: Proven Methods for Middle and High School Classrooms*, New York, Teachers College Press.

Bakhtin, M. M. (1986) *Speech Genres and Other Late Essays*, Austin, TX, Austin University Press.

Barton, D. (1994) *Literacy: An Introduction to the Ecology of Written Language*, Oxford, Blackwell.

Burgess, A. and Ivanič, R. (2010) 'Writing and being written: Issues of identity across timescales', *Written Communication*, vol. 27, pp. 228–255.

Christensen, T. S., Elf, N. F. and Krogh, E. (2014) *Skrivekulturer i folkeskolens niende klasse*, Odense, Denmark, Syddansk Universitetsforlag.

Erickson, F. (1977) 'Some approaches to inquiry in school-community ethnography', *Anthropology & Education Quarterly*, vol. 8, pp. 58–69.

Gee, J. P. and Green, J. (1998) 'Discourse Analysis, learning, and social practice: A methodological study', *Review of Educational Research*, vol. 23, pp. 119–169.

Gundem, B. (2000) 'Understanding European didactics', in Peretz, B. M., Brown, S. and Moon, B. (eds) *Routledge International Companion to Education*, pp. 235–262, London, Routledge.

Ivanič, R. (1998) *Writing and Identity: The Discoursal Construction of Identity in Academic Writing*, Amsterdam/Philadelphia, John Benjamins Publishing Company.

Ivanič, R. (2006) 'Language, learning and identification', in Kiely, R., Rea-Dickens, P., Woodfield, H. and Clibbon, G. (eds) *Language, Culture and Identity in Applied Linguistics*, pp. 7–29, Sheffield, Equinox.

Kress, G. (1997) *Before Writing: Rethinking Paths to Literacy*, London, Routledge.

Kress, G. (2010) *Multimodality: A Social Semiotic Approach to Contemporary Communication*, London, Routledge.

Krogh, E. (forthcoming) 'Crossing the divide between writing cultures', in Spelmanmiller, K. and Stevenson, M. (eds) *Transitions in Writing*, Leiden, Holland, Brill.

Krogh, E., Christensen, T. S. and Jakobsen, K. S. (2015) (eds) *Elevskrivere i gymnasiefag*, Odense, Denmark, Syddansk Universitetsforlag.

Lemke, J. L. (2000) 'Across the scales of time: Artifacts, activities, and meanings in ecosocial systems', *Mind, Culture, and Activity*, vol. 7, pp. 273–290.

Lillis, T. (2009) 'Bringing writers' voices to writing research: Talk around texts', in Carter, A., Lillis, T. and Parkin, S. (eds) *Why Writing Matters: Issues of Access and Identity in Writing Research and Pedagogy*, pp. 169–187, Amsterdam, Benjamins.

Lillis, T. (2013) *The Sociolinguistics of Writing*, Edinburgh, Edinburgh University Press.

Mojé E. B. (2008) 'Foregrounding the disciplines in secondary literacy teaching and learning: A call for change', *Journal of Adolescent and Adult Literacy*, vol. 52, pp. 96–107.

Prior, P. (2006) 'A sociocultural theory of writing', in Macarthur, C.A., Graham, S. and Fitzgerald, J. (eds) *Handbook of Writing Research*, pp. 54–66, New York/London, Guilford Press.

Rogers, P. (2010) 'Longitudinal studies and writing development', in Bazerman, C., Krut, R., Lunsford, K., Mcleod, S., Null, S., Rogers, P. and Stansell, A. (eds) *Traditions of Writing Research*, pp. 365–377, New York/London, Routledge.

Street, B. (1984) *Literacy in Theory and Practice*, New York, Cambridge University Press.

Vygotsky, L. (1986) *Thought and Language*, Cambridge, MA, MIT Press.

Wellington, J. and Osborne, J. (2001) *Language and Literacy in Science Education*, New York, Open University Press.

Wertsch, J. V. (1993) *Voices of the Mind: A Sociocultural Approach to Mediated Action*, Cambridge, MA, Harvard University Press.

13

WRITING REFLEXIVELY

Students and teachers shaping texts and identities

Mary Ryan

Introduction

Written language is a powerful communicative tool. It enables us to bring something into existence, to create a snapshot that we can ponder on, to which we can attend and relate to other ideas or understandings (Halliday and Hasan, 1985). Recent research in writing confirms and extends the idea that the writer is an active designer of text, shaping meanings and representing self within a social context (Ryan, 2014a; Myhill et al., 2013). Research also shows that developing students' abilities to make effective and satisfying textual decisions within specific conditions is crucial (Ryan and Kettle, 2012; Ryan, 2014b). Effective choices are contingent upon a repertoire of textual knowledges and skills, including metalinguistic and communicative knowledge, and the skills to negotiate audience, modes and medium (Ivanic, 2004; Macken-Horarik and Morgan, 2011). Students not only need to develop a deep knowledge of these repertoires, but importantly, a high level of awareness about the implications of their writing choices – both in and out of school.

Too often, school writing is abstract, depersonalised and context-reduced. Myhill (2009) warns that process writing has, in many instances, been institutionalised as a programmatic approach to writing, which assumes all students undertake the composing process in similar ways. Turvey (2007) argues that over-attention to forms and features of writing dictated by external strategies and assessment systems has led to a corresponding neglect of the importance of developing the writer's ideas and voice (Elbow, 2000) to establish a relationship with the reader. Hilton (2006) and, more recently, Ryan and Barton (2014) similarly argue that writing pedagogy, and particularly genre pedagogy, often assumes a mechanical texture and is bound by the priorities of standardised assessment and system demands. There is an urgent need to consider the ways in which we might position writers as agentic and reflexive. It is important that teachers enable young writers to weigh up both personal and structural considerations to make decisions and produce writing that is both satisfying and powerfully intentional.

In this chapter, I use Margaret Archer's (1995, 2012) critical realist theory of reflexivity to argue that the teaching of writing must account for the different ways that students manage and make decisions in their writing. Further, I suggest that teachers are highly influential in the ways in which students consider writing as a reflexive pursuit. Data from linguistically and culturally diverse primary students in Australia are used to illustrate how four distinct reflexive modalities (communicative, autonomous, meta, fractured) are evident in students' approaches to writing. These data are interpreted in relation to the ways in which teachers enable or constrain particular kinds of reflexive modalities in writing. Based on these findings, I offer recommendations for teaching writing that enable a *meta-reflexive approach* to the identity work that happens in writing. I argue that developing students' reflexive writing identities is an imperative for contemporary times, which require new forms of reflexive teaching identities to manage the complex and highly visible conditions of young people's writing development.

Performing identity through writing

Writing is a social performance: young people write to communicate, to get things done, to please others and negotiate relationships, to portray themselves in particular ways, and to influence thinking about social issues (Lillis and McKinney, 2013). Written texts carry powerful and sometimes unintended messages, and the access to networked digital technologies has seen the rise of instantaneous and impulsive written communication, akin to oral language (Maybin, 2013). In these unpredictable, participatory contexts of writing, knowledge of audience and medium and, significantly, knowledge of self have claimed a new importance (Ito et al., 2010).

School writing is assessed for its rhetorical structures, correct grammar and appropriateness for (often) hypothetical audiences. What is more difficult to assess is the identity work that happens through writing and the reasons why students make particular authorial decisions. These less visible elements of the writing process need to involve reflexive self-assessment and dialogic discussions to make them visible and open for transformation. Given that young people are prolific in their use of digital technologies and social media (Donoso and Verdoodt, 2014), it is vital that the teaching of writing in schools enables students to navigate incongruous and highly visible contexts to make writing decisions that represent self, others and things in appropriate and intended ways.

Research has shown that diversity and identity matter in writing (Athanases et al., 2013; Canagarajah, 2006; Cremin and Myhill, 2012). Linguistically and culturally diverse writers, who are proficient writers, can switch their languages, discourses and writing identities in response to contextual change. Canagarajah (2006) strongly argues that multilingual writers are not passively conditioned by their language and culture, but rather they make choices as writers for different texts and contexts. For diverse writers to have the repertoires from which to choose, and a self-awareness of the implications of writing choices in different contexts, they need to be enabled as reflexive writers.

A new approach to writing: the reflexive imperative

Margaret Archer's (1995, 2012) approach to reflexivity through realist social theory provides the conceptual tools to investigate reflexivity in diverse and/or unpredictable writing contexts. This approach, using Archer, extends the work of Flower and Hayes (1980) and others such as Sharples (1999) who theorised cognitive models of writing, acknowledging the external and internal conditions that influence writing. Archer's work provides a framework for understanding *the ways* in which individuals manage choices and make decisions in different contexts. Reflexivity involves deliberating about possible courses of action, deciding what might be feasible at this time in this writing situation and then choosing a way forward. Reflexive processes might include planning, rehearsing, reliving, mulling over, imagining, deciding, prioritising, clarifying and holding imaginary conversations (Archer, 2012). Through these reflexive processes, we mediate our subjective concerns and the objective structures that shape and are shaped by our actions. Making oneself the object of study through reflexivity is a powerful way to interrogate the decisions one makes and the ensuing consequences.

Effective individual writers are seen as active decision-makers and designers of text who mediate their *subjective considerations and agency* (interests, emotions, beliefs, creativity, priorities, language and cultural resources and capabilities) and their particular *objective circumstances* (for example, school curriculum and assessment requirements, teacher and text-type expectations, social media norms, peer relationships) to write in certain ways. Archer suggests that we have 'internal conversations' in which we reflect upon and weigh up (multiple) possible options, taking *agency and structure* into account. The causal powers of these external or *objective structures* are exercised as enablements and constraints, and even the anticipation or perception of particular enablements or constraints can serve as a deterrent or an encouragement (Archer, 2007). In this way, the writing conditions that teachers create or promote can have an enormous and differential effect on students' engagement with writing.

In contextually congruent or static conditions (such as highly structured and formulaic writing conditions in some classrooms), students have less need (and potentially less encouragement) to reflexively weigh up their options. However, in contextually incongruent or unpredictable conditions that have less formal structure and/or privacy and/or more potential for misinterpretation (such as out-of-school writing on social media sites, instant messaging, blogs or email), reflexive processes, which go beyond reflective thought to include action and *re*-action, are more important than ever in weighing up good decisions.

Different people deliberate their concerns in different ways. Archer (2012) suggests that we tend to develop and practise a particular mode of reflexivity, which may change at different times in our lives, but often stems from our experiences along the way. These modes are 1) communicative reflexive, 2) autonomous reflexive, 3) meta-reflexive and 4) fractured reflexive. For communicative reflexives, decisions need to be confirmed and completed by others before they lead to action. For example, constant checking-in with the teacher or peers about writing decisions or following the teacher's ideas and structures without injecting personal style or voice. Autonomous reflexives, on the other hand, are clear about their pathway and goal and their deliberations lead to direct action. For example, setting a writing plan and following it no matter what might develop in the process or through interactions with others. Meta-reflexives tend to critically analyse past deliberations and actions by them and others to make decisions that will best serve the common good. For example, meeting the expectations of the teacher while also serving one's own interests and priorities as a writer. Fractured reflexives, however, cannot use their deliberations to lead to purposeful action. Deliberation only serves to distress and disorient them, and they can't work out how to put things right or make effective decisions. For example, disaffected writers who are paralysed by language requirements or the perceived enormity of the task. Each of us can adopt all of these modes at some point and in some contexts, but Archer argues that we generally have a dominant mode. Understanding our mode of reflexivity is a crucial step in becoming self-aware. If teachers also understand their own and students' modes of reflexivity, they can create enabling pedagogic conditions that engender satisfying and successful writing practices for themselves and their students.

Research context and design

Student data (interviews and writing samples) from two linguistically and culturally diverse primary schools in an Australian metropolitan area are used to illustrate the four reflexive modes that were evident in students' writing in an exploratory study (see Ryan, 2014a, 2014b; Ryan and Barton, 2014 for more about this project). At both participating schools around a third of students spoke languages other than English at home and comprised 45 nationalities. The students were in Years 5–7.

I demonstrate how writers can be identified as using particular modes in their decision-making and action. I used Archer's (2012) descriptions of these modes across the life projects of generations of people as a starting point, and then applied these to writing.

Conditions of writing: enablements and constraints

For each reflexive mode (communicative, autonomous, meta-reflexive, fractured), I outline the indicators that constitute that mode, using illustrative examples of student data; I discuss conditions that may produce and/or perpetuate the mode; and I consider potential constraints for students who enact that mode. These conditions indicate that some modes are more effective than others for particular writing events. I argue that meta-reflexivity is the mode that will most enable students to negotiate variable conditions of writing and develop identities as writers with something to say.

Communicative reflexives

Communicative reflexives are 'identifiers' (Archer, 2012). In relation to writing development, these are students who have most likely had continuous contact and support for writing from teachers they trust. Writing tends to be seen as related to school and is undertaken, for the most part, to please the teacher. Maintaining relationships and having common goals with these trusted teachers are key foci for communicative reflexives, so they are happy to 'do school' (Ryan, 2014c) and are reliant on teachers for direction.

Communicative indicators were evident across data sets (Ryan, 2014a) as follows: parrots teacher talk and discourses; checks in with friends, teachers, parents; use of modals to show uncertainty; writing conforms to structures but does not show confident command of language, rhetorical devices or styles.

Tahlia (second-generation Australian who speaks English), in Year 7, demonstrates the influence of objective structures (teacher and text-type expectations) as she tries to explain the difference between persuasive texts and biographies:

> Well you're trying to persuade people to, like, read the autograph thing [referring to a letter to the editor] and that, and then in, like, a biography you're not really persuading anybody, you're just doing what you've been told, just doin' that.

She understands a persuasive text in terms of persuading an audience to read it, which is one legitimate textual purpose. However, she doesn't move beyond this idea to engage in a more subjective concern for the subject matter and her own stance in the argument. Her persuasive text about caging animals, with a position that this constitutes animal cruelty, shows definite paragraph structure organised around key points. However, she is clearly following the formula and appropriate phrasing provided by her teacher during a brainstorm session pre-writing (Figure 13.1): 'needs to be noted . . . On the surface of this matter . . . ' Despite her use of these features, she struggles with morphosyntactic elements of the text.

Tahlia uses linguistic and structural moves that have been provided by her teacher for this task; however, she shows limited engagement with the subject matter or with the idea of herself as a writer with something to say on this subject.

Parti, in Year 6 (born in India, speaks Gujarati and English and some Hindi), similarly demonstrates how she follows the structures provided by her teacher to

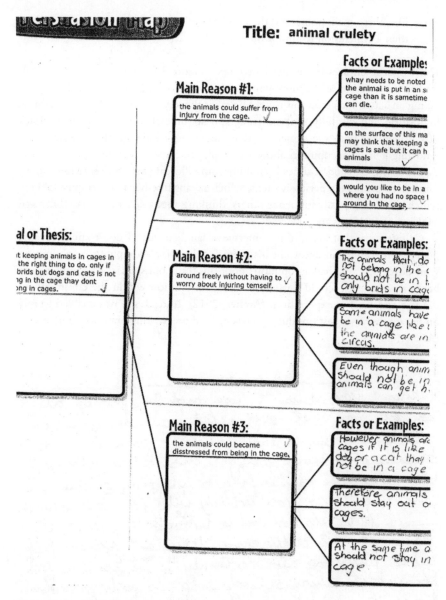

FIGURE 13.1 Tahlia's persuasive plan

produce texts that are mostly for test preparation rather than for a real audience and purpose.

> We did a bit of persuasive text and planning it for NAPLAN . . . most of the time it is just trying to convince Miss L. or the other students . . . you have to have an introduction like taking a position and then you have to have,

> like, three main points and then each write some sentences to back it up and then a conclusion to sum it up.

Her language choices in her persuasive text (Figure 13.2) indicate that she is following endorsed ideas, 'I know you mustn't use mobile phones . . . ', rather than taking an actual stance on this issue. She takes the key points from the pre-writing brainstorm and dutifully writes a paragraph about each one. Yet there is a lack of engagement with the subject matter and little positioning of self as someone who might have an opinion about this topic. She states: 'it's really easy to start cyberbullying . . . and at times it could become illeagal [sic]'. She is following the formula to produce a persuasive text, which means that her voice (Elbow, 2000), which could potentially influence others' thinking about this social issue (Lillis and McKinney, 2013), is absent.

Of interest is that Parti, in her interview, laughed that, 'I don't know because people sometimes can cheat but it's pretty cool to have computers or phones on your desk . . . '. She had an opinion about this topic but she lacked confidence in being a writer who could pursue or voice this opinion within the constraints of the task and teacher expectations (Archer, 2012). Instead, she was enabled to rely on her teacher's suggestions during a teacher-led pre-writing brainstorming session (Archer, 2012).

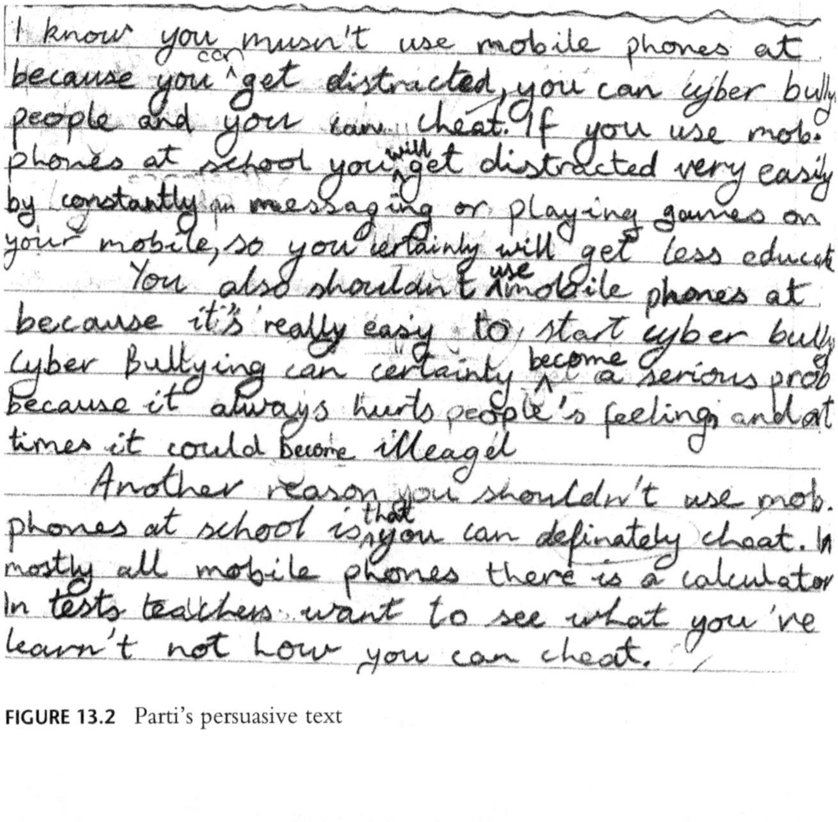
I know you mustn't use mobile phones at
because you can get distracted, you can cyber bully
people and you can cheat. If you use mob.
phones at school you will get distracted very easily
by constantly messaging or playing games on
your mobile, so you certainly will get less educat
You also shouldn't use mobile phones at
because it's really easy to start cyber bully
Cyber Bullying can certainly become a serious prob
because it always hurts people's feelings and at
times it could become illeagel
Another reason you shouldn't use mob.
phones at school is that you can definately cheat. In
mostly all mobile phones there is a calculator
In tests teachers want to see what you've
learn't not how you can cheat.

FIGURE 13.2 Parti's persuasive text

Communicative reflexives are 'enabled' in this mode when they are provided with constant guidance about every aspect of writing. Such enablement is not desirable if we want students to be able to make choices without teacher intervention. Teachers might enable communicative decision-making in these ways:

- Modelling most aspects of writing prior to students 'having a go';
- Providing little opportunity for students' own knowledge construction;
- Providing templates or recipes for *the* way to plan and write specific texts;
- Directing topics and/or text types for most writing opportunities; and/or
- Planning writing tasks with no real audience outside the classroom or school.

Pragmatically, there is not always a formula that will work for writing, and sometimes writers need to make decisions 'in the moment' that may have far-reaching effects. In this sense, by enabling students in this mode, teachers may also be constraining them:

- Students become reliant on the teacher and cannot make decisions without help – untenable in less predictable contexts outside of school (Ryan, 2014a);
- Students can only operate in stable conditions – if conditions change, support is withdrawn or relationships break down, these students may become fractured reflexives (Archer, 2012).

Autonomous reflexives

Autonomous reflexives are interest-driven and self-reliant (Archer, 2012). They may have had an absence of strong relationships with teachers. They tend to be quite intense and practical, and don't see the point of things that are not in line with what they want. They get on with things, but do not necessarily accept that the teacher's ways are their ways, so they are selective about what to invest energy in or how they might dovetail their own concerns. For example, they may get compulsory tasks finished quickly with little care, so they can get onto things that they consider more important. Autonomous reflexives are least likely to turn into fractured reflexives.

Autonomous indicators were evident across data sets (Ryan, 2014a) as follows: keen to finish tasks; focused on most efficient way to get the task done; approaches all writing in similar ways; writing is structured according to expectations but shows a command of the genre; high linguistic modality and use of definite articles to show certainty.

Alice, in Year 6 (Australian-born with parents who speak Greek as L1 and English as L2 at home), says, 'I just like coming up with the story and writing it out – originality is my favourite part'. Writing narratives is her main subjective concern (Archer, 2013) and she tended to respond to questions about writing in reference to narratives. This was in contrast to the communicative reflexives who tended to discuss whichever text type their teacher was focusing on at the time (mostly persuasive for the upcoming national test). For example, when asked about the purpose of paragraphing, she said, 'sometimes I forget about them, but . . . they kind of put out the different scenes in the story'. She was interested in dramatic or comedic vocabulary and engaging the reader with her imaginative plotlines and, in particular, setting the scene:

Death by Barnacle

> As the ferocious, angry waves smashed against the strong rocks, my boat The Tiki was smashed against the rock and splintered into what looked as though a million tiny pieces. As my boat crumbled into the sea I leaped out with terror from my boat in to the icy, blue sea. The water slapped my skin the first moment I hit the water I was PETRIFIED . . .
>
> I'm going to die! Will I be smashed against the rocks or be eaten by shark? The possibilities are endless. My freezing hands tread the very unforgiving sea, my blood-shot eyes caught site of a very mysterious and disturbing figure it was about five meters long lurking behind small rock and slowly but surly creeping towards me. I can almost imagine its three rows of razor sharp teeth slicing threw my body like a huge blender.
>
> But I couldn't leave my loving wife and three children behind, how would they cope without me? I WILL SURVIVE I hope . . . I swam for dear life as fast as my terrified body could take me I scrambled frantically onto the biggest barnacled rock the barnacles ripped my body they shredded my skin. I felt I couldn't go on but I just kept on fighting for life. When I reached the top of the rock my whole body was bleeding. The man only lived for a few more painful minutes . . . he bled to death!

Alice created impact in her short story 'Death by Barnacle' with her use of interesting vocabulary, variety of moods (declarative, interrogative) and degrees of modality moving from definite statements to hesitation and doubt – all effective elements in a short narrative. After a tense and exciting beginning that foregrounds her dramatic voice (Elbow, 2000), Alice goes on to describe a 'mysterious and disturbing figure lurking behind a rock' in her second paragraph. So far, so good; however, she concludes with a final paragraph that has the main character thinking about his loving wife and three children, determined to survive, climbing onto a barnacled rock and dying. Alice's switch of tenor from *I* to *the man*, her tantalising threads that are not revisited, and her quick and unsatisfying ending suggest that she is constrained (Archer, 2012) in terms of her investment in the story. She is determined to set the scene in a compelling way, yet she said, 'personally I'd like it to be longer but the teacher said it had to be short, so . . . ' She managed to satisfy her own subjective desire (Archer, 2012) to set a dramatic scene but then abruptly finished her text to meet the objective conditions (Archer, 2012) of the classroom task so she could move onto her next priority.

Autonomous reflexives are 'enabled' in this mode when they are left to their own devices and not asked to account for their choices or weigh up the effects of such choices. Such enablement is not desirable if we want students to interrogate their choices. Teachers might enable autonomous decision-making in these ways:

- Assuming that students who have strong metalinguistic or textual knowledge and skills are able to 'get on' with writing and require little assistance;
- Providing little opportunity for dialogic events where students have an opportunity to articulate and justify their choices in writing;
- Valuing the product over the interplay of person, context and product (Wardle and Roozen, 2012); and/or
- Planning writing tasks with no real audience or platform outside the classroom or school.

A misreading of purpose, roles and relationships, context or audience can be risky when one commits words to a page or screen. In this sense, by enabling students as autonomous reflexives, teachers may also be constraining them:

- The single-minded approach is almost untenable as we are much less able to predict outcomes in ever-changing contexts (Archer, 2012);
- If choices are not self-interrogated, students won't learn from poor choices;
- Students develop no real sense of audience or platform or potentially real effects of their writing choices.

Meta-reflexives

Meta-reflexives are value-driven and analytical (Archer, 2012). They have most likely had teachers who didn't present themselves as having all the answers and have had opportunities to analyse, critique and engage in active learning and generation of knowledge. They often have a cause or are concerned about social good and tend to respond to variety and new ideas. For example, they have lateral and unconventional takes on writing topics and hybridise text-types for novel effect. They see writing as an opportunity to explore ideas and options and are able to project mental scenarios about the effects of writing choices and action for moving forward.

Ged, in Year 7 (born in the USA and moves between there and Australia), demonstrated a high level of self-awareness about his writing and the strategies he uses to achieve particular outcomes. He is prepared to question the teacher about feedback: 'Sometimes I think the feedback is very anti . . . like it's against what I'm trying to do, which I would explain to them and they get it . . . it's not like that happens frequently.' His explanation of the feedback with the descriptors *anti* or *against* indicates his understanding that teachers are readers who look for particular things when they give feedback, but that they are not necessarily the authority on his writing. He is also quick to modify his statements so that he does not give the interviewer the wrong idea about his teachers. This indicates a meta-awareness of roles, responsibilities and authorities of participants in this context, including the university researcher.

Meta indicators were evident across data sets (Ryan, 2014a) as follows: mediates appropriateness and creativity; uses unusual or interesting language and techniques; subverts genre; hybridises; talks about self as writer; writes outside school; pleases others and self; questions teacher.

Ged shared a narrative that he wrote in Year 5 called 'Raining Cats and Frogs' in which he demonstrates his playfulness with and command of language, and his ability to improvise techniques from junior fiction that he has read. He is confident to address the reader and assume that they can fill the telling gaps, for example 'well, you get the point':

Raining Cats and Frogs

So my fifth grade class and my fifth grade teacher, Mr Kanshagrin, headed outside for a view of the weather. By the time we noticed the cloud over our own heads, we heard the huge croak. Then a bang, a scream, a hand gesture, and we were all inside, watching it rain giant frogs. After a long wait the raining stopped. Following the town tradition we hopped on top of the giant beasts which was harder than expected because of the frogs' slimy bodies. "Each kid to their own frog!" announced the teacher.

. . .

The trees by themselves, appear to us as a world, no, an alien world and with alien animals too and colourful vines stretching far up the leafy plateaus. And the floor was covered in leaves of all different sizes. One of the children actually thought that it was raining leaves right down from the clouds. There were more animals on the floor that there were trees in the rainforest and of all sizes and colors. Frogs too, lots of frogs, so many frogs that well, you get the point.

. . .

Oh well, looks like a weather change. I wonder what's brewing?

Ged's more recent narrative shows maturity in his choice to engage with difficult experiences. He draws on memories of visiting his grandfather who has dementia, including a flashback element remembering stories from his grandfather's childhood. The narrative is engaging and realistic, exploring the relationship between the two characters, strategies for dealing with difficult emotions, and his knowledge about dementia and its effects. He uses humour, creative wordplay and figurative language to foreground his recognisable style. Ged is a writer who can mediate subjective and objective concerns (Archer, 2012) on his own terms. He has shaped an identity as a writer with something to share and comment on (Lillis and McKinney, 2013), rather than someone who is going through the motions of a school task – evidenced in his narrative:

Push On

"This is a nice place you've got," announced Ryan's grandfather, suddenly waking, "Do you live here?"

"Do you know who I am?" questioned Ryan.

"Yes, you're jam and toast!" replied his grandfather.

"Sure, that's me!" said Ryan, letting it go, "Do you need your medicine?"

"Oh yes, I love my purple shirt!" exclaimed his grandfather.

Ryan was about to respond when the nurse walked in announcing that dinner was ready and that he would have to go.

"Come on, Netsook, let's go and have some lovely dinner," she said, taking his hand.

"Yes, Mother!" he replied, like an obedient child.

The nurse, who was now completely used to this sort of thing, ignored him.

"Come on, up you get!" she exclaimed, cheerfully hiding her frustration. But Netsook had attached himself firmly to his bedcovers. It took five minutes to pry the covers free from his hands and get him to stand up. Netsook's walking was almost as unsteady as his mind. He would stumble every five or so steps, would turn left when he was supposed to turn right and vice versa, and talk to inanimate objects, which included complimenting an upright fan on its hairdo.

. . .

As he remembered this story, Ryan felt himself a little older and wiser, not too much but just enough. He thought of his grandfather now and of how he used to be. The cheekiness of his grandfather remains, Ryan thought to himself, but not much more. And just like his grandfather Ryan would be determined to push on.

. . .

"We must not forget what our elders past lives were like," said Ryan aloud, "or we will forget our own past".

Ged indicated in his interview that he was drawing on his family background for this story, using his own memories and those of his parents to paint a vivid picture of his Inuit grandfather. His connectedness to the subject matter and the narrative style to entertain and make social comment is obvious as he draws the reader in, and maintains interest using narrative techniques of flashback, characterisation and interesting vocabulary. Ged is able to explain how he changes his style depending on audience and purpose: 'If I was trying to write for a teacher to read and for their feedback I would probably make it more formal or scientific. For a class audience like if I wanted their applause or their feedback I'd make it humorous.' He is aware of how he mediates the subjective and objective conditions (Archer, 2007) when he writes. His use of comparison/contrast shows that he understands that there are particular expectations in school writing, yet he is also able to satisfy his own desires and pique the interest of his peers in writing. Ged is a writer who is able to weigh up different contexts and considerations without needing a formula or guidelines. He is open to learning new skills and knowledge. However, he is well aware of how he can use those new skills and knowledges in new and different ways across platforms and contexts.

Meta-reflexives are 'enabled' in this mode when they are encouraged to experiment, to critique and to take up identities as writers who have something to say. This mode is the most desirable if students are to negotiate complex and variable conditions of writing. Teachers enable meta-reflexive decision-making in these ways:

- Presenting themselves as writers to their students;
- Providing opportunities for dialogic and contemplative events, where they and their students articulate and justify their choices in writing;
- Valuing the student as a writer rather than just valuing the texts they produce; and
- Planning writing tasks with real audiences, authentic purposes and for a variety of platforms in and out of the classroom or school.

Analysing the potential effects of writing on people and places can engender powerful deliberations for action that subvert the status quo and provide leadership for others in performing as a writer in new ways. However, there is a danger that meta-reflexives can become fractured as teachers can potentially constrain them:

- The weight of expectation and reliance upon such students to help others can cause them to be overwhelmed and fractured (Archer, 2012);
- The encouragement to strive for improvement may mean that they become hypercritical of their own performance.

Fractured reflexives

Fractured reflexives are dependent on others and overwhelmed by their circumstances (Archer, 2012). They may have experienced negative contexts (poor relationships with teachers, little encouragement for writing) or expectations that are too high so they give up. They are focused on the present moment rather than longer term; for example, they can't see how skill development or vocabulary or planning can be used to improve their writing. Self-talk is primarily expressive rather than action-oriented, with little personal investment in subject matter. Identity as a writer is not evident.

> *Fractured* indicators were evident across data sets (Ryan, 2014a) as follows: does not apply pre-writing activities (vocabulary development, brainstorming) in writing; can't answer questions about writing or decision-making unless very direct; does not elaborate on reasoning for choices; can't see self as writer; tends to dislike writing; makes inappropriate writing decisions related to audience, structure, vocabulary, context; writes very little and follows a provided formula.

Aaron, in Year 5 (a Vietnamese student who began school in Australia and whose parents speak Vietnamese as L1 – Mum speaks little English), is a reluctant writer. In his interview he was unable to elaborate on his writing choices or preferences, giving mostly one or two-word answers. His narrative (Figure 13.3) demonstrates the use of basic vocabulary and is mainly composed of additive clauses. He doesn't invite the reader to invest in his story through characterisation (no characters are named) or wordplay or interesting plotlines. He relies on action scenes in an attempt to keep the reader, and potentially himself, interested.

Aaron stated in his interview that he liked *writing stories* but indicated, when asked about a recent book review he had written, that he liked that kind of writing because 'you don't have to get like really long'. Learning about features of a narrative text has provided Aaron with some writing resources. However, this approach alone does not engender a creative discourse (Kramsch, 2000) which encourages students to transpose or appropriate linguistic and cultural resources to construct new textual identities. Aaron is not able to mediate his subjective concerns or the objective structures (Archer, 2012) of school writing to develop writing practices that are sustaining or sustainable.

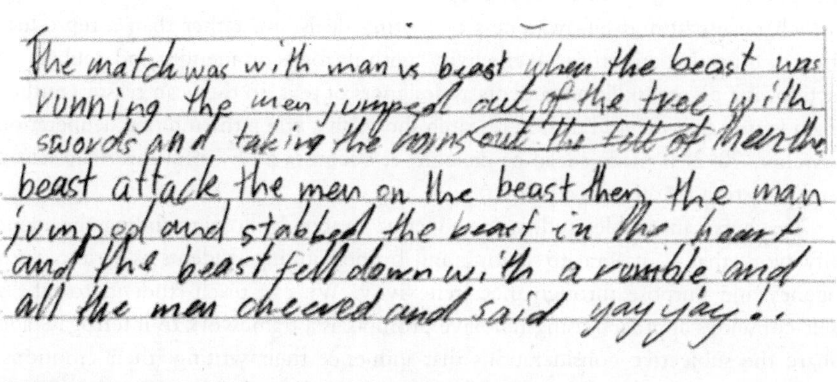
The match was with man vs beast when the beast was running the men jumped out of the tree with swords and taking the horns out the ~~fell of them~~ the beast attack the men on the beast then the man jumped and stabbed the beast in the heart and the beast fell down with a rumble and all the men cheered and said yay yay!.

FIGURE 13.3 Paragraphs from Aaron's narrative

Fractured reflexives are 'enabled' in this mode when they are taught about skills and text-types, but do not learn about themselves as writers (Ryan, 2014a). This is the least desirable mode and one that teachers may inadvertently enable in these ways:

- Invoking time pressure as part of most writing events;
- Providing little opportunity for dialogic events where students articulate their desires and motivations and justify their choices in writing;
- Position themselves as teachers, not writers/teachers;
- Valuing finished products as a priority;
- Providing feedback that is not specific or not checking that it is understood;
- Planning writing tasks with no real audiences or authentic purposes outside of the classroom or school; or
- Providing little choice of different types of writing events for students.

Fractured reflexives are unable to commit to decisions or actions and feel a lack of control. By enabling fractured decision-making, teachers constrain students as writers:

- Students do not develop identities as writers;
- They cannot articulate what matters to them;
- They are passive in that they can't envisage or take action;
- Writing is seen only as a school task.

Reflexive enablements

Current conditions in writing classrooms in Australia, the United States, Canada, New Zealand and the United Kingdom engender reductionist approaches to form and feature at the expense of identity and voice (Comber, 2012; Enright and Gilliland, 2011; Turvey, 2007) as teachers negotiate the current policy environment of standardised assessments and accountability regimes. There is growing evidence, however, that writers, including multilingual writers, need to be enabled as active designers of text (Myhill et al., 2013; Ryan and Barton, 2014; Canagarajah, 2006), which necessitates a self-awareness of writing decisions, rather than a reproduction of formulaic structures. Reflexivity, with its focus on identity and deliberated action, is a pivotal skill for students as designers of text, so they can reassert authorial identity in writing. Further, research shows that when the internal deliberation (Archer, 2012) is made social or dialogic, it becomes a powerful force for action and re-action (Moffatt et al., 2015).

Teachers can enable students as effective writers by foregrounding the identity work that is integral to writing and by positioning students as writers with agency and purpose through meta-reflexivity. We can teach students to take a self-conscious approach using reflexive prompts as a framework to interrogate and share the subjective considerations that influence their writing (their emotions, experiences, knowledge, beliefs, mood) and how their choices and manipulation of rhetorical tools and textual strategies afford them voice for particular objective structures or contexts, purposes and audiences. These strategies can stimulate the creative aspects of writing through such self-awareness and dialogic reflexivity to elevate the writer's performance.

Teachers can scaffold the use of these reflective strategies using prompts for dialogic reflection and reflexive action. For example, I use Archer's three Ds of reflexivity – discernment, deliberation and dedication – as a framework (see Table 13.1) for

TABLE 13.1 Reflexive prompts for self-assessment in writing (Ryan, 2014a)

Stage	Questions to get started
Discern: *Identify choices made*	• Identify some key choices that you, as a writer, made. For example, who or what is being written about and how did you intend them to come across? Or, what role did you take on as a writer – to explain something or show your knowledge to an expert or make people laugh or voice your opinion? Or, why is it set out that way? • How do you feel about this piece of writing? Why? Who do you think will read it? How do you think they might respond? Why?
Deliberate: *Weigh up personal concerns*	• Are you interested in this topic? Do you know much about it? What do you know about it? • Have you done this kind of writing before? What do you think makes this kind of writing enjoyable? Do you like writing in this way? Why? • How did you go about it? How did you know what to write? • What is your opinion about this topic? Who would you really like to read this writing? Why?
Weigh up expectations	• What choices did you make to help you to represent the participants/topic/things/text or yourself in this way (refer back to Discern)? Give some examples. Do you think they work? Why? • What are some other ways you could have done this? • What response do you think your teacher would have if they read this? Why? What response do you think your friend/parent/sibling would have? Why? • How do you think they would think about you as the author of this writing? Why? • What do you think are important features of this kind of writing? Why are they important? How do you know they are important?
Dedicate: *Make an action plan*	• Look back over your writing and think about how you approached it. What are some different strategies you could try in this kind of writing? • What could you change about this writing to make it clearer/more exciting/more convincing for your ideal audience? • Where could you get some ideas for how to do this? • What kind of writer do you want to be? What can you do to make this happen?

specific prompts that promote a reflexive approach to writing. These prompts can be modified according to the type of writing that is being undertaken.

These prompts can help students to articulate reflexive deliberations so that they can be made visible and opened up to dialogue and analysis. Prompting *discernment* is a way to encourage students to 'notice' things about their writing and have some kind of response to what they notice. Questions related to *deliberation* include both personal concerns and contextual expectations. Questions related to personal concerns bring self to the forefront so students can see that they are in this text and can represent their identities and personal considerations through the decisions they make. Prompts for expectations can encourage a deeper interrogation of the reasons for and effects of particular choices in this context, including consideration of other possibilities. Prompts to encourage *dedication* can lead to new understandings or plans for action based on these reflections.

For *communicative reflexives*, the scaffolded interrogation of one's own work in relation to the variety of responses from others can enable one to weigh up choices in a more agentic way than simple confirmation of courses of action. This means the communicative reflexive takes more responsibility for abstracting their ideas and interpreting others' reactions, and they start to learn about making decisions with less reliance on specific advice from others.

For *autonomous reflexives*, the single course of action can be tempered by considering others' responses and by weighing up the potential effects of novel alternatives. In today's society, the single-minded approach is barely tenable, as we are much less able to predict outcomes in ever-changing contexts (Archer, 2012). Thus having the opportunity to stop, reflect and weigh up the impact of one's choices can provide the catalyst for new ways of imagining and performing one's writing.

For *meta-reflexives*, reflexive self-assessment of writing provides morphogenetic possibilities, particularly in relation to expected norms and the interactions with the reader of the work. Analysing the potential effects of the writing on people and places can engender powerful deliberations for action that subvert the status quo and provide leadership for others in performing as a writer in new ways.

Fractured reflexives (who are unable to commit to decisions or actions) can benefit most of all from reflexive and social self-assessment of writing. Dialogic and contemplative strategies that are carefully scaffolded can help to abstract the core issues and feelings from the fractured context and make appropriate action clearer. Responses from others can provide inspiration, and a plan of action can help these students to reassert some control in their writing. In this way, dialogic reflexivity can facilitate transformation and a deeper engagement with writing, which takes time, but gives students ownership of their choices as they develop identities as writers (Ryan, 2014a).

Conclusion

Meaningful writing requires a purposeful shaping of text in context. When young writers produce texts with little understanding about how or why they made particular choices, they are unlikely to be able to negotiate new and uncertain writing contexts. The time invested in robust dialogic reflexive strategies is well spent in providing students with the confidence and skills to negotiate uncertain writing conditions. These reflexive strategies are not merely focused on producing writing according to the teacher's criteria. Rather, they encourage students to draw on and share their productive and diverse personal resources to find a sustaining and effective way to perform their identities as writers in different contexts. Self-awareness through dialogic reflexivity is imperative in the teaching of writing to prepare students for contemporary writing contexts.

References

Archer, M. (1995) *Realist social theory: The morphogenetic approach*, Cambridge, Cambridge University Press.

Archer, M. (2012) *The reflexive imperative in late modernity*, Cambridge, Cambridge University Press.

Athanases, S. Z., Bennett, L. H. and Michelsen Wahleithner, J. (2013) 'Responsive teacher inquiry for learning about adolescent English learners as developing writers', in De Oliveira, L. C. and Silva, T. (eds) *L2 Writing in Secondary Classrooms*, New York, Routledge.

Canagarajah, A. S. (2006) 'Toward a writing pedagogy of shuttling between languages: Learning from multilingual writers', *College English*, vol. 68, pp. 589–604.

Comber, B. (2012) 'Mandated literacy assessment and the reorganisation of teachers' work: Federal policy, local effects', *Critical Studies in Education*, vol. 53, pp. 119–136.

Cremin, T. and Myhill, D. (2012) *Writing voices: Creating communities of writers*, London, Routledge.

Donoso, V. and Verdoodt, V. (2014) Social media literacy: Time for an update [Online]. Available: http://emsoc.be/wpcontent/uploads.

Elbow, P. (2000) *Everyone can write: Essays toward a hopeful theory of writing and teaching writing*, Oxford, Oxford University Press.

Enright, K. A. and Gilliland, B. (2011) 'Multilingual writing in an age of accountability: From policy to practice in U.S. high school classrooms', *Journal of Second Language Writing*, vol. 20, pp. 182–195.

Flower, L. and Hayes, J. R. (1980) 'A cognitive process theory of writing', *College Composition and Communication*, vol. 31, pp. 365–387.

Halliday, M. A. K. and Hasan, R. (1985) *Language, context, and text: Aspects of language in a social-semiotic perspective*, Burwood, Victoria, Deakin University Press.

Hilton, M. (2006) 'Reflective creativity: Reforming the Arts curriculum for the information age', in Burnard, P. and Hennessey, S. (eds) *Reflective practice in arts education*, Amsterdam, Springer.

Ivanič, R. (2004) 'Discourses of writing and learning to write', *Language and Education*, vol. 18, no. 3, pp. 220–245.

Ito, M., Baumer, S., Bittanti, M., Boyd, D., Cody, R., Herr-Stephenson, B., Horst, H. A., Lange, P. G., Mahendran, D., Martinez, K. Z., Pascoe, C. J., Perrkel, D., Robinson, L., Sims, C. and Tripp, L. (eds) (2010) *Hanging out, messing around, and geeking out: Kids living and learning with new media*, Cambridge, The MIT Press.

Kramsch, C. (2000) Linguistic identities at the boundaries. Annual convention of American Association for Applied Linguistics, Vancouver, Canada.

Lillis, T. and McKinney, C. (2013) 'The sociolinguistics of writing in a global context: Objects, lenses, consequences', *Journal of Sociolinguistics*, vol. 17, pp. 415–439.

Macken-Horarik, M. and Morgan, W. (2011) 'Towards a metalanguage adequate to linguistic achievement in post-structuralism and English: Reflections on voicing in the writing of secondary students', *Linguistics and Education*, vol. 22, no. 2, pp. 133–149.

Maybin, J. (2013) 'Working towards a more complete sociolinguistics', *Journal of Sociolinguistics*, vol. 17, pp. 547–555.

Moffatt, A., Ryan, M. E. and Barton, G. (2015) 'Reflexivity and self-care for creative facilitators: Stepping outside the circle', *Studies in Continuing Education*, vol. 38, pp. 1–18.

Myhill, D. (2009) 'Becoming a Designer: Trajectories of Linguistic Development', in Beard, R., Myhill, D., Riley, J. and Nystrand, M. (eds) The SAGE handbook of writing development, London, Sage, pp. 402–414.

Myhill, D., Jones, S., Watson, A. and Lines, H. (2013) 'Playful explicitness with grammar: A pedagogy for writing', *Literacy*, vol. 47, pp. 103–111.

Ryan, M. E. (2014a) 'Reflexive writers: Rethinking writing development and assessment in schools', *Assessing Writing*, vol. 22, pp. 60–74.

Ryan, M. E. (2014b) 'Reflexivity and aesthetic inquiry: Building dialogues between the arts and literacy', *English Teaching: Practice and Critique*, vol. 13, pp. 5–18.

Ryan, M. E. (2014c) 'Writers as performers: Developing reflexive and creative writing identities', *English Teaching: Practice and Critique*, vol. 13, pp. 130–148.

Ryan, M. E. and Kettle, M. (2012) 'Re-thinking context and reflexive mediation in the teaching of writing', *Australian Journal of Language and Literacy*, vol. 35, pp. 283–300.

Ryan, M. E. and Barton, G. (2014) 'The spatialized practices of teaching writing in elementary schools: Diverse students shaping discoursal selves', *Research in the Teaching of English*, vol. 48, pp. 303–329.

Sharples, M. (1999) *How We Write: Writing as Creative Design*, London, Routledge.

Turvey, A. (2007) 'Writing and teaching writing', *Changing English*, vol. 14, pp. 145–159.

Wardle, E. and Roozen, K. (2012) 'Addressing the complexity of writing development: Toward an ecological model of assessment', *Assessing Writing*, vol. 17, pp. 106–119.

AFTERWORD

Teresa Cremin and Terry Locke

As editors of this volume, we sought a range of viewpoints, including examples of new empirical research, to illuminate the nature of writer identity and its relationship to the teaching of writing. In reflecting on the contributions published here, we draw a number of implications which, taken collectively, constitute a kind of call for action – for teacher education and research.

It is clear that all of us, who are members of literate societies, have histories as writers which contribute to the process whereby we construct personal narratives about what it means to write and be a writer. Some of these narratives are stories of struggle, classroom alienation, indifferent response and failure. Others are stories of writing as a portal to self-realisation, empowerment and mastery in relation to various domains of learning. There is, of course, a wealth of hard and anecdotal evidence linking the classroom experiences of students, the behaviour and practices of teachers, and the narratives of writing identity that form and reform in our students as they travel through the compulsory school sector and into adulthood – where some of them decide to become teachers.

These personal narratives matter for a range of reasons. They constitute the baggage that teachers take into their pre-service education, and will for good or ill impact on their formation as teachers of writing. They also matter because they will shape the predispositions of all adults, who have been subject to the formal education system, in respect of writing as an activity (personal or professional) and as a potential dimension of their identity. These predispositions will inevitably have a role in determining the nature of the literacy practices in many homes, and in part may determine the relationship between these and local school practices.

Let us be clear that while all of us have writing identities of one sort or another, based on our personal narratives and our subscribed-to discourses or stories about what it means to be a writer that are implicit in our beliefs and practices, *positioning* ourselves as writers in our relationships with others, especially in our work settings, is a different matter – an assertion of a different order. We might call this our performed or enacted writing identity; it involves the subtle or overt claiming of a dimension of self that asserts that writing is a crucial element of who we are (ontology) and how we come to know (epistemology). It is also political, because it signifies that *being* a writer, and *articulating* my understandings as a writer, are a warrant for my claiming that what I say is valid and worthy of note.

As a number of studies in this volume testify, there is evidence for the transformative effect on teachers of engagement in sustained, systematic writing workshops, both in pre-service and in-service settings. There is thus a case for the development of courses in the tertiary education sector that provide undergraduates (including pre-service teachers) with opportunities to engage in writing, investigate their own writing histories, learn from the practices of established writers, and reflect critically and productively on the processes they engage in when writing different kinds of text. Many university and college campuses, it should be noted, have developed policies that privilege the development of writing-across-the-curriculum programmes, especially given the current, global realisation of the importance of fostering disciplinary literacies, including disciplinary writer identities.

There is also clear evidence of the importance of framing (professional) writing development as participation in a community of practice. The identities we develop as constituting our complex, contemporary selves are always socially situated, and responses to the challenges and resources characterising the times in which we live. Sociocultural understandings of literacy and learning, which underpin most of the contributions to the book, highlight the fluid and dynamic nature of identity formation. It is not surprising then that the stories about professional learning in the context of writing workshops documented in this volume, emphasise the key role of participants sharing and responding to their own and each other's writing.

However, the role of formative assessment and metalinguistic understanding in the development of writing and the enactment of writer identities warrants further attention. The importance of both formative teacher and peer response in the development of writers is routinely acknowledged in the research literature, as are strategies such as self-reflection and goal-setting. Also acknowledged is the long and contentious history related to the place and propriety of grammar in the service of writing pedagogy. We suggest, therefore, that the nature of the language that both novice and expert writers employ as they reflect on their own writing during the various stages of production is an area worthy of investigation. This metalinguistic understanding will both contribute to and constitute a component of their writing identity, and will also have a role to play in the performance of writer identity in the context of a community of practice – for example when a teacher uses think-aloud protocols to reflect with students on the first draft of a poem.

While many, though by no means all, of our contributors have focused on teachers' identities as writers, we believe there is more work to be done on the question of what it *means* to perform a writer identity in the classroom context and invite educators and researchers to respond to our call for action. We consider more research studies need to observe teachers in action and interaction with their students, so that the complex positioning and repositioning of both as writers within lessons and over time can be examined. In the high-school context, many teachers still resist the mantra that all teachers are teachers of writing, so we hope the book will also prompt more classroom-based research and practical support in a range of disciplines. Future research might valuably explore questions such as: What is the nature of the interplay between teachers and student writer identities? How do teachers share and validate their own and their students' writer identities from beyond school and to what extent, if at all, might this make a difference to the community of writers in the classroom? Additionally, what does it look like to perform a writer identity as a chemistry (or other subject) teacher? What kinds of texts (genres) would such a teacher model and what metalanguage might be particularly pertinent in different disciplinary contexts?

And then there are our students. What we can say is that influenced by their own engagement and experience, and by the identity positions made available to them in schools, their writing identities will be in flux. All of them will bring their own 'funds of knowledge and identity' from their own homes and community settings which will either be capitalised on or marginalised, depending on the ethos of the formal schooling situation in which they find themselves. Whether their teachers enact and perform identities as writers will be a matter of chance, of course. This raises another range of questions for further investigation, including: what are the consequences of writer identity positioning for teachers' pedagogic practice, and the quality of student writing, their motivation, attitudes and outcomes? To what extent is writing identity age- and/or discipline-specific? If teachers position themselves as writers and draw on their own writing identities to teach, does this make it more likely that students will also either develop positive writing identities and/or begin performing identities as writers themselves? We perceive this is possible but recognise the salience of personal, interpersonal and institutional influences which are uniquely present in each context. We would like to see more studies that specifically investigate these questions.

To conclude, we consider this volume, drawing on studies of professional writers' identities and those of teachers and students, makes a new and strongly theorised contribution to the field. However, we are the first to acknowledge that it is effectively a work in progress. While collectively our contributors have done a fine job of mining the present moment, offering nuanced understandings of how writer identities are shaped and formed, we are left with tantalising glimpses of research that is yet to be done and theoretical understandings that await us over the horizon.

INDEX